SUMMA PU [barcode] D0864592

Thom

P

Norris J. Lacy
Editor-in-Chief

ORDERS:
  Box 20725
  Birmingham, AL 35216

EDITORIAL ADDRESS:
  1904 Countryside
  Lawrence, KS 66044

Parables of Theory

Jean Ricardou's Metafiction

Parables of Theory

Jean Ricardou's Metafiction

by

Lynn A. Higgins

SUMMA PUBLICATIONS, INC.
Birmingham, Alabama
1984

For Edward M. Anthony and Ann T. Anthony
Parents, mentors, friends

CONTENTS

Acknowledgments

It is a pleasure to express my appreciation of the many friends who helped shape this book. The project began at the University of Minnesota, where Peter Lock, Eileen Sivert and Tom O'Donnell read early versions and provided valuable guidance. Initial research was supported by an Alliance Française de New York Fribourg Foundation Fellowship.

Portions of the text have previously appeared in published form: as "Literature 'à la lettre': Ricardou and the Poetics of Anagram," *The Romanic Review* (Fall, 1982), and "Typographical Eros: Reading Ricardou in the Third Dimension," *Yale French Studies* 57 (1979). I thank the editors of these journals for their permission to reprint.

During the process of rewriting and since, my colleagues and students at Dartmouth have tested my understanding, challenged me to refine my thinking, and continue to sustain the excitement of intellectual inquiry. A special debt of gratitude is due to Colette Gaudin, Marianne Hirsch, Neal Oxenhandler and Don Pease; I have benefited from their specific suggestions and helpful criticisms. I wish also to thank Camille Smith for her editorial advice.

Finally, Roland Higgins knows how much I have depended on his encouragement.

Hanover, New Hampshire
January, 1983

Introduction: Reading Ricardou

> Nous sommes tous des réalistes,
> Picasso aussi bien que Botticelli, et les
> auteurs du nouveau roman aussi bien,
> pas plus mal en tout cas, que les
> romanciers traditionnels.
>
> —Claude Mauriac

As the self-appointed advocate and spokesman for the New Novel, Jean Ricardou is better known as a theoretician than as a novelist. While at first glance his fiction seems hopelessly inaccessible, his essays are models of highly logical argumentation. The aphoristic style of his critical formulations have made him highly quotable and a convenient reference in discussions of postmodern literary texts. Because his essays are more accessible and more easily applied to other critical endeavors, and perhaps also because Ricardou himself more actively promotes his theoretical activities, his fiction has not been given the attention it deserves.

Fiction and theory cannot be seen as separate domains in Ricardou's writing, however. John Sturrock calls him "one of the most perceptive critics and rigorous practitioners of the New Novel." Leon Roudiez devotes most of the last chapter of his *French Fiction Today* to Ricardou, giving him "a leading position in the development of textual fiction and the concept of generative scription." A critic and avid reader of French literature, Canadian writer Margaret Atwood playfully remarks that "The French are about the only people who do the theory first and then write the works that will prove it's true."[1] If her statement calls to mind any contemporary French writer, it evokes Ricardou. Always sensitive to the flow of words, he manifests in his theoretical works some of the lyrical qualities evident in his fiction. Conversely, his novels and "*nouvelles*" are replete with theoretical frameworks and elaborate metafictional clues to guide the reader, often cast as a detective or questing voyager. They simultaneously tell a story—or more often a complex interweaving of improbable stories—while at the same time calling attention to themselves as stories by reflecting explicitly on the mechanisms that make fiction possible.

Ricardou is a "second generation" New Novelist. When his first novel, *L'Observatoire de Cannes* appeared in 1961, Alain Robbe-Grillet had already published four novels: *Les Gommes* (1953), *Le Voyeur* (1955), *La Jalousie* (1957) and *Dans le Labyrinthe* (1959). Michel Butor also had four novels to his credit: *Passage de Milan* (1954), *L'Emploi du temps* (1956), *La Modification* (1957) and *Degrés* (1960). Claude Simon's *Le Vent* and *L'Herbe* appeared in 1957 and 1958 respectively, and in 1960 he published *La Route des Flandres*, which Roudiez considers Simon's first "textual fiction."[2] Nathalie Sarraute's career was launched well before any of the others by her *Tropismes* (1939) and *Portrait d'un inconnu* (1947). Robert Pinget, Claude Ollier and Marguerite Duras were already writing. The New Novel is generally considered to have acquired its name, by accident, as these things often happen, in 1957[3] and been designated as a "phenomenon" (a movement? a collective? a school?) in a 1958 special issue of the review *L'Esprit*.

A writer's place in literary history emerges from tensions between traditions and rebellions and in light of the adversaries and precursors he chooses for himself. As is made clear by the titles of two of his essay collections—*Problèmes du nouveau roman* and *Nouveaux Problèmes du roman*—Ricardou's thinking developed in response to perceived "problems" in fiction, many of which were suggested by the writings of his older colleagues. Ricardou began his writing career as a critic; among his earliest published writings are articles on Robbe-Grillet and Ollier.[4] His fiction explores some of the same narrative problems and ideological implications of writing as theirs; his *Les Lieux-dits* (1969), for example, imitates *Les Gommes* and *L'Emploi du temps* in staging a subversion of detective plot conventions. It poses similar questions but comes up with different solutions.

If Ricardou is indebted to other New Novelists, it is equally clear that he has developed a vision of his own and has in turn influenced them. First, and in a purely practical way, he provoked greater interaction among New Novelists by being the first to bring them together as a "collective" of writers. In 1971, Robbe-Grillet, Sarraute, Pinget, Butor, Simon and Ollier chose to align or at least ally themselves with the designation "Nouveau Roman" by accepting Ricardou's invitation to participate in a colloquium at Cerisy-la-Salle on the topic "Nouveau Roman: Hier, aujourd'hui." Although differences in their approaches to fiction and in their writing techniques prevent the group from "collecting" except very loosely into a school, there was enough common ground for ten days of productive discussion.[5]

While continuing in the line of earlier New Novels, Ricardou's own writing has in turn produced echoes in his colleagues' more recent work. While *L'Observatoire de Cannes* experiments with themes and techniques proposed earlier in *La Jalousie* (such as vision distorted by obsession), Ricardou's novel uses comico-erotic wordplay that later reappears in Robbe-Grillet's *Projet pour une révolution à New York* (1971). And while Ricardou's theories continue in some of the directions outlined in Robbe-Grillet's *Pour un nouveau roman* (1963), they also diverge from it in important ways. Robbe-Grillet categorically rejects metaphor, for example, while Ricardou has defined and put into practice elaborate structuring metaphors useful for reading not only his own fiction but Robbe-Grillet's as well.

Ricardou agrees with Michel Butor that the novel is a form of research into the nature of reality and the properties of language;[6] his novels incorporate both fictional searches and theoretical researches. Ricardou has gone beyond the others in applying a materialist conception of art to the novel. Seen in terms of production rather than communication, the text becomes "à la fois le lieu et l'effet d'un certain travail."[7] His aphorism that fiction is not only "l'écriture d'une aventure" but also "l'aventure d'une écriture"[8] can be heard echoed in a recent preface by Simon, who explains that "C'est seulement en écrivant que quelque chose *se* produit dans tous les sens du terme." For Simon, a novel is not a story about a hero or heroine, "Mais cette toute autre histoire qu'est l'aventure singulière du narrateur qui ne cesse de chercher, découvrant à tâtons le monde dans et par l'écriture."[9]

But Ricardou's most significant contribution to contemporary thinking about fiction in general and the New Novel in particular lies less in individual instances of influence than in his exploration of the relationships between fiction and theory, in what can be called his metafictional vision. His three novels—*L'Observatoire de Cannes* (1961), *Les Lieux-dits* (1969) and *La Prise* (or *Prose* on the back cover) *de Constantinople* (1965)—and the *nouvelles* of *Révolutions minuscules* (1971) and *Le Théâtre des métamorphoses* (1982) are all metafictional in the usual sense that they are self-conscious and self-reflecting: they are fiction about fiction. *All* novels are metafictional to some degree, however, when they either explicitly, or more often implicitly, reflect on their own use of generic conventions, or when they point to their own fictionality. Ricardou's writing is metafictional at another level as well: his is fiction about *theory*. To talk about fiction today, it usually proves necessary at the same time to analyze the properties of language and the operations that make reading possible and to make general statements about what literature is or should be. Ricardou, more than any other New Novelist, has formulated a sustained theoretical discourse on these problems.[10]

What is more, this discourse unfolds most richly not in his essays, which seek to redefine the shifting tension between fiction and theory, but in his fiction, where these new definitions are put to the test. More than his colleagues, Ricardou has had a hand in the recycling of theory back into fiction. At his best (*La Prise/Prose de Constantinople*, certain stories in *Révolutions minuscules*), he creates a dialectic in which fiction and theory sustain or resist each other as the book progresses. Theory attempts to structure the text, but the fiction escapes the confines of theory, throws a rock in its limpid pool, exposing its limits and contradictions. At his worst (*Les Lieux-dits*), he demonstrates the dangers of a fiction too terrorized by theory. Everywhere, the struggle between the two constitutes the fiction's plot and is responsible for Ricardou's habitually high level of abstraction. It is the purpose of this book, therefore, to take a close look at Ricardou's novels and *nouvelles* as a case study of the meeting, within fiction, of fiction and theory.

Most recently, Ricardou has made explicit his project of creating what amounts to an intermediate genre. *Le Théâtre des métamorphoses* is called neither fiction nor theory, but bears on its cover the label *mixte*, defined within as "une souple textualisation d'écrits divers sous l'emprise d'un x."[11] The "x" suggests several ideas. Symbolically, it is the unknown, the focus of the (re)search that motivates writing. Graphically, it marks the spot at which heterogeneous threads intersect in a text intended not as a "mélange" but a "tissage." The "x" also refers back to Ricardou's other books, where crosses represent the principle of overdetermined structural and thematic elements. Most importantly, the "x" and the generic *mixte* designate the articulation and alternation of binaries structuring this and all Ricardou's writing: Prise/Prose, realists/poets, presence/absence, fiction/theory, and so on. The *Petit Robert* dictionary reveals that among things that can be called *mixte* are trains that transport both passengers and merchandise. The example provides an appropriate image for

Ricardou's novels, which are vehicles for both theory and storytelling. In fact, *L'Observatoire de Cannes* opens with a train that conveys the idea that Ricardou's fiction is best seen not as a product but as a process where fiction and theory transform each other reciprocally.

"Theater" and "theory" are related etymologically; the latter is a mental spectacle, while the former is a visual one. Ricardou's writing is a unique theater (even in the military sense as well) where a drama or battle of fiction and theory is staged. While *Le Théâtre des métamorphoses* does not live up to the definitions of *mixte* it profers (its fictional components are overshadowed by its theoretical thrust), the term is applicable to the four volumes previously published under the rubrics *roman* and *nouvelles*, the four books to be studied here. But before examining each of these in turn, it will be helpful to look briefly at Ricardou's general theoretical concerns and become acquainted with his vocabulary.

1

Extremely concerned about social and political implications of a writing career, Ricardou sees his work as profoundly *engagé*. Given the content of his novels, this claim seems somewhat surprising. In his critical essays, the word "idéologie" occurs frequently, usually in the phrase "idéologie dominante" which, translated into our jargon, refers to the "establishment." Because he is a writer and an intellectual, the establishment with which Ricardou most often interacts is a literary one. In his novels as in his essays, he is dedicated to dismantling ideologies responsible for the belief that language can reflect reality. Invoking in support of his arguments such critics as Gérard Genette, Roland Barthes, Jacques Derrida and Philippe Sollers (before Ricardou's 1971 split with *Tel Quel*), he explores implications of a material, polyvalent and self-transforming textuality, and he shares their ideological project of challenging the literary notion of mimesis and the Western metaphysics of logocentrism on which it is based. If his fiction is to be seen as *engagé* at all, it must be considered in terms of its form and its concern with language.

The most nefarious element of the ideology of literary representation is, Ricardou believes, the imperialism of the signified, the unquestioned importance of what is said ("le quelque chose à dire"), which leaves writing and the writer in a subordinate position at the mercy of "un sens institué."[12]

This by no means implies that society tells the writer what to say, at least not directly. Rather, and more insidiously, the writer understands *that he must have something to say*. The text thus becomes the mere expression of a predetermined message. Ricardou's scorn for this dogma is conveyed with missionary zeal:

> Repérable en français au XIIe siècle, le verbe exprimer vient on le sait du Latin *premere*, presser. Quelles qu'en soient les nuances, ses diverses acceptions se ressentent chacune de cette idée, venue d'ailleurs en plein jour au XVIe, qu'exprimer, c'est faire sortir par pression. Le plus fréquent exemple de cette pratique est offert, on s'en doute, par le citron et son jus. L'expression suppose donc, avant sa manoeuvre même, la nécessaire abondance d'un suc, la présence obligée d'une substance, l'inéluctable existence d'un 'quelque chose à dire.' Pour cette doctrine, l'essentiel est ce qui précède le texte et le contraint à n'être qu'un moment second et secondaire: le moyen de son expression.[13]

This doctrine of expression gives rise to two kinds of literature, which Ricardou calls "Romanticism" (expressing the writer's subjective inner self) and "Realism" (reflecting realities of an objective world outside). Both involve representation or mimesis, and they are two faces of the same: "Il n'y a guère de bien grand hasard si l'hugolien poème—'miroir d'âme'—trouve son parallèle irrécusable en le stendhalien roman—'miroir que l'on promène le long d'une route.' "[14] These oppositions in turn support other dichotomies on which bourgeois culture depends: self and world, words and things, prose and poetry, fiction and theory. Suppressed, however, is the distinction between life and literature; the second is subordinated as a vehicle of the first. Such an approach privileges what Ricardou calls literature's "dimension référentielle."

Several related beliefs, according to Ricardou, reinforce the dogmas of romanticism and realism. Since the message is all that counts, it can be translated, summarized or debated at will without being affected in its essence. Expression itself is simply translation of perceived reality into words. A second belief exalts the role of inspiration. In its extreme form, belief in inspiration sees the author as *vates*—as someone in a hypnotic trance or mystic frenzy, transformed into a passive vehicle for transmitting a message coming from beyond. The writer is thus alienated from the processes and materials of literary production.

To the imperialism of referentiality that characterizes the traditional novel, Ricardou opposes emphasis on the text's "dimension littérale." Literal and referential dimensions of a text are inversely proportional. Predominance of either constitutes an "illusion." When the reader identifies with characters and marvels at the reality of descriptions and events, an "euphorie du récit" turns words and text into a transparent window on reality. Conversely, when the text insists on its own presence, it becomes opaque, and the story's reality is put into question.[15] The text is thus an unstable terrain: on one side lies the dominant ideology which would erase the text in favor of its message; on the other lurks unintelligibility of a language too detached from reference. Ricardou's fictions attempt to thread a precarious course between the two dangers, but in his theoretical writings he tends to emphasize, even overemphasize, the evils of referentiality in an attempt to counteract widespread assumptions about writing and reading. As a result, the novels paint a much more complex and subtle picture of the dynamics of representation.

Instead of communicating a message, then, Ricardou intends to play a sort of zero-sum game with his readers. The reader reared on romanticism and realism, seeking a reassuring illusion of reality, attempts to reduce the text to a story. The text, however, with its contradictions and polyvalences, resists such an aggression, maintaining language's material presence. In this struggle, the text usually wins, as becomes clear with any attempt to summarize its story. A summary is by nature an attempt to express the story's events in other words. But the New Novelists refuse to accept this separation of form and content. Their stories aim neither to "express" ideas nor to "create" a fictive reality in the traditional sense. Rather, writing is seen as an activity of working with materials, and the events that "produce" a story are linguistic ones. The phrase "textual production" underlines the primacy of work with language over ideas of expression, creation, inspiration, and imitation of reality.

The text's resistance to the reader's (and ultimately its own) referential tendencies takes several forms. As narration unfolds, anti-representational strategies sytematically obliterate referential touchstones. Illusion and contradiction create a reality which can only exist in a novel, forcing the reader to consider a coexistence of incompatible meanings and to ask questions about where meaning comes from. Supporting anti-representation are auto-referential internal mirror devices. Two types of auto-representation resist the assimilation of a novel to reality outside: Ricardou uses the term "auto-représentation horizontale" to designate aspects of a fiction that correspond to each other in ways unlikely outside a novel; objects group according to shape or the spelling of their names, for example. "Auto-représentation verticale," on the other hand, describes aspects of a fiction which dramatize mechanisms of narration,[16] providing a metafictional or self-reading dimension.

2

If the position just outlined in many ways reflects and formulates theoretically the research carried on by other New Novelists, the literary context in which Ricardou can be understood is much larger. He is aware that to write is always to rewrite, and his choice and reworking of subtexts offer an instructive laboratory for the study of poetic and intellectual influence. Beyond the immediate context of the New Novel, Sartre, Valéry, Mallarmé, Raymond Roussel, and even Balzac and Ferdinand de Saussure are among the precursors with or against whom Ricardou has forged his identity as a novelist.

One of his favorite targets of criticism is the "traditional novel," that is, the nineteenth century realistic novel, which he often personifies as Balzac. In defense of Balzac, let it be said that for polemical reasons Ricardou oversimplifies the works he chooses to call Balzacian. Furthermore, it is often clear that Ricardou speaks as a writer who would not care to have written Balzac's novels.[17] Recent readers have made the distinction between traditional and modern writing more problematic, seeing in novels by Balzac, Stendhal, Zola and others, many of the same forces at play which the New Novel self-consciously exploits. Although a bad reader of Balzac, Ricardou's adversary attitude helps in the articulation of his theories.

His unsympathetic view of the so-called traditional novel has an important implication. Ricardou's entire theoretical apparatus, which he uses quite fruitfully to write his fiction, is actually more accurately seen as a description of modes of *reading*. Understood in this light, we need no longer distinguish between mimetic and anti-referential *writing*, but instead accept an invitation as we *read* to resist realistic illusions by turning our attention to the play of the text. The various reader *personae* sprinkled through the novels serve as models. Although his polemical tone tends at times to cloud the issues, Ricardou's desire to educate the public for a re-reading of old stories (except Balzac's) constitutes a sincere commitment.

Another adversary figure is Jean-Paul Sartre. For Sartre, commitment means involvement in a class struggle, which most often takes place outside writing. For Ricardou, as for the younger less disillusioned Sartre, there are still struggles that can be carried on within a literary vocation. Their conflict crystallized in late 1964 at the Mutualité building in the Latin Quarter, where six writers were invited to debate the question: "Que peut la littérature?"[18] Sartre's speech was largely an attack on the New Novel, which, he claimed, was gratuitious and self-indulgent, imposing an absolute world devoid of chance. In the New Novel's aggression, he asserted, the reader receives security (a comforting verbal world) in exchange for freedom. Engrossed in this rather surprising assessment (It is still difficult to think of the New Novel as reassuring), Sartre neglected to ask the question posed by the debate. His implicit answer was: "Nothing."

Ricardou's argument baited Sartre as much as Sartre taunted the New Novel, and in a rather ingenious way. According to Ricardou, rather than being a transparent vehicle for publication of ugly realities such as hunger, literature proposes a separate verbal world which contests those realities:

> Si l'écrivain—donc—n'a rien à *dire avant son livre*, cela n'assure nullement que le livre, *lui*, ne dise rien. Soyons plus précis. La structure du langage ne correspond apparemment pas à la structure physique du monde; ou pour oser une excessive simplification, disons qu'un *objet* et un *objet décrit* n'ont pas la même structure . . .
>
> Comment donc explorer la structure du langage, sinon en écrivant, en essayant de le constituer selon un fonctionnement intégral? Mais cela, cet *acte d'écrire* fait surgir un monde nouveau dont la structure est celle même du langage.

This second verbal world exists in opposition and as a challenge to already-known worlds.

> Et ce monde fictif, obtenu par l'exercice de l'écriture, oppose sa structure propre à celle de notre monde—et ainsi le met en question. La littérature est ce qui dit au monde: "Es-tu ce que tu prétends être?" ou, si l'on veut, comme on l'a remarqué, elle nous le fait mieux voir et comme le révèle.[19]

In answer, then, to the question implied throughout the debate—What can literature do when children are starving?—Ricardou suggests the following eloquent answer:

> Mais ces considérations ont-elles une valeur dans un monde qui a faim? . . .
>
> J'ai dit plus haut que deux théories me semblaient inadmissibles: l'art pour l'art, l'art pour l'homme. Car l'art, c'est l'homme même, c'est la qualité *différentielle* par laquelle un certain mammifère supérieur devient *homme*.
>
> Alors, au sens où nous l'entendons, *qu'est-ce qu'écrire*? sinon dire que l'homme doit exister (ou a un niveau banal, doit pouvoir lire), c'est-à-dire doit ne pas mourir de faim.
>
> La littérature, par sa simple existence, c'est ce qui fait que la faim des hommes est un *scandale*.[20]

Such optimism about literature was in itself a bit scandalous in the context of the gloomy appraisals offered by other participants at the Mutualité. But, as Ricardou remarks aphoristically in his own review of the debate, "Tout pessimisme sans motif est une attitude réactionnaire." In his review he calls literature "ce qui nettoie ma vision," and repeats that it is thanks to an "écart essentiel que la littérature intérroge le monde."[21]

Ricardou was not only alone in offering an optimistic answer to the question "Que peut la littérature?", he was the only debater who answered the question at all. Sartre's attitude was basically that of a guilty white liberal: starving people cannot read, even less eat a novel; writers write because that is all they know how to do, but writing offers no solution whatsoever to starvation. For him, commitment is often the task of a writer rather than a text. His stand assumes language to be transitive, and therefore must act directly on the world if it is to have an effect.

Ricardou's stand, on the other hand, was based on his claim that language is intransitive and opaque. Rather than lamenting the fact that oppressed people do not read novels and cannot be helped by them, Ricardou chooses to teach his readers to "clean" their own vision. He accepts the fact that only an elite intellectual minority will read his novels, but suspects that that minority will be disproportionately influential. This is the strategy of consciousness-raising. The "idéologie dominante" holds sway largely because its assumptions are taken for granted. Not only are certain beliefs espoused (such as that language accurately reflects reality), but they are not even seen as beliefs. A censorship is protected by another censorship as a crime is hidden by a cover up. Ricardou's *engagement* goes in the direction of Barthes's *Mythologies* (1957), revealing the received ideas at the foundation of intelligibility of texts and the world.

The opposition between Sartre and the New Novelists is not as clear as both sides would make it seem, however. It was Sartre, after all, who approvingly coined the term *anti-roman* to characterize the self-examination found in some novels emerging just after the war. In his preface to Sarraute's *Portrait d'un inconnu* (1947), Sartre maintained that the very kinds of experimentation that led to the New Novel were neither a foreboding of artistic decadence, nor did they toll the death of the novel or of literary commitment. Rather, such writings "marquent seulement que nous vivons à une époque de réflexion et que le roman est en train de réfléchir sur lui-même." He argued that such fiction turned novelistic categories against themselves the better to jolt the reader out of complacency.[22] By the time of the Mutualité debate, Sartre had found that self-reflection had gone too far and had become narcissistic. What had intervened, in addition to nearly two decades of novelistic experimentation, was structuralism, with its highly technical and linguistically-oriented methods. Ricardou was arguing, ironically, a Sartrean conception of commitment, but through a structuralist conviction that literature could not act directly on the world. Where Sartre would teach his readers to see a certain oppression (a laudable effort, which Ricardou refused to appreciate), Ricardou would teach his readers quite simply *to see*. This statement must be taken literally when reading his novels, which rely on the visual sense to demonstrate the relativity of perception. Describing minuscule worlds cleans the vision as effectively as large doses of disaster, he might argue. Describing a painting or the surface of a pond, Ricardou uncovers the conventions unconsciously espoused in traditional modes of reading.

For Sartre, whose 1948 question "Qu'est-ce la littérature?" was an implicit subtext at the Mutualité eighteen years later, language should be transparent, implying "qu' on puisse à son gré le traverser comme une vitre et poursuivre à travers lui la chose signifiée." When people speak, they use language instrumentally, and therefore, "L'homme qui parle est au-delà des mots, près de l'objet." The poet, on the other hand, does not "speak" but rather sees words as things instead of signs. "Les poètes sont des hommes qui refusent d'*utiliser* le langage."[23] Because of this distinction, Sartre sees poetry and *engagement* as mutually exclusive.

Paul Valéry is another writer whose views Ricardou has read to help formulate his own, but this time he adopts no adversary stance. Although Valéry's evaluation differs, his separation of poets from novelists corresponds to Sartre's distinction between committed literature and poets. Like Sartre, Valéry sees the poet as an artisan who manipulates a material: words. To him, however, it is the novelist who abuses words by making them disappear in favor of referential reality:

> Superstitions Littéraires
> J'appelle ainsi toutes croyances qui ont de commun l'oubli de la condition verbale de la littérature.
> Ainsi existence et *psychologie* des *personnages*, ces vivants *sans entrailles.*[24]

Valéry was especially concerned about the deceptions of transitive language that ignores its own conventions. This use of language replaces words with the world signified: "Son office est rempli quand chaque phrase a été entièrement abolie, annulée, remplacée par le sens."[25]

If Ricardou developed his view of literary commitment in the context of questions like "Que peut la littérature?", his valorization of poetic language is informed by his reading of Valéry, who was less concerned with commitment to social or political ideologies. About Valéry's "novelist" and Sartre's "écrivain engagé" who see language as a window on reality, Ricardou says:

> Pour ma part, puisque, en telle occurrence, le langage est considéré comme *le pur véhicule d'une information*, je me propose de les appeler les *informateurs*—et leurs produits, *informations*.

He has another name for what Valéry (approvingly) and Sartre (pejoratively) call "poets":

> Et puis, il y a d'autres gens. Ceux-là n'admettent nullement le langage comme ce véhicule par lequel se transmettent un enseignement ou un témoignage; ils ne l'envisagent nullement comme un instrument. Ils l'acceptent plutôt comme une sorte de *matériau*, et ce matériau, ils le travaillent avec un soin, une patience infinis. Pour ces gens-là, l'essentiel n'est pas hors du

langage; *l'essentiel, c'est le langage même.* Ecrire, pour eux, est non telle volonté de communiquer une information préalable, mais ce projet *d'explorer le langage entendu comme espace particulier.*

Ces gens-là, avec Barthes, je propose de les appeler écrivains—et leurs écrits: *littérature.*[26]

Valéry, too, frequently used words like "bâtir" and "travailler" to describe his relationship to language and poetry. And before Ricardou, he mocked the notion of inspiration:

L'idée d'*Inspiration* contient celles-ci: *Ce qui ne coûte rien est ce qui a le plus de valeur.*
Ce qui a le plus de valeur ne doit rien coûter.
Et celle-ci: *Se glorifier le plus de ce dont on est le moins responsable.*

Art et travail s'emploient à constituer un langage que nul homme réel ne pourrait improviser. . . . C'est à un tel discours que se donne le nom *d'inspiré.* Un discours qui a demandé trois ans de tâtonnements, de dépouillements, de rectifications, de refus, de tirages au sort, est apprécié, lu en trente minutes par quelque autre. Celui-ci reconstitue comme *cause* de ce discours, un auteur capable de l'émettre spontanément et de suite, c'est-à-dire un auteur infiniment peu *probable.* On appelait *Muse* cet auteur qui est dans l'auteur.[27]

Ricardou's conception of the work itself is also similar to Valéry's. Both are more interested in reproducing perceptual processes and psychological mechanisms than in creating characters who think about such things. In describing scenes seen by a hypothetical, disembodied point of view, Ricardou might even be realizing Valéry's dream of a novel or poem which would have a sentiment or perception as its main character.[28] Above all, the work expresses a desire to write: as Valéry remarks, "La littérature est pleine de gens qui ne savent au juste que dire, mais qui sont forts de leur besoin d'écrire."[29] Characterized by overdetermined internal connection—"Les parties d'un ouvrage doivent être liées les unes aux autres par plus d'un fil"[30]—the work's shape results from its repetitions.

With help from Valéry, Sartre and others, Ricardou has brought into question the convention that separates poetry from prose. He rarely uses the word *poésie* except to refer to *poèmes*. When not using the word *littérature* (as above), he speaks of *prose*. Here again, Ricardou is saying nothing new; Mallarmé's "proses" (which are poems), and the very existence of prose poems or poetic prose amply demonstrate that the distinction is vague at best. One can speak of Ricardou's "poetics" without implying that his novels, unbeknownst to him, are actually poems, but rather to point to an attitude toward and use of language that he, Valéry and even Sartre have described and that can be called poetic. Interestingly enough, the word *poem* comes from a Greek verb meaning to do or to make, reminding us of Ricardou's contention that instead of being "quelque chose à dire," literature should be (for the reader, as for the writer) "quelque chose à faire."

3

Ricardou's narrative techniques are designed, then, to subvert readers' expectations that literature mirror "real" people in lifelike situations. His improbable stories have the appeal of fairy tales or detective stories. His prose evokes scenes infused with an eroticism that is sometimes lyrical and sensual, sometimes sinister and perverse. But no sooner are these fictions displayed before us than they crumble under the mocking gaze of their own self-readings, and we are transported, sometimes against our will, to another level of reality. This is their didactic dimension: the text turns back on itself and away from the world in order to stress the arbitrary nature of the linguistic sign. This is what makes possible the production of purely textual meaning.

There is, however, a fundamental contradiction that pervades all Ricardou's work and will be a major focus of ours. His novels contradict their own position by aiming to dramatize a theory by means of a transparent fiction. So rather than concluding too hastily that Ricardou's fiction does not represent reality because it does not depict war, love, or psychological conflict, we would do better to ask *what* reality he portrays. Put this way, the question answers itself: the fiction represents theory. The term "auto-representation" only begins to suggest the complications inherent in writing that sets out to represent...anti-representation. At the level of its metafictional reality, Ricardou's fiction is not anti-mimetic at all.

It thus falls within the category *roman à thèse* as Susan Suleiman defines it:

> a 'realistic' novel possessing stylistic and formal qualities that place it in the category of 'literature' (as opposed to *sous-littérature* or simple propaganda), but in which the aesthetic function is in strong 'competition' with a clearly discernible ideological (communicative) function. In other words, it is a novel that seeks, through aesthetic means, to persuade its readers of the validity of a particular ethical, social, political or religious doctrine.[31]

While setting out to demonstrate in fiction the arbitrary nature of language, Ricardou's texts ironically work against him by undermining that very assumption on which they are based. It is their *roman à thèse* dimension that prevents the fictions from being simply the consequence of their linguistic manipulations. And even this would not be contradictory were it not that the message is that there is no message.   .

Ricardou's narrative devices—description, metaphor, *mise-en-abyme* and anagram are a few that will be encountered—create an illusion that the text can be accounted for in terms of its structural and linguistic raw materials. Such strategies are called "generative": the text is ostensibly "generated" from a *jeu de mots*, a metaphor, a series of anagrammatic transformations, or from microcosmic interior duplications of the larger containing work. Generative devices—and the decipherment activity required of the reader—give Ricardou's and other New Novelists' fictions their riddle-like constructions. Critics have often been satisfied with locating and identifying generative kernels, thereby contributing to a general tendency not to take the New Novel seriously.

But riddles often only *seem* frivolous, as Oedipus knew, and Ricardou's theories and fictions reveal a persistent anxiety that takes the form of a riddle. The riddle is this: where does the text come from? This fundamental and unresolved question about origins emerges from close reading of all his fiction. If inspiration and reality are no longer acceptable sources for fiction, if expression of self and world are illegitimate (or impossible), what *is* the fiction's reason for existing? In light of this question, theory—the metafictional message—can be seen as the most potent generative device that attempts to account for or motivate the text.

What the theories systematize and the novels attempt to demonstrate is the possibility that words, not the world, are at the origin of fiction. But while insisting that the relationship between words and world is arbitrary, Ricardou's fiction attempts to justify its existence by creating another kind of mimesis; it consistently and in varying ways suggests the concept of a natural or motivated language.

Gérard Genette's reading of Plato's *Cratylus*[32] will help situate Ricardou's position more clearly. In the *Cratylus*, Socrates discusses the nature of language first with Hermogenes, then with Cratylus. Hermogenes maintains that conventions or agreements within human society determine what meanings are conveyed by given linguistic forms. His is the Saussurean view of the arbitrary relationship linking signifier to signified. Cratylus, on the other hand, professes belief in the "justesse des noms" (Genette), the "natural fitness of names" (Plato). According to him, language as it exists demonstrates that expression derives (or is motivated) directly from ideas. Genette calls his position "Primary Cratylism," or "Primary Mimologism" because of its belief in a mimetic character of language.

More interesting for our purposes than the position of either Cratylus or Hermogenes is that of Socrates, who participates in both arguments, first seeming to argue on the side of Cratylism, finally seeming to adopt Hermogenes' conventionalist thesis. Far from being indecisive or contradictory, Socrates' position is, according to Genette, coherent and distinct from the other two. Allowing that words imitate reality only in exceptional cases, Socrates nevertheless attributes that sad fact to a failure on the part of a primal "Giver of names." "For I believe," he says, "that if we could always or almost always use likenesses which are perfectly appropriate, this would be the most perfect state of language. . ."[33] In other words, Socrates sees signifiers as arbitrarily assigned to their meanings (Hermogenes' position), but maintains a nostalgic belief in the *capacity* of words to mirror meanings. Language as it exists is thus, in his view, imperfect and fallen, holding out only a promise of return to a "paradis linguistique perdu" (Genette). It is in this gap between defective language as it is (Socrates) and as it could be (Cratylus) that Genette elsewhere locates the compensatory task of poets.[34] And it is in light of this third, Socratic stance, described by Genette as a "cratylisme déçu et . . . mécontent" that we can understand the contradictory nature of Ricardou's fictions.

There too, words are "no longer" the natural reflection of ideas. Inherent in Ricardou's writing is a struggle between two mutually exclusive conceptions of language, both of which must be taken into account if we are to understand his work. On the one hand, he bases his ideological, theoretical stance on a rejection of the Cratylian viewpoint, seeking instead to demonstrate after Hermogenes, that language is arbitrary or unmotivated. He begins to subvert his own argument, however, by going beyond Hermogenes to establish a sort of reverse mimesis, where stories follow the initiative of words. Characters, often playing the role of readers, sometimes even intervene by deciphering riddles or pointing out the inevitability of textual production of meaning. Ricardou's analytical essays complete the task by demonstrating, step by laborious step, how the story follows necessarily—almost mechanically—from its linguistic raw materials. Thus undermined by its own confirmation, the original reversal turns ironically on itself, becoming a strategy to bridge a grief by constructing a new poetic "justesse." Far from incorporating the arbitrary nature of language into an anti-representational view of writing, Ricardou actually emerges, like Socrates, a disappointed Cratylist in search of a lost linguistic paradise.

Other writers and theoreticians have faced the same dilemmas. An important precursor of Ricardou's thinking, the Swiss linguist Ferdinand de Saussure built his *Cours de linguistique générale* on the observation that linguistic signifiers are only arbitrarily paired with their signifieds, and he showed how arguments in favor of the sign's motivation are demonstrably fallacious. The simplest of these is onomatopoeia, where the word seems an echo of an original sound. But if one looks at how examples of onomatopoeia vary with translation from one language to another, it becomes clear that no necessity binds sound to sense. Another more complex but equally illusory argument for the 'justesse des noms" is etymology. Here, a word's form is justified as necessary through recourse to previously existing forms. On closer examination, however, etymology is actually a form of intertextuality for, as Saussure succinctly summarized:

> L'étymologie est donc avant tout l'explication des mots par la recherche de leurs rapports avec d'autres mots . . . En linguistique, expliquer un mot, c'est le ramener à d'autres mots, puisqu'il n'y a pas de rapports nécessaires entre le son et le sens.[35]

This argument for the motivation of signs, like onomatopoeia, depends then, on infinite deferral of their arbitrariness, affording but uneasy respite to the disappointed Cratylist.

But the problem of motivation resurfaces outside Saussure's course if we consider his study of anagram—what a recent issue of *Semiotexte* called Saussure's "curse."[36] In his reading of Greek and Latin poetry, he repeatedly detected the presence of key theme words—the name of a mentor, for example, or a God to whom the poem was addressed—fragmented and dispersed as "hypograms" throughout the poem. The problem was like a tantalizing peripheral vision or an optical illusion that vanishes when gazed at head on. Were the names there by chance? By conscious design? Were they a figment of the reader's imagination? Or were they simply, as Jean Starobinski suggests in his book on Saussure, "an aspect of human speech (*parole*) as it unfolds itself, in a way which is neither haphazard nor fully conscious?"[37] Saussure looked endlessly for a motive behind the phonetic correspondences he found. If his inconclusive studies do not reveal a new motivation for poetic language, Saussure was operating on Socrates' assumption—or at least on a suspicion or a hope—that such motivation was possible, and so was undertaking the same project that can be seen in Ricardou's "generative scription."

Another precursor to whom Ricardou often refers is the surrealist poet and novelist Raymond Roussel. Toward the end of his life, Roussel decided to divulge the devices (he called them "procédés") he had used to create several of his novels and stories. In his *Comment j'ai écrit certains de mes livres*, he confessed that he had frequently begun a story by finding two sentences which, although differing in form by only one letter, had totally different meanings, thanks to semantic polyvalence of each word. The story was elaborated as an itinerary from one of the sentences to the other. The two sentences, which he calls "metagrams," function like rhymes. Like rhyme, this method of composition makes use of phonetic combinations to generate texts. Between the story's metagrams, a device Roussel called the "à peu près" made use of small phonetic displacements whereby words from a familiar sentence served to suggest other similar words. The folk tune "J'ai du bon tabac dans ma tabatière" yielded a lexical reservoir—*jade, tube, onde, aubade* and so on—from which a fiction could be "produced." If Roussel had not finally revealed his *procédé*, it is doubtful that readers would have found the secret generative mechanisms in *Impressions d'Afrique, Locus Solus*, and others of his books. It is worth wondering whether someday Roussel would have had his Saussure, annotating inexplicable patterns in Roussel's works and wondering about his own sanity.

Roussel's system, like Ricardou's, creates only an illusion of motivated language, however. Like Mallarmé before him, but in spite of himself, Roussel ultimately reveals that "un coup de dés n'abolira jamais le hasard," for if a story derives from calculated manipulation of a sentence, that sentence itself is chosen arbitrarily. "Une phrase quelconque," says Roussel. And as he parenthetically but significantly admits about his system, "Encore faut-il savoir l'employer. Et de même qu'avec des rimes on peut faire de bons ou de mauvais vers, on peut, avec ce procédé, faire de bons ou de mauvais ouvrages."[38] In spite of theory, poetic inspiration, subjective intentionality, chance, and other banished categories return, and the question of narrative origin, like etymology, is never resolved but only deferred.

4

Ricardou uses a panoply of terms to designate the presence of a theoretical signified in his fiction. *Mise-en abyme*, "metaphor," "fable," and "myth" are a few that will be encountered along the way. I will use Ricardou's terms when appropriate and to quote him. But in order to group together all his devices that convey a theory by means of an image, I propose here another term: parable. It is a rhetoric of parable, I maintain, that articulates fiction and the metafictional impulse in Ricardou's fiction.

Parable is a term that Ricardou would not like, but that cannot be helped. It is appropriate because it evokes both the ingenious, poetic and puzzle-like aspects of his byzantine storytelling that fascinate his readers and also the didactic moralizing tone that drives them away. Although he repudiates theological and hermeneutic conceptions of writing where a textual corpus embodies an abstract soul, this is exactly what his fictions purport to do. There is no avoiding the fact that Ricardou sets himself up as a sort of self-righteous prophet of the Word. His theories go beyond describing what literary texts and readers *do* in order to prescribe what they *should* do.

But the choice of the term is not intended to belabor this or to suggest a snide put-down of writing that is far richer and more complex. As Frank Kermode tells us, a parable is first of all a comparison, an illustration, or an analogy. Kermode goes on to say that in the Greek *Bible*, *parabolè* is equivalent to Hebrew words meaning "riddle" or "exemplary tale."[39] In exactly these ways, Ricardou's fictions are illustrations of problems in literary theory. Reading his novels is often in part a process of solving riddles, deciphering puzzles and ferreting out hidden structures that elucidate the fiction's theoretical dimension. The word is also related to the English *parabola*, suggesting the way in which Ricardou uses spatial representation: his essays reveal a fondness for diagrams, charts, graphs and geometric configurations, which reappear in the fiction as maps, grids, and structured internal correspondences.

More significant, the word *parable* is related to *parole*. This is understandable if one remembers that in French in addition to being the Word, *parole* is also, for Saussure, a speech act, a production of language from which the rules of language (*langue*) can be deduced. The cyclical relationship between *langue* and *parole* can be seen as a model for Ricardou's parables, which set up a dialectic between theory (the rules and concepts) and the fiction based on those theories but which also acts to transform them. An important difference between Ricardou's writing and the workings of language is that while *langue* can be known only deductively from *parole*, Ricardou's theories are spelled out in his essays and made explicit even within the fictions. And if his fictions are a theater for theory, they function as parables in that they stage a "performance" of theory, both in the sense that transformational grammarians assign to the term and also in the more familiar theatrical sense. "Performance" is more accurate still if we think of music; a fiction is performance of theory in the way a musician "interprets" a musical score. The interpretation does not follow the music, nor is it subordinate: it *is* the music.

We must therefore take care to insist that Ricardou's parables do not hide "secret" meanings or recondite doctrines. By means of the novel's self-reading, both terms of the comparison are on the surface of the text. As a kind of allegory, parable differs from metaphor, according to Fontanier, in that the former

> consiste dans une proposition à double sens, à sens littéral et à sens spirituel tout ensemble, par laquelle on présente une pensée sous l'image d'une autre pensée, propre à la rendre plus sensible et plus frappante que si elle était présentée directement et sans aucune espèce de voile; et cette définition montre assez qu'il ne faut pas la confondre avec la *Métaphore continuée, . . .* qui n'offre jamais qu'un seul vrai sens, le sens figuré.[40]

In Ricardou's parables, then, the story is not a husk to be discarded when the kernel is found. Both the theoretical sense and the imaged sense coexist in the fiction. They are auto-representational in that the latter represents the former.

What I am arguing then is that Ricardou's fictions are illustrations—Kermode calls parables an "incarnation"—of theory. But if this were all, we could just as well (and more easily) read the essays instead. The fact that a parable is "une proposition à double sens" points the way toward what keeps Ricardou's novels fascinating and problematic even when theoretical doctrines and textual devices have been understood. In spite of all the generative strategies, including theory, that justify and explain the text's origin from words and render it transparent, the fiction remains opaque and mysterious. It generates its own excess which cannot be assimilated by the theory it purports to illustrate. This excess can be perceived in the fact that the specific images which *dramatize* theory are not *motivated* by theory. From the point of view of theory, any image would do.

What is particularly superfluous, if one compares the theories to the fiction, is the eroticism in the latter. The representation that is suggested only to be erased for didactic purposes is more often than not the semi-nude body of an alluring female. At the core of Ricardou's parables is the personification or allegorization of Reference as a desirable woman and the relation between reader and text as erotic. The referential illusion is thus described as a tease, a come-on, a seduction. But Ricardou's view of literature is highly puritanical, and his parables are cautionary tales of temptation imperfectly resisted. The coin has two sides: Referentiality is erotic and difficult to repress; at the same time, Eros is referential. The two are resisted together. Ricardou writes to reeducate traditional habits of reading where desire *is* desire for mimesis. In his fiction, the female image is transformed from a desired signified into a signifier in a theoretical formulation. The result is not only a poetics but also an erotics of theory.

It is thus the points where fiction exceeds theory that are the true riddle of Ricardou's fiction. Parable does not *only* incarnate theory. In fact, as in the shifting of an optical illusion, it comes to seem that the fiction is not there to illustrate the theory, but rather that the theory is there to keep the fiction under control. Here is a delicate balance hovering or hesitating between theory and madness. It is not by accident that Ricardou's narrators find themselves menaced by madness in their stringent pursuit of theoretical

coherence and scriptural origin. The hybrid text, half theory, half fiction—
the *mixte*—is in fact a menacing monster posing a riddle that all of New
Novel theory can neither answer nor repress.

In reading Ricardou it therefore becomes necessary to examine, first,
how his fiction represents theory, and secondly, at what points and with
what consequences the contradictions of such a project are no longer
tolerated by the text. The excess generated by the fiction—what is left over
and cannot be appropriated by the theories represented—proves that the
fiction is both transparent and opague. Theory is both right (literature does
not, indeed cannot, express a pre-existing reality; it creates a reality of its
own) and wrong (it cannot account for the text). Even this aporia is recycled
back into the fiction, giving us some of the *oeuvre*'s most striking images of
infinite regress: a striptease where layers (of clothing, of text) are repeatedly
peeled away only to reveal more layers; a character whose desires can never
be satisfied because at the threshhold of fulfillment he must read his own
story from the beginning. Fiction leads to theory leads to fiction leads to
theory . . .

CHAPTER I

Fiction as Illusion: *L'Observatoire de Cannes*

> Je venais de les glisser dans le stéréoscope intérieur à travers lequel, dès que nous ne sommes plus nous-mêmes, dès que, doués d'une âme mondaine, nous ne voulons plus recevoir notre vie que des autres, nous donnons du relief à ce qu'ils ont dit, à ce qu'ils ont fait.
>
> —Proust

L'Observatoire de Cannes[1] is a systematic reeducation in reading. Characters, story and setting are introduced only to be dismantled, revealing novelistic conventions on which they rely. Rather than constructing a believable fictional world, the novel skillfully—and often comically—encourages *dis*belief. The reader's referential expectations are continuously teased and then unmasked, the better to analyse them. Instead of entering an imaginary but recognizable world, we are invited to peer into a series of funhouse mirrors, where our own distorted form tells us that the image is a fiction, and fiction is an illusion.

Ricardou's 1961 novel evokes already-known New Novel techniques and motifs, using them in new ways. Emphasis on description and the visual sense to reveal mental obsessions is indebted to Robbe-Grillet's *La Jalousie*, and the perverse but absent traveler-observer of *L'Observatoire de Cannes* is akin to Mathias of *Le Voyeur*. Presence of a train is no surprise to New Novel fans. But Ricardou exploits both the humorous and the structuring potential of wordplay more extensively than his colleagues. The opening pages of *L'Observatoire de Cannes* describe groups of tourists preparing to board a funicular railcar that will take them to the top of a lookout tower. A series of objects are infused with impatient energy as if ready to traverse the space of the ascent and the book and undergo numerous transformations:

> Un courant d'air traverse la gare dans toute sa longueur. Il entraîne la vapeur de la locomotive en nuages effilochés qui se dissolvent bientôt. Ces nuées blanches effacent cependant ici et là, au passage, les arcades de fer, les murs crépis de jaune, les photographies touristiques et les portes des bureaux de la S.N.C.F.
> L'annonce du départ est émise par les haut-parleurs. (p.11)

The novel is already underway (*en train*) emitting sparks in all directions. Energies generated here recur throughout: "nuages," immediately changes shape to become "nuées," both words hiding the latent "nu(e)," as erotic content is veiled in the entire novel. The clouds erase (or screen) what is behind them, as each photograph will screen the next in an album, and as visual obstacles will frustrate an ardent *voyeur*. Vision cannot penetrate opaque objects (in spite of locutions) any more than we can see through pages to a reality behind. Robbe-Grillet's venetian blinds sliced visual fields into strips in *La Jalousie*; in Ricardou's novel, opaque objects mask, and transparent ones distort or frame. The photos and doors will return numerous times as will the station (*gare*, and perhaps re-*gare/regard*). Train and novel take off almost simultaneously, and will be mutually metaphoric: the traveler thus personifies a reader, the landscape is assimilated to the book, and the train to the process of reading.

1.

L'Observatoire de Cannes has no fixed point of view—it *is* one. The novel is set in a city called Cannes, which closely resembles the city of the same name where Ricardou was born. Its story, insofar as there is one, inheres in the various objects within a precisely delimited field of vision: an observatory offers a sweeping view over a circular panorama, in which no point is privileged and no hierarchy exists. Circumscribed by the horizon on all sides, the novel moves from scene to scene "dans l'ordre du regard," following the gaze of a shifting—and shifty—observing eye.

From the top of the observatory, the landscape is visible in all directions. Upon insertion of a coin into one of four telescopes around the observation deck, the sightseer can focus on a series of spots in which various scenes unfold: to the north are mountains and dense vegetation except in a clearing where a young girl wrings out her clothing after a storm. Also to the north is a water tower on whose door are scratched graffiti. To the east and west are hills. Turning southward, between an apartment building and a Citroën garage, one can see the beach, where characters from the train, or their doubles, engage in the usual seaside activities: swimming, sunbathing, playing beachball and ogling. From the upper observation platform can also be seen the upper and lower stations where vacationers buy tickets and postcards and prepare to board the train. This entire panorama is visible from the observation deck and its four telescopes and from an upper tower, accessible via a spiral staircase. A glassed-in elevator leading from the upper station to the observation deck provides a sweeping southern coastal view. The train and the elevator, both in motion, create an illusion of a moving landscape, what Proust would have called somewhat pejoratively a "défilé cinématographique."

Most of the novel consists of descriptions of scenes visible from one of the points of view on the deck, although it is often difficult or impossible to localize the viewpoint. Several major sequences take place in the train compartment. Although many views are seen by the naked eye, most are framed by telescope, window, camera, or scuba mask. Such framing has the advantage of eliminating the eye's movement and reducing the panorama to a series of more manageable "stills." Ricardou recognized this advantage in his analysis of Claude Ollier's *Description panoramique d'un quartier moderne*, in which segments of a panorama are reflected in a window whose position changes periodically.[2] Ricardou sees this strategy as a compromise between two mutually exclusive possibilities for rendering the panoramic: enumeration, which renders the movement but not the objects, and description of objects, which fails to account for their mobility. The moving window offers mobility analyzed into fixed but arbitrary components. *L'Observatoire de Cannes* plays with similar solutions. The panorama appears through the optical devices in successive immobilized "frames." Conversely, pages of a photograph album, when flipped rapidly, create the illusion of movement. A further consequence of these treatments of the panoramic and the problem of movement is that having eliminated the movement of eye and object as it might occur in reality, the text is freer to deploy its own kind of mobility, and even to impose it on the story.

There are recognizable characters in *L'Observatoire de Cannes*, although they are nameless, and they tend to overlap and blend, or split into doubles. Six characters occupy a train compartment. A young man and woman sit face to face, entirely preoccupied with each other. He wears a white shirt, she a pink lace-edged dress and her dark hair in a knot at the nape of her neck. There is also "un touriste d'un certain âge, la figure rouge, le crâne chauve" (p.13). He can be identified by these features, his camera, carried on a strap around his neck, and by his wrinkled raincoat. A little blonde girl is in the charge of a "grosse dame," apparently her mother or grandmother, who wears a blue dress covering a red bathing suit. In one passage the bald tourist, the little girl and the fat lady appear to form a family. The most important character, however, judging by sheer number of pages devoted to her and her avatars, is a "jeune fille blonde" dressed in a semi-transparent white blouse, green striped slacks and yellow sandals. Beneath this outfit, she wears a green and white checkered bikini swimsuit. She is further identified by her photo album and a green canvas beachbag she carries.

Our training in the conventions of reading teaches us to sort out the characters in a novel, to keep them separate, to recognize them when they reappear and to assume they continue to exist while the text deals with other things. All these habits are brought into question by *L'Observatoire de Cannes*. Characters have no names. Their attributes (in the iconographic sense) are of singular importance, for it is only by these that we recognize them when they reappear. Little besides clothing, the green beachbag and certain repeated descriptions links this "jeune voyageuse" with her transformations into the "jeune fille" of the photographs and of a striptease sequence, a "jeune cover-girl", "jeune Scandinave" and so on. The word "jeune," like her beach gear, induces the reader to compose a sketchy character from the reappearances of a figure who is different (the designation changes with each situation) but the same. (Repetition of adjectives, descriptions, objects and the definite article indicate that we have seen her before). She and the others are not characters in any usual sense. Rather, they are allegorical figures in a parable of reading, and this is where their significance lies.

In addition to the six characters in the train compartment, there is an empty seat, reserved by the beachbag which occupies it. French train compartments invariably contain eight places: six characters plus an empty seat leaves one place unaccounted for. In a darkened moving train, with no indication of anyone looking in from the corridor, it is likely that the eighth spot will be occupied by the "point of view," a narrator. The existence of a perceiving consciousness in the novel is undeniable, although our knowledge of the narrator is entirely mediated by the visual field onto which his preoccupations are projected. All aspects of this reduced and hypothetical narrator must be deduced from what is seen. Neither absence nor plenitude, the narrator does not bear even the minimal tags of characterhood required in this novel. The wandering gaze is initially no more than the logical consequence of the narration, as a view implies a viewer. This postulate I choose to call the narrator-eye. Olga Bernal's remarks about the narrator of *La Jalousie* are equally applicable to *L'Observatoire de Cannes*. Robbe-Grillet's novel, Bernal explains,

> . . . n'a pas de véritable narrateur. D'abord parce que ce récit n'est raconté ni à la troisième ni à la première personne. L'extrême subjectivité du récit appellerait le 'je' narratif, ce qui pourtant n'est pas le cas dans ce roman. Mais le roman ne se raconte pas non plus à partir d'un 'il'. C'est un roman qui n'est raconté ni à la première ni à la troisième personne. C'est donc un roman où il n'y a pas de personne qui raconte . . . A la place du 'je' et du 'il' traditionnels, nous avons donc un 'regard narrateur'.[3]

La Jalousie was perhaps, as Bernal states, the representation of a passion in the New Novel. *L'Observatoire de Cannes* is narrated by a *regard* in a much more literal sense. The eye and what it sees are the novel's material points of departure. And Ricardou's novel finds vision productive because of its capacity to mislead. Its narrator-eye (often an "I" in other kinds of novels) is itself an illusion or mirage of our reading—a convergence of rays (repetitions, obsessions, assumptions) on a point where something seems to materialize but is never satisfactorily confirmed and which may even disappear.

Vision and visual distortion are translated onto the page by means of description. Conventions of reading are undermined when they are conveyed in terms of visual perception. The world of *L'Observatoire de Cannes* is seen through various optical devices—camera, telescope, windows in a moving train—which frame and distort objects, revealing the ways our eyes adjust to conform to what we assume is "reality." If the novel's central metafictional message is that fiction is illusion, this message is illustrated and developed into a theory by unmasking the manipulations of description. So crucial is the modulation of description to an understanding of *L'Observatoire de Cannes* that Philippe Sollers has said of Ricardou's novel that "la description trouve là son épopée."[4]

Description as a component of any writing is discussed by Gérard Genette in an important article entitled "Frontières du récit."[5] A distinction between description and its traditional counterpart, narration, appears to exist even at the level of the sentence, a sort of micro-*récit* where verbs indicate actions and nouns refer to people or things. Genette convincingly argues, however, that "pure" narration and "pure" description are impossible. On the one hand, any verb hides a potential action. Description can never shed action entirely unless perhaps by eliminating all but the single verb "to be." Even other rhetorical equivalents of *être* stray dangerously close to becoming events: *se trouver, être posé, apparaître*, etc. Perhaps the most successful attempt at pure description is Robbe-Grillet's short story "Le Mannequin."[6] Viewed as a struggle to repress latent story potential of verbs, this five-page description is quite a show of acrobatic dexterity. It is doubtful, however, that even Robbe-Grillet could persevere long enough to produce an entire novel similarly composed.

Narration in turn becomes description as soon as a noun appears; mere denomination is an "amorce de description," says Genette. If "La marquise sortit à cinq heures" delimits an action and launches a story on a temporal trajectory, it also unfolds a describable topology. "Marquise" is already more descriptive than a less colorful label, "female human" for example. Even the verb *sortit* itself harbors potential for description of a house, a destination or a motive. According to Genette, however, description, although "plus indispensable que la narration" remains subordinate in the sense that it is ornamental and dependent on the imperatives of recounted events. "La description est tout naturellement *ancilla narrationis*, esclave toujours nécessaire mais toujours soumise, jamais émancipée." (Genette, p.60)

The New Novel's interest in exploring the possibility of description "emancipated" from story is well known. Ricardou, with typical zeal, proclaims the necessity of endless description and eye-crossing detail as a method of training (or punishing) the reader who, addicted to the hypnotic effects of reading, skips the descriptions to find out what *happens*. Genette expresses scepticism about this aspect of the New Novel; contemporary writers attempting to "libérer le mode descriptif de la tyrannie du récit," he claims, are actually doing no more than generating stories from descriptions. They amount to un effort pour constituer un récit (une *histoire*) par le moyen presque exclusif de descriptions imperceptiblement modifiées de page en page, ce qui peut passer à la fois pour une promotion spectaculaire de la fonction descriptive, et pour une confirmation éclatante de son irréductible finalité narrative. (Genette, p.59)

The language used in description is indistinguishable from that used for narration; any such dichotomy is based on differences between types of signified realities. There is, however, an important distinction to be made regarding the way signifiers correspond to the events or objects presented. That is, description and narration produce qualitatively different spaces between the *récit* and the visible world.

La différence la plus significative serait peut-être que la narration restitue, dans la succession temporelle de son discours, la succession également temporelle des événements, tandis que la description doit moduler dans le successif la représentation d'objets simultanés et juxtaposés dans l'espace. (Genette, p. 60)

Rendering an object, a description cannot avoid conferring on that object a characteristic it lacks: time. An apple may be simultaneously round, red and delicious, but enumeration of these features decomposes the apple into parts and attributes. By tacit agreement, the reader reassembles in its simultaneity what the description has taken apart. This is one of the conventions of reading Ricardou intends to unmask. Only in repressing awareness of this convention *as convention* dare we say that a written apple bears any resemblance at all to the real one.

Various techniques have been used to make reality fit the exigencies of description, since the reverse is often impossible. Experiments have capitalized on the spatial dimension of the page to represent objects. Apollinaire's *Calligrammes* and Maurice Roche's arrangements are attempts to compensate for the temporality of the *récit*. The fact remains that reading time has not been altered, and thus seeing and reading still diverge. In an article entitled "De natura *fictionis*" Ricardou points to a solution Flaubert found for Emma Bovary's wedding cake, described via what amounts to a flashback to a bakery. Parts of the cake are named in the order they might have been added to the structure, Ricardou notes; temporal sequence, indicated by words like "d'abord," "puis," and "enfin" reveal that the cake is being *narrated*. Thus the "referential dimension" (our mental image of a cake) and the "literal dimension" attain an equilibrium where neither totally obscures the other.[7]

Genette and others before him have examined the *récit* in order to assess its aptitude for representing, thus assuming the primacy of the represented world. In theory and practice, Ricardou goes beyond Genette in exploring the features characterizing description. Ricardou does not deny that descriptions have springboards in the real: anything from a cigarette package to an erotic fantasy or especially a theoretical problem visually conceived or allegorized can serve to launch writing. Once underway, however, language can create its own fictions.

Instead of attempting to render simultaneity, Ricardou lets description become narration, and he refuses to permit his reader to recompose the objects he offers. If description frames, fragments or confers temporality on objects, the story incorporates these deformations, inducing us to see frames, fragments and temporal progression. Few characters in traditional novels, for example, are actually dismembered by the fragmenting effects of description, but this is exactly the sort of thing that comes to pass in Ricardou's fiction. His objects, when written, take up time, thus attaining the status of events and erasing distinctions between narration and description. To allow us to imagine otherwise would be to permit the text to disappear. Subverting our habits of reading for the referential illusion involves making us conscious of our attempts to adjust the words we read to correspond to a known reality.

2

L'Observatoire de Cannes opens with two epigraphs, both pointing to the notion of illusion. The first is a dictionary definition: "Illusion d'optique, erreur du sens de la vue sur l'état des corps." Contrasted to this conception of illusion as error is a reminder from Paulhan that perceived reality may itself be no less illusory: "Que dire du cas où notre idée implique en soi l'illusion, et ne supporte, pour ainsi dire, point d'autre contenu?"

The most familiar definition of the word *illusion* as perceptual error is reinforced and enriched by its etymological origin in the Latin verb *ludere*, to play. As a sphere of human activity, *ludere* differs from the French word *jeu* in important ways, as John Huizenga indicates:

> We should observe that *jocus, jocari* in the special sense of joking and jesting does not mean play proper in classical Latin. Though *ludere* may be used for the leaping of fishes, the fluttering of birds and the plashing of water, its etymology does not appear to lie in the sphere of rapid movement, flashing, etc., but in that of non-seriousness, and particularly of 'semblance' or 'deception'...The idea of 'feigning' or 'taking on the semblance of' seems to be uppermost. The compounds *alludo, colludo, illudo* all point in the direction of the unreal, the illusory. . .
>
> It is remarkable that *ludus*, as the general term for play, has not only not passed into the Romance languages but has left hardly any traces there, so far as I can see.[8]

The French word *illusion* as Ricardou uses it reveals those traces. Deception or semblance is certainly apparent in *L'Observatoire de Cannes*, as is the validation of the illusory or unreal. There are several explicit references to phenomena of optical illusion. The novel falls under the rubric of *ludere* insofar as it sees itself as separate from ordinary reality. It evolves in a clearly delimited space; it involves voluntary submission to arbitrary formal rules which give it its own reality. *L'Observatoire de Cannes* also participates in the larger definition of *ludere*, Huizenga's "fluttering," "plashing" and "leaping." These are movements within defined limits, in the sense that a rope has a certain amount of "slack" or "give," or focus on an object seen through a lens may be adjusted. At the limits of its range the rope breaks, the object risks slipping totally out of focus and becoming fuzzy or ambiguous, language loses intelligibility.

The lens example is not gratuitous. Roger Shattuck has studied Proust's use of optical imagery as a metaphor for time. Proust's memories come into full relief only when seen side by side with significant analogous images from the present. Similarly, Shattuck argues, the two slightly disparate images offered by our two eyes (or two lenses of binoculars), are the source of what is called "depth perception," or perspective. The images differ because the two lenses, although focused on the same object, are slightly separated in space. "Two slightly different versions of the same 'object' from our two eyes are combined subjectively with the effect of relief," says Shattuck,[9] explaining the basis for Proust's optical metaphor which appears in the epigraph to this chapter. Such a combination of two-dimensional images is an adjustment we make automatically because we know that real space exists in three dimensions.

According to Ricardou, material or psychological "depth" in a novel is part of its referential illusion. Play with depth perception and with figure-ground ambiguity in *L'Observatoire de Cannes* constitutes the novel's parable of theory. Illusion, including all of Huizenga's definitions of *ludere*, is both form (first epigraph) and content (second epigraph) of *L'Observatoire de Cannes*. Peering through the two O's in *L'Observatoire* on the cover, we find two disparate definitions of illusion. While producing an "in-depth" experiment on a theoretical issue (vision, reading and illusion), the novel systematically withdraws the possibilities of depth we habitually take for granted. Although not as concerned as Proust with the reality of memory, Ricardou uses an optical framework to demystify two of the major conventions contributing to the traditional suspension of disbelief in the novel: Shattuck's "cinematographic principle" appears in a sequence where the "jeune fille" flips quickly through the album, producing in the photographs an illusion of movement; his "stereoptic principle" is demonstrated wherever the text plays with illusions of depth.[10] The Greek root *stereos* means "solid." Three dimensional space, as emblematic of realism, is the primary target of Ricardou's deconstruction.

The notion of optical illusion is clearly applicable to the written word if we redefine it in semiotic terms. An optical illusion is a visual sign in which the signifier hesitates or vacillates among multiple signifieds. In other words, optical illusion is to the visible much as semantic polyvalence is to the *lisible*. Both exploit a particular kind of ambiguity to produce their effects.

The above figure can serve as a first example of optical illusion. Here two possible perceptions of figure and ground allow more than one meaning. When the shaded areas are seen as foreground, the figure shows two identical faces: the lines are seen as foreheads, noses, lips and chins. When the white area takes prominence, the same lines are seen as the arbitrary symmety of a vase. Thanks to careful framing, nothing permits a decision as to which, the vase or the faces, the figure "really" represents, nor is it possible to establish a hierarchy of the two. While they coexist in the image, it is impossible to see both simultaneously. E. H. Gombrich explains that when we are confronted with equivocal images such as the one above, it is easy to discover both readings, but less easy to know what happens when we switch from one interpretation to the other; the shape is somehow transformed as we stare at it. What he finds compelling in such tricks of illusion is their "power of metamorphosis."[11]

It is just this power of metamorphosis that New Novelists exploit by creating, then exposing the workings of semantic illusion. Robbe-Grillet, for example, uses ambiguity in *La Jalousie*, whose title evokes the emotion of the narrator-husband spying on his wife and the blinds on the windows through which he surreptitiously watches her. But as Bernal points out, and unlike the figure above, the two meanings reinforce each other: both the blinds and jealousy are distorting filters through which the narrator observes.[12] Ricardou also establishes multiple possibilities for certain signifiers in *L'Observatoire de Cannes*, but his illusions do resemble the figure in that their various interpretations exclude each other, and he is thus able to point to the illusion *as illusion*. A fresco map of Cannes in the train station is marred by "une trace foncée, indéfinissable, sur la plage." Like the ambiguous spots of *La Jalousie*, this mark is seen as a variety of different objects depending on context: it also appears as a shirt thrown on a rock and as an octopus in the sun. Such objects, allowing the imagination to create optical illusions, also serve as transitions from one narrative unit to the next, with the effect that apparent continuity is built on the shifting of an illusion.

In other cases an identical description returns and materializes a different object at each repetition. The words "dentelle," "dentelé," and "mousse," and the descriptions that contain them refer to lace on the young wife's dress, the bather's teeth, or foam on the waves. As a result, when any one of these signifieds appears in the fiction, the others are evoked obliquely. In a network of mutual metaphors related according to Ricardou's principle of "qui se ressemble s'assemble," these descriptions form a circuit in which each is both signifier and signified in relation to the others.

Similarly, a single description serves to evoke a bather on the beach and a photograph of the same bather. The rule of the game is to maintain the ambiguity as long as possible. The goal is, as always, to subvert the illusion of reality. Length of the narrative sequences helps obscure our memory of the level of reality being described, until a final jolt brings the edges of the frame back into view. Division into chapters arbitrarily breaks the continuity of the description, further blurring the "frame of reference."

An example of this occurs in chapters XVI to XVIII. The fat lady, holding her little girl tightly by the hand, selects vacation postcards to be sent to friends. One of the cards depicts a young girl (*the* young girl) writing postcards on the beach. Another shows "une énorme dame, en maillot rouge" watching a "fillette blonde" on the beach. Six pages of description of the two scenes follow, through two chapter breaks. A dramatic incident occurs near where the girl sits: an adolescent, emerging from the water, finds a rusty tin can on the sand. An octopus crawls out of the can. A crowd assembles to watch the young man pick up the creature, rinse it off in the sea and replace it on the rock. When the crowd begins to disperse, the adolescent, "comme pour ranimer leur intérêt," (and the reader's) seizes the beast and bites it squarely between the eyes. The fat lady, however, doesn't seem to have noticed all the hubbub. Then this:

> En observant plus attentivement le maillot rouge de la mère, on constate qu'il est fait d'une simple pièce de carton amovible, terminée par une languette insérée dans une fente de la carte postale.
> Soulevé par un ongle, le maillot découvre toute une série de minuscules vues. (p.89)

The personage examining the card and the pictured fat lady are, it turns out, one and the same. The falsely innocent "on" and the indefinite article for "ongle" help maintain the illusion of difference. The passage continues: "La dame commence alors à déployer sur ses genoux, sur sa robe bleue piquetée de pois blancs, la longue bande de papier plié en accordéon" (pp. 89-90).

Several conclusions emerge from this round of trickery. First, it is clear that the displacement of the frame is designed to provoke a suspension of disbelief, that is, a progressive shifting, under the guise of continuity, from postcard reality to "real" people. At the outset we know the description refers to a postcard: it is named; we can see its edges. As the point of view comes closer, the frame disappears, and the reader enters the scenes depicted on the cards. From sentence to sentence the progression is logical, so it does not seem impertinent that the scenes should become animated. Since description and narration overlap, object risks becoming event at each verb, and there is slippage from description appropriate to a postcard to description of activity impossible at that level of reality.

Description of another postcard photo—of a young woman writing postcards—creates similar transformations and transgressions of logic. At first the sentences, full of suggested activity, are nevertheless devoid of actions: "les pieds, en extension complète, sont enfouis sous un dome de sable," and "les mollets sont ramenés sous les cuisses . . . elle écrit." Past participles used adjectivally, passive constructions, the present tense all produce a description hovering on the threshold of movement. Finally, "la tête se relève" (pp.84-85) transporting us imperceptibly from the improbable to the impossible, and we can no longer be contemplating a postcard. Ambiguity about the level of reality confers double meaning on further details: the girl's laughter is "silencieux" because no sound emerges, but also because it is a pictured smile.

A further complication helps obscure the shift in the description away from the postcard. The scene involving the young girl interrupts the sequence with the fat lady. The logic of a "real" scene is imposed on pictured ones. Although actions can interrupt and overlap, two postcards cannot; thus when the fat lady from one card fails to notice the octopus in the other, it is implied that she *could* have noticed. Postcard logic has been transgressed and the frames broken. It is the description which operates this metamorphosis step by step. Transformation is arrested when the text reminds us that the fat lady is made of cardboard. This unexpected and comic turn highlights several of Ricardou's metatextual preoccupations regarding characters. The "grosse dame" on the card is an "être en papier," and we are not allowed to forget it for long. The comedy becomes subtle slapstick on the next page; like Queneau's Icarus, Ricardou's paper people exist in a world which has its own laws. With the appearance on the scene of a ticket-taker, twisted bodies and tortured syntax materialize the reaction of these special characters to a most formidable weapon—a paper punch.

The scene's function as parable can be heard this time as a chuckle directed at the "real" woman unfolding scenes hidden in the bathing suit of her paper double. As a kind of comic parody of the introspective novel, she recalls Valéry's remarks about the silliness of assuming that characters had hidden depths:

> Quelle confusion d'idées cachent des locutions comme 'Roman psychologique.' 'Vérité de ce caractère', 'Analyse'! etc.
>   —Pourquoi ne pas parler du système nerveux de la Joconde et du foie de la Vénus de Milo?[13]

Here, "depth" is strategically transformed into the inner folds of paper surfaces.

The description of the women, and indeed the entire sequence, is an example of illusion as I have defined it. The signifier (the narration itself) sends us alternately to the "real" woman and the postcard one, with neither winning final supremacy over the other. Except relative to each other, neither is real, and we are left with illusion as the only content of perception.

A second figure will illustrate another important type of optical illusion:

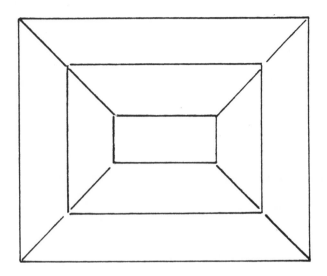

Here too, the same figure (sign) can be read two ways. The eye can perceive a series of concentric squares on a flat page or the illusion of three-dimensional space. Unlike the figure-ground ambiguity, however, there exists a hierarchy of meanings: clearly depth is illusion. This is precisely the trick used by painters to create spatial perspective. This model of optical illusion, like the other, is applicable to *L'Observatoire de Cannes* in discussing both theory and structure, and thus, here again, vision is a model for reading.

Illusions of perspective serve to illustrate the classical conception of *mise-en-abyme*. I will have much more to say in subsequent chapters about Ricardou's refinement of the concept. *Mise-en-abyme* in its most straightforward form (as demonstrated in *L'Observatoire de Cannes*) consists of a special type of repetition: it is a reduced model of a larger version of the same, in which it is usually contained. The optical illusion above shows a square within a square; internal reduplication continues in a logical sequence, each square containing another which is the same (also a square) but also different (smaller). Although Gide was the first to use the term *mise-en-abyme* for what Bruce Morrissette renames "interior duplication," the phenomenon is much older: one is likely to think of the baroque play-within-a-play such as can be found in Shakespeare's *A Midsummer Night's Dream* or Corneille's *L'Illusion Comique*. Gide's discussion refers to optics; he mentions in particular Velasquez' painted mirrors and interior reflections in *Las Meninas*.[14] Use of *mis-en-abyme* usually has two major functions, one structural, the other theoretical. As a form of repetition, it organizes the relationship of parts to the whole *récit*. In addition, it articulates fiction and theory, as the smaller version usually offers clues for a reading of the larger containing version.

In *L'Observatoire de Cannes*, consistent with the overall project of the book, examples of internal reduplication abound as illustrations of visual phenomena, especially optical illusions. The multiplication of objects at progressively reduced scale, establishing the proportions of the whole, uses symmetry to highlight the literal dimension of the novel. The most obvious examples organize the geography:

—The Lérin archipelago, seen from the south side of the observatory, consists of two islands: "une première île, d'un vert sombre, précède, dans l'ordre du regard, une seconde île de proportions semblables, mais plus réduite" (p.16).

—From the lower station, looking up at the obsevatory building, the tourist sees two platforms: above the main observation deck, "la seconde plate-forme, et son socle haut de sept à huit mètres, constituent une tour plus petite" (pp.15-16).

These two features of the landscape determine the "ordre du regard" itself. Perceiving two elements in a series, the eye learns to look beyond the second term for a third version, even more reduced: "le regard, machinalement se porte plus loin, comme s'il escomptait découvrir une troisième île, semblable encore et encore plus petite" (p. 17). The *mise-en-abyme* is thus a didactic tool, training the eye to look for structure. By establishing a parallel between disparate geographic features (island and towers) the reader produces a structured or metaphoric reading, what Ricardou calls a "lecture virtuelle."

The visible world and the *lisible* share the same systematic arrangement. The tourist can easily identify points of the landscape on a ceramic map affixed to the observatory guardrail near the telescopes: "à ce paysage [the surrounding geography] correspond exactement un paysage semblable, factice et plus petit" (p.17). Obeying the habit inculcated by the two examples above, we are encouraged to look for a third version, which can be found in the book itself, where the pictorial aspect of the map disappears completely, and we are given the landscape to *read*. A requisite of the Gidian definition of *mise-en-abyme* lacking in the first two cases above (islands and towers)—namely that the larger version contain the smaller—is met here: the book contains the landscape as a fiction. Between a described scene and an actual landscape, the map is an intermediate state between reading and seeing. Rather than establishing a hierarchy of reality and description, however, and thanks to a structured series of *mises-en-abyme*, each is here at the origin of the other.

If we remember that a single scene is described from "reality" (seen through a telescope) and from flat surfaces such as photographs, postcards and the written page, the juxtaposition of similar objects at progressively reduced scale demonstrates a further feature of the illusion structure we are discussing. On a flat surface, distances are represented by means of adjustments in size. To represent a tree-lined alley, for example, the painter skilled in the art of illusion will show identical trees graduated in size, in order for the smaller ones to appear more distant. Visual perception of depth in painting is one of the conventions of the medium. Parallel lines intersect in the distance: visual perspective can be schematized in a triangular configuration, as the two eyes focus on a single object. In *L'Observatoire de Cannes* a single description is repeated in reference to a real scene and a pictured one. This fact leads to a paradox: in the real scenes, more distant objects appear smaller. However, according to the laws of perspective, on postcards and photographs, smaller objects appear more distant. Without clear reference to a frame indicating level of reality, we cannot know whether a branch, for example, or a building in a series appears small because it is far away (as in reality) or appears far away because it is small (as in a painting). The two illusions are mutually reinforcing and have the effect of undermining the representation of depth. Even in the so-called "real" scenes, depth perception is denied in many cases. Through a camera sight, through the observatory telescopes, the observer peers with one eye, as the text specifies. Since it is binocular vision that permits perspective, the landscape, losing its relief, comes to resemble the postcard. From real to postcard to scriptural landscape marks a progression away from depth.

3

The many abyssal structures in *L'Observatoire de Cannes* are somewhat dizzying. What is more, the landscape just discussed has parallels in a proliferation of other reduplications: the 360-degree panorama visible from the observatory's four telescopes finds its miniature analogy in a postcard display rack—a rotating stand offering in each of its quadrants paper views of the same landscape. Mountains to the west face hills in the east, and the sea to the south is reflected by a smaller body of water to the north: a water tower. This water tower, particularly its metal door, repays closer examination in a discussion of *mise-en-abyme*, because it offers the most complete guide to reading available in Ricardou's fiction.

The spectator's gaze, focused through the observatory's northern telescope, pauses to scrutinize in detail a multitude of graffiti scratched with a sharp instrument on the painted door, revealing the metal beneath. Here is the way the graffiti appear to perception, before the eye begins to seek pattern:

> Les lettres, signes, chiffres, dessins—obscenités, coeurs, initiales . . .—, aucun emplacement vierge n'étant plus libre depuis longtemps, ont été gravés les uns par-dessus les autres, se chevauchant, s'entrecroisant, se complétant, les plus anciens graphismes, errodés, oxydés, étant presque indiscernables, recouverts par les sillons plus récents, plus nets, plus tranchés, qui seront visibles encore pendant quelque temps. (pp.61-62)

If we keep in mind the overlapping roles of tourist and reader/writer established from the first page of the novel, it is not surprising to find this metaphor for the book within the book.

As the many "touristes de passage" leave their written traces on the door, each layer of graffiti complicates the layers below by contributing new lines to previous designs, or by obscuring old patterns so as to make them unrecognizable. The buildup of successive layers—paint and then superimposed designs—fails to produce even the effect of depth. That the graffiti have been added over a long history is stressed by the accumulated effect of phrases like "depuis longtemps," "plus anciens graphismes," "plus récents," and "qui seront visibles encore pendant quelque temps." Past, present and future are represented on a two-dimensional surface.

Although the graffiti are obscured by subsequent scratchings and by erosion and oxidation—time made visible—it is significant that none is removed. The result is an intertextual archive of sorts, where all traces are permanently recorded. Similarly, the book itself must be seen as a "volume" composed of superimposed surfaces. Reading these pages, one perceives pattern in the form of memories of previous pages or as traces of earlier writers. The door is a new patterned surface produced as a collage by a series of scriptors. Similar "holes" cut in Ricardou's text reveal intertextual fragments of predecessors. The logical consequence of this collective collage is the fading of the author as an identifiable personage, the emergence of the text as surface.

The text goes on to describe manners of organizing or reading the graffiti. In particular,

Il y a, par exemple, à mi-hauteur, toute une série de gros hiéroglyphes d'une facture assez particulière, de formes diverses, au tracé très appuyé. Il est impossible, à première vue, de déceler les préoccupations auxquelles ils répondent et l'imagination, tout à loisir, peut leur prêter les significations les plus variées. (p.62)

This group of hieroglyphs includes: a cylinder to which has been added "une ligne ondulée qui fait songer à une cordelière;" a rectangle; two lines forming a reversed "V" which might represent "les deux jambes d'un pantalon" or "le schéma d'une tente indienne;" two ovals "semblables à des haricots, à des raquettes, à des semelles de spartiates;" a figure formed from two triangles that meet at their angles, and a third triangle pointing downwards; and a more enigmatic figure, "un écheveau inextricable de lignes entrecroisées figurant peut-être des pistes embrouillées dans une forêt, les plis d'un corsage froissé ou des tourbillons d'écume autour d'un groupe de roches." Finally, an eighth figure, not a geometric form, represents a pocketknife, probably the one used to scratch the graffiti and which can thus be read as a signature.

Each item begins as a geometric shape, a pure form which can be named. Describing the shapes, however, inevitably begins to generate stories; immediately, the forms refer to a fiction and become categories of organization. A cylinder evokes a beachbag as soon as "ligne" becomes "cordelière." The imagination transforms geometry into fable by means of

phrases like "fait songer à" and "semblable à." The inverted "V" recalls
the photo album propped open or suggests the legs of the pretty young
baigneuse. Other forms are merely named, but it is clear that the reader is to
participate actively in the construction of the fiction by filling in the blanks
and completing comparisons. Photographs, postcards, windows form a
group of rectangular objects. Besides evoking wrinkled fabric and paths
crossing in a forest, the tangled lines also call to mind the checkered
pattern on the girl's bikini and scribbles drawn on a postcard by the young
wife. Triangles are almost omnipresent; under this rubric belong the sails as
seen on the horizon, the course for the regata, the beach itself, articles of
laundry on a line and a whole series of erotic indices including the neckline
of the young girl's blouse, which widens as she unbuttons it, as well as her
green and white bikini, composed of "les deux triangles de la piece
supérieure du maillot de bain et enfin le slip, triangle lui-même, en tissu à
carreaux verts et blancs, ourlé des minuscules festons de la dentelle
blanche" (p.31). Finally, the octagonal distribution of the eight figures
recalls the eight ball players, the directions of the compass, the shape of the
observatory, and other eight-sided or octopartite objects, like the octopus,
as well as the frequent occurrences of the number eight itself.

A final paragraph describing the door remarks that several items in the
series seem to have been crossed out. This observation suggests the
hypothesis that

> ces huit dessins font partie d'un jeu scout, d'un jeu de piste,
> d'une course au trésor. Chaque graphisme représenterait sché-
> matiquement différents objets à chercher, le couteau à lames
> multiples étant le trésor lui-même, caché dans les environs de la
> tour. Les biffures obliques indiqueraient alors, au passage, que
> les premiers trésors ont été découverts . . . (pp. 63-64).

If the author of the drawings is left unidentified, the process and tools used
for producing them are elaborately presented. First, the eye arranged and
selected designs in an octagonal motif and the imagination lent meaning to
each of the figures. Here, in a subsequent movement of the description, the
imagination undertakes a critical interpretation. The suggestion that the
graffiti are clues in a treasure hunt or signposts in a quest invites the reader to be
an active seeker or researcher. The treasure is the knife itself—not the
anonymous pretextual origin of the graffiti, but the one which appears on the

door, the eighth angle of the octogon. It is worth noting that this quest is not a religious one; no transcendent or extratextual truths will be revealed. Rather, reading the signs is to gain entrance into the special space of *ludere*. "Jeu de piste," "jeu scout," "course au trésor," "caché," indicate the rules of the game.

In this process, it is important to note that the intentions of an absent scriptor are not known, and so it is the viewer/reader who is supposed to name and imagine—in other words produce—the story. The suggestion is that the reader group the objects scattered throughout the book according to their form. Since pure geometric shapes have no referential meaning, the reader must read interrelationships by means of the signifier alone. Grouping scattered objects according to their shape, Ricardou's *lecture virtuelle*, is a process of metaphorization; elements belonging to the same geometric classification become mutually metaphoric. The fact that the elements are geometric forms as opposed, say, to numerical concepts, taxes the *eye* to assemble them, making pattern out of apparent disorder. The eye alone cannot suffice to produce fiction, however; an imagination is necessary to add pattern to random events recorded by the eye.

But whose imagination? If we ask where the story comes from, the answer is supposed to be: the reader. We are not that reader, however, and cannot take credit for the stories produced any more than we are responsible for the anonymous act of vandalism by which the signs were carved in the first place. The novel offers a parable of *how* but not of *what* to read. Claiming to be generated by its reader, the text begs the question of its origin.

4

It is possible, however, to identify the preoccupations that inform this intratextual self-reading. Although the narration describes only objects within a limited visual field, whether sweeping the panorama or zooming in to focus on a young woman disrobing, its gaze, though disembodied, is neither objective nor dispassionate. Illusion structures furnish a context conducive to mistaken perception, which, much like an inkblot test, serves to identify a narrator. Selection and repetition reveal his preoccupations. Obsessive return to the young girl, for example, and to details of her clothing and body, imply a masculine perspective. A character with a camera confirms this hunch when he displaces the narrator from his post at the telescope in one episode, calling him "monsieur" (p. 35).

The narrator almost names himself on this and several other occasions. Looking downward from the upper platform at the tourist who is focusing his camera upwards, we read

> L'Observatoire entier doit figurer dans le viseur, ou, simplement, peut-être, l'ultime plateforme, et, penché sur la grille de fer . . . (p. 23, Ricardou's punctuation)

Thus ends chapter four. If we needed any further confirmation of the sexual identity of the narrator, the masculine adjective supplies it. Ricardou's ellipsis is a safety device, like the iron railing, that retains the narrator who risks and avoids self-designation as he avoids falling over the balcony into the camera of the other *voyeur*. Instead of designating the protagonist in mirror confrontation, we read only three periods. These do, in fact, name the narrator, who is no more than a *point de vue* and who is here suspended over the rail, a quite literal *point de suspension*. The humor of this scene is important. Equally significant is the fact that in a visually structured world where naming and seeing are mutually dependent, only the object can be named—the eye (subject) cannot see itself.

The eye does, however, see doubles of itself in various mirrors. Characters contemplate themselves on postcards or reflected in shop windows. The fat lady unfolds her paper self. The young man and woman of the train compartment gaze lovingly into each other's eyes and stroll together through the novel accompanied by an endless parade of reflexive verbs. They provide a vivid example of the internal self-reflection of the New Novel. Referring again to Shattuck's analysis of Proust's optical imagery, it is as if a reverse procedure occurs in *L'Observatoire de Cannes*: if Marcel inserted two similar experiences into a mental stereoscope in order to experience time more fully in a single in-depth image, Ricardou's narration removes the cards from the machine (also known as a stereopticon—or "stereOb. de Cannes" possibly?). Ricardou's novel thus contains a multitude of paired, almost identical flat images. Playing with the same properties of binocular vision that interested Proust, Ricardou's doubles thus frustrate traditional readings and the desire for coherent personalities and lifelike depth.

Writing about Robbe-Grillet and metaphor, Ricardou states the impossibility of describing an uninhabited world. Writing always presents "le monde orienté par un projet, un point de vue dans les deux sens du terme et en même temps ce projet lui-même." Objects betray what Ricardou calls the "infraconsciousness" of an implied but necessary narrator.[15] In *L'Observatoire de Cannes*, the narration's infraconsciousness reveals latent violence and eroticism which can be read in the lexical choices and in mechanisms of projection, dreamlike displacement and condensation. The text manifests characteristics that cannot, though clearly present, be fixed to any character, however, either as attributes or as projections. Banal objects such as twigs and rocks bear the most erotically charged descriptions. Attributes circulate from one character to another. Personal subjects and objects of desire and of violence are progressively erased or overlap and blend irretrievably with other signifieds. Such shifts have the purpose and effect of forcing the reader to examine desire and violence in the text rather than in the characters.

The graffiti were scratched with a knife—writing is graphically associated with potential violence via that description. Seeing can be violent too, a photograph ("une prise de vue") a form of rape. The only two violent events in the story (one could say the only two events of any sort) are trivial or comic. The scene in which the adolescent bites an octopus is surprising and grotesque, but has as little aftermath as preparation, and serves largely to shock us into forgetting the level of reality described, and to demonstrate the extremes of the narration-description continuum. When the fat lady slaps the little girl, the event is rendered sinister by the elaborate melodrama surrounding it, yet it too is a short and isolated incident. This is the only violence that occurs in the book, and yet the effect is so strong that one critic has called *L'Observatoire de Cannes* a novel in which erotic violence "éclate avec une cruauté néantissante."[16]

A long central sequence of chapters describes a young girl lying on the beach and/or photographs of the same scene. The sudden rise of a storm, and the title of the album—"un corps dans la tempête" (p.92)—give credibility to the possibility that the girl is not simply sleeping; she may be dead. The tempest and the brutality of the waves slapping the rocks materialize the probability of a violent death. Violent images displaced onto innocent objects maintain ambiguity through the long sequence.

Exploiting the ambiguity of photographs, the description materializes an elaborate optical and semantic illusion. Since Antonioni's *Blow-up*, we know that a vague photographed spot might be a corpse, and *La Jalousie* demonstrates that a trivial spot can take on monstrous proportions in an obsessed imagination. The description in *L'Observatoire de Cannes* wants the reader to be aware of the possible interference of illusion:

> Est-ce une illusion d'optique provoquée par cette mèche diagonale de la tempe à la lèvre? Il semble que la bouche, entrouverte, soit étirée, un peu, en une sorte de sourire, de rire recouvert par le fracas de la tempête. (p. 57)

The photograph with its ambiguous silent laughter is already an illusion of reality, and we are meant to remember that the text offers analogous illusions in another medium.

The idea of death is explicit, but attached to anodine signifieds; the waves, described as *lames* (blades) scrape a branch to a bare skeletal whiteness:

> On ne distingue plus cependant sur la plage ni les cartes postales, ni le sac vert et sa cordelière jaune, ni le pantalon aux fines rayures alternées, ni le ballon rouge criblé de triangles blancs, ni la serviette éponge qui ont été emportés, probablement, par la tempête, cette fois déchaînée.
>
> La limite atteinte par chaque lame est dessinée sur la pente de la grève par une frange—recoupée, effacée, recomposée—de minuscules débris, fragments d'ulves et de liège, bouts d'allumettes, morceaux de papier argenté, brindilles de toutes sortes.
>
> Une petite branche morte,   décapée et blanchie par le sel, émerge de cette zone humide, sur la bordure supérieure du cliché.
>
> La jeune fille est allongée . . . (p.95)

Morbidity contaminates the young girl by spatial contiguity and the metonymic movement of reading. It is never clear whether she is dead or sleeping. She is "decomposed" into pure geometric forms (p. 108) and recomposed as the waves wash over her. The obsessive but evanescent young girl is a true floating signifier, an illusory (and elusive) prey in a meticulously articulated description. Rather than describing an actual person, the description itself has killed her, this being a way in which description produces fiction. The cumulative effect of many examples is overwhelming: "La vague . . . submerge la branche morte, le corps abandonné." (p. 107); "la peau violemment colorée" (p. 106); "Le corps de la jeune fille, entièrement submergé" (p. 97); "Le visage est méconnaissable." (p. 98); "Elle dort, peut-être." (pp. 101, 102, 105). Creative description, through its use of verbs, does not remain static—it transforms. A liberal sprinkling of carefully loaded words heightens the effect: "arraché" (three times on pp. 100-101), "assauts" (p. 96), "branche morte" (pp. 95, 107, 98), "déchets déposés" (p. 99), "rabattu" (p. 100), "déformé" (p. 103), etc. Not even the subsequent reappearance of the live girl resolves ambiguity, since the time of the text bears no clues as to the sequence of fictional events.

Progression from one still photograph to the next is motivated by desire, as is made clear in their sequence in the album:

> De cliché en cliché, l'opérateur a progressé suivant une trajectoire rectiligne qui élimine successivement tous les accidents dont la surface pouvait faire écran, qui le rapproche du seul objet convoité. (p.92)

Each page in the album is a screen that hides the ones that follow. All the pages are a series of veils that remove the desired object from view. Ricardou's purpose is to show the screens. The "corps bronzé" of the young girl, is never actually displayed. Optical ambiguity prevents identifying her with certainty; fragmented or decomposed by the description, she remains hidden. Since the "opérateur" never seizes the object, which continuously disappears into the folds of illusion, it is again the quest itself which is the only content. (The word "opérateur" points to any or all of the following: the narrative eye, the photographer, the tourist, the reader or the writer.)

Words themselves act as screens and reveal displaced violence and eroticism. Play with words, although less pervasive and less structuring than in Ricardou's later novels, is nonetheless present in L'Observatoire de Cannes. Like geometric shapes, words bring together dispersed elements of the text; they are superimposable or decompose into syllables that migrate like charged molecules, toward other receptive particles. One comic and important example occurs in the long tempest description, where the girl's body is decomposed into the discs, ovals, and triangles that form its contours. Then we read:

> Sur le ventre, au point de convergence des deux cuisses, est
> inscrite une trace oblongue, en forme de losange, sombre, trop
> sombre pour ne pas être une ombre déformée par la réfraction ou
> une algue, une simple ulve arrachée à quelque pierre sous-
> marine, par la tempête déchaînée, et posée là, miraculeusement,
> à la base du pubis. (pp.108-109)

The current—or text on which the signifiers float—has detached an "ulve"
(or should it be "-ulve"?) and superimposed it on the "V renversé" formed
by the girl's legs, forming a word never said by the text. Since there is
nothing surprising about the presence of bathers or algae on a beach, the
word "miraculeusement" is a puzzle. It can only refer to the rebus-like
marriage consummated between a geometric form and a phonetic unit to
produce the word "vulve."[17]

Both the V and the "ulve," no longer joined but still associated
with the girl's pubis, are elsewhere the objects of aggression: the "lames" of
the thrashing waves tear and mutilate the seaweed, leaving "morceaux
d'ulves déchirées" and rip off the branch of a tree, which hangs at an angle to
the trunk, thus forming "les deux montants d'un V renversé" (p. 109). The
inverted V is already associated with graffiti carved on the water tower door
with a pocketknife (which, like the waves, has a "lame"). The knife as a
weapon and as writing instrument both come to play in an implicit rape of
the young bather. Violence is displaced to innocent objects, however, and
the violent potential of eroticism is masked.

The girl is doubly unattainable. The series of photographs or screens
in the album, removed one by one as the quest proceeds, never yield up the
"objet convoité." The object of desire, the ultimate repressed signifier,
when submitted to close scrutiny, is broken down by the description into a
succession of body parts, geometrical shapes, words. It is in the nature of
description, then, to do violence to its object by fragmenting it, and thereby
leave it forever hidden, even to the last word of the novel: "disparu." The
screen that hides the object of desire intensifies the mysterious eroticism of
the book, for, as Starobinski succinctly puts it, "le caché fascine."

The reader can only seek, but never find. The young woman can only
be suggested to the imagination; she cannot be materialized by the
description. She is literally beyond description, being virtual as well as

presumably virtu*ous*. Both absolutely unattainable and also paradoxically forbidden, she is—in her absence—at the heart of the fiction's parable. As an allegorical figure for Mimesis, she represents an unattainable reality beyond the text. She is there to make illusion frustrating.

Ricardou has drawn the frustrations of description into a composite image that functions as a theater of theory: the striptease. A long sequence of the novel (pp.162-180) is an extended *mise-en-abyme* which simultaneously tells a story and demonstrates the conditions that make that story what it is. This sequence has wide application to Ricardou's whole work, and indeed it recurs in some form in all his books of fiction.[18]

In an analysis of Herodias, Ricardou argues that Flaubert's description itself produces a striptease effect:

> dans *Hérodias*, la silhouette vêtue de Salomé est-elle *à la fois immédiatement offerte et peu à peu révélée*, de haut en bas, selon cette 'découverte par degrès' dont parle Léonard de Vinci à propos de la description et qu'on pourrait nommer le *striptease scriptural*. Ici commence alors un domaine passionnant et méconnu: celui, emminemment paradoxal, de l'*inénarrable*. Ce strip-tease irrécusable est, en effet, à la lettre, impossible à raconter: la jeune fille est restée vêtue. Il a eu lieu et n'a pas eu lieu. Qu'il hante le récit, nous en tenons, si besoin est, pour preuve, la phrase que Flaubert ajoute aussitôt: 'Sur le haut de l'estrade, elle retira son voile.' Le strip-tease inénarrable a produit son inverse: un strip-tease dont il est possible d'assurer la narration.[19]

This is precisely what happens in *L'Observatoire de Cannes*. I have shown how the tempest sequence illustrates the essential aggressiveness, even sadism of description as it dismembers in successive time what exists simultaneously. Any of the novel's descriptions illustrates how language decomposes objects into parts or abstracts them into pure forms. The striptease chapters are composed of a description, minutely detailed, of a young woman removing her clothing. By tracing the temporal dimension of the narrator's gaze, the sequence shows how description can become a projected striptease in the sense that one might say "he undressed her with his eyes."

The chapters are set at the intersection of two separate spaces—a train compartment and a cabaret—which, when superimposed, produce the scene of the striptease. This composite space contains a luggage net and a seat with armrest from the train and the "salle," "cliquetis des verres," whispers and commotion of a cabaret theater. The word "batterie" could apply either to an orchestra or to the rhythms of the train's movement. Persistent flashing of light in the dark could indicate the train's motion or suggest a strobe light. In this way the setting combines on the one hand the cabaret features of spectacle and socially-managed erotic fantasy, and on the other hand the dangerous appeal of illicit voyeurism (and a tribute to Robbe-Grillet's *voyeur* who is a "voyageur").

The stripper herself is also a condensed image. Wearing a pink dress, she includes the image of the young bride and the *fillette*, both of whom had pink dresses. The major ingredient composing the figure of the stripper is the blond young girl, whose beachbag, shoes and checkered bikini (with sequins added for the cabaret milieu) identify her with the character earlier viewed on the beach.

The polyvalent scene and character, concentrated in the short and relatively autonomous striptease sequence have the features of yet another kind of illusion: dream. Dream images, because condensed, are overdetermined, that is, each element is an intersection in a network of meanings. An important feature of dream is the polyvalence of its elements, which produces a density common to dream and literature. According to Freud, "From every element in a dream's content, associative threads branch out in two or more directions; every situation in a dream seems to be put together out of two or more impressions or experiences." This is certainly true of the elements of the striptease sequence (and the rest of the book as well), although the "impressions or experiences" are strictly limited to those provided by other parts of the book. The resulting network is entirely contained in the limited ludic space of the book.

Furthermore, the logic of dream is strikingly different from that of waking life in a way which is applicable to the striptease sequence, and refers us back to the dynamics of optical illusion. As Freud points out:

> This method of production [of dreams] also explains to some extent the varying degrees of characteristic vagueness shown by so many elements in the content of dreams. Basing itself on this discovery, dream interpretation has laid down the following

rule: in analyzing a dream, if an uncertainty can be resolved into an 'either—or,' we must replace it for purposes of interpretation by an 'and,' and take each of the apparent alternatives as an independent starting point for a series of associations.[20]

Like the psychoanalyst, the reader of Ricardou's fiction must avoid deciding, for example, whether the space is a cabaret or a train, or who the characters are. Making a critical choice of this kind would be a reduction of a text that capitalizes on the economy of condensation of mutually exclusive (either—or) elements. Unlike the analyst, however, we do not discard the manifest content in favor of a latent meaning. "Elle s'endort peut-être." "Elle dort peut-être." "Elle rêve peut-être." These sentences, repeated several times each, add credibility to a dream analysis of the sequence. But if it is a dream or a fantasy, *who* is dreaming? As before, the answer to this question is obscured to prevent a resurgence of the notion of character. The New Novel consistently puts the emphasis on operations, not origins, and this perspective is not so different from Freud's as would appear at first glance. Freud speaks of "production," and he defines dream not as the latent or manifest content, but as the dream *work*, the processes of transformation.

But it is certainly not the sleeping woman herself who dreams. She is everywhere, but we do not share her vision. Rather, she is part of the panoramic sweep onto which are projected (in the optical as well as psychological sense) the obsessions of a hidden eye. As a dream contains its dreamer, this semantic and visual field constitutes a coherent point of view. Lacking only presence, this narrator-eye, perhaps the title observatory itself, is the novel's only identifiable character.

The striptease offers a two-part attempt to describe the young woman without destroying her. First, the simultaneous appeal of all her attractions is transmitted into action (disrobing). Second, the description tries to capture slow motion in successive still "frames," a reversal of the cinematographic principle defined by Shattuck and seen when the album pages are flipped rapidly: a train moving past lights or a cabaret strobe light are variants of the *minuterie* principle that regulates other framing devices and divides continuity into segments. But each of these two phases negates the other. However close the focus and however small the fragment of action may be, description cannot capture it without transforming it. The alternation is between two ways of translating visual into readable space. Description can attempt to capture an object which is closely focused and small enough to eliminate the temporality of writing/reading. This proving impossible, one can try to expand the temporality of the object so it can be narrated. The line between the two is artificial anyway, and neither extreme satisfactorily materializes the "objet convoité," and so, as in particle-wave theory, alternation of the two proves to be the best possible compromise. The text thus plays with the literal and referential veils of description, rendering the girl alternately accessible and inaccessible. She is covered with a sort of grid which is alternately transparent and opaque. This pattern is found on the checkered bathing suit she wears and in other similar geometries: the design drawn on a postcard by the young couple, the cross-hatched graffiti lines, and so on.

In another version of this sequence published separately under the title *Improbables Strip-teases*, accompanying drawings are framed in an actual grid, some of whose squares are blacked out. There, the girl's image degenerates into a *Playboy* puzzle with pieces missing. The text's interest is to be found in its hypogram: scattered throughout are upper-case letters that demand to be assembled into a hidden message. To crack this strange but easily accessible code, readers must imitate Saussure when he recomposed syllables of a secret name dispersed throughout a poem. Here the resultant message is itself a poem, a doggerel deformation of Mallarmé's "Le Vierge, le vivace et le bel aujourd'hui," that serves primarily as a vehicle for restatement of theoretical tenets:

Cette improbable vierge et son ptyx orangé
Vont-ils donc déchiffrer avec un coup de livre
Ce passage oublié que chante entre les lignes
Le symbolique oiseau au plumage étranger?

Un signe d'autrefois se souvient que c'est lui
Magnifique mais qui sans espoir se délivre
D'avoir inauguré tout le chapitre
Ou lire quand du stérile hymène a resplendi l'écrit.

Ses lettres secoueront cette blanche agonie
Par les pages infligée aux plumes qui les nient
Même l'horreur du mot où le secret est pris

Hypogramme en ce lieu si son pur éclat l'ose
Il s'immobilise au songe blanc de l'inscrit
Du précis souvenir de la prise enfin prose.[21]

It is a better joke than a poem, but its implications are interesting. By means of a Roussellian *à peu près* (Mallarmé's "déchirer avec un coup d'aile ivre" becomes "déchiffrer avec un coup de livre") we are warned once again against the kind of reading which disdains the material aspects of literature ("l'horreur du mot"), thus missing the point ("ou le secret est pris"). The danger is the referential illusion which induces the reader to conjure the woman and the "prise," neglecting the "prose," or, in the terms of this analysis, to underestimate the foreign reality of the *lisible* in favor of the more comfortable visible world.

Improbables Strip-teases does not yield a "secret" meaning, but rather another abyme-like text within a text. As when contemplating the towers and islands, the trained eye looks beyond the second for a third, which it finds in Mallarmé's sonnet. Like the multiple screens which hide the "objet convoîté" on the beach, each successive intertextual layer represses ordinary reality one step further. If there is a pre-textual reality, let it be another text. This kind of writing replaces referential depth with a series of underlying surfaces. In place of a meaning or a realistic image, we have another signifier in a chain. The chain is not infinite, however: it ends with the articulation of theory.

In similar fashion, the striptease sequence as it appears in *L'Observatoire de Cannes* is a *mise-en-abyme* of a more pervasive global operation. Sollers calls the young girl a "paysage dans le paysage,"[22] and indeed the larger landscape, like the girl, is alternately masked and revealed. Buildings, mountains and trees are visual obstacles that screen the views behind. The elevator and train, by an illusion of transferred motion, unveil the countryside. The word *effeuilleuse* (stripper) articulates an analogy of girl, landscape and book: the panorama becomes accessible to the eye as the foliage (*feuillage*) falls away during the elevator's ascent; the striptease consists of the removal of layers of petals or leaves, a kind of visual and literal "defloration;" finally, the pages (*feuilles*) of the book also fall away, as reading pursues its own "ordre du regard." Each referring to the others, not one of these stripteases yields any secret meaning or naked truth. Rather, their total configuration suggests Barthes's description of the text as an onion, whose layers can be pulled away one by one until nothing remains.[23]

Yet, it would be a mistake to reduce *L'Observatoire de Cannes* or any of Ricardou's fictions to an underlying theoretical formulation, even when Ricardou himself would encourage us to do so. It should be possible to approve the fictions as a challenge to logocentric conceptions of reading while remaining aware of the specific metaphors into which that challenge is cast. Ricardou's stories do evoke realistic characters, if only momentarily, and the puzzling mixture of eroticism, violence and theory is not fully explained by didactic intentions or by notions of textual pleasure.

The evanescent blond bather in *L'Observatoire de Cannes* is only the first in a series of seductive but inaccessible female images that haunt Ricardou's fiction. She reappears as a crowd of redheads in *La Prise/Prose de Constantinople*, as a comely but dangerous reader figure in *Les Lieux-dits*, and as a bevy of golden-haired goddesses in *Révolutions minuscules*. In all cases, she is called forth by the story only to serve as an object lesson in the deconstruction of the referential illusion by the mechanisms of description. But before she is fragmented and disappears, she is the focus for the narrator's erotic fantasy. If, as Norman Holland proposes, every artist has a sort of personal myth which contributes to the organic unity of the entire *oeuvre* and defines its specificity,[24] this omnipresent female image must certainly provide a major clue to Ricardou's fictional imagination.

Especially insistent is the relationship of this female image to a landscape. *La Prise/Prose* closely documents a woman's metamorphosis into a geography, her hair into a cataract. This metaphoric equivalence permits a voyage resulting in "la prise de Constantinople" to be superimposed on an anatomical itinerary and a playful but sinister "prise du con."[25] In *Les Lieux-dits*, both woman and landscape are compared to a chessboard, where opposing factions wage war over literary doctrine. (Sharing many themes with *La Prise/Prose*, *Les Lieux-dits* is more schematically formalized and will be treated in the next chapter before the earlier but more complex novel.) Assimilation of a female character and a seaside decor is a feature of several stories in *Révolutions minuscules* as well.

Fusion of woman and landscape is a common theme in Western literature, often embodied in metaphor. In a study of the American pastoral novel, Annette Kolodny[26] argues that a "land-as-woman" metaphor is associated with archetypal patterns and reflects a collective dream of regression to a protective environment while at the same time justifying myths of exploration and mastery and ultimately a disastrous "rape of the land." Kolodny's argument that a culture's pervasive metaphors actually create an ambiance for their realization is ironically consonant with

Ricardou's view that a fiction is generated by the interplay of its literal and metaphorical levels. Ricardou's analogy is the reverse of the one Kolodny discusses, but his woman-as-landscape striptease supports many of the same images. Thanks to this metaphor, *voyeur* and *voyageur* merge, as a scene is described in close detail, broken into attributes or geometrical fragments, and then transformed into a parable or *mise-en-abyme* of textual functioning.

Thus to the *voyeur* and traveler must be added the figure of the implicit reader persona. Erotic fantasy, geographical decor, and linguistic or metafictional discourse merge, each referring to (or masking) the others. All three are manipulated by a hidden but aggressive *homo ludens*, who travels across the book/landscape and is titillated by its images. The knife as instrument of writing indicates the potential violence of his game.

As the narrator peeps through the observatory telescope, the coins he inserts into the viewing machine are a monetary analogy to his libidinal investment in his voyeurism, and the *minuterie* principle that functions as a tease in the striptease sequences is itself an apt image of the relationship between the mimetic urge and the distancing of theory. The unity of Ricardou's writings underlines the extent to which it is essential not only to study the fiction in light of the theory, but also the reverse. To see the fiction exclusively as a *mise-en-abyme* of textual processes is to erase the literal dimension of his images in favor of the theory they supposedly embody. Rather than returning to the referential illusion through a back door, as Ricardou invites us to do, we should be wise to the seductions of theory, for, as Robbe-Grillet teasingly points out, "tout se passe [...] comme si la théorie n'avait jamais servi à rien, qu'à repousser le sens un peu plus loin."[27]

CHAPTER II

Les Lieux-dits: A Structuralist Quest

> Il y a plus affaire à interpréter les
> interprétations qu'à interpréter les
> choses, et plus de livres sur les livres
> que sur autre sujet: nous ne faisons que
> nous entregloser. Tout fourmille de
> commentaires.
>
> —Montaigne

Like *L'Observatoire de Cannes*, *Les Lieux-dits*[1] dramatizes a tension between the temptations of mimesis and an ideology of non-representation. And referential reading is again portrayed as an alluring—and this time dangerous—female. Olivier, the novel's hero, spends the first three chapters in quest of a mysterious woman in red. When he finally finds Atta, he attempts to distract her from the "ombres chinoises" she is projecting on the ground. In order to attract her attention, he asks, "Est-ce à moi que vous destinez les étranges signaux de vos mains?" "Non, bien sûr," replies Atta, to which Olivier responds, "C'est dommage; rien ne me passionne davantage que déchiffrer des signes" (p. 63). Olivier is the exegete and champion of the novel's literal dimension. It is he who explains the anagrammatic transformations that produce the story, and he condemns any intrusion of heretical referentiality or extratextual motivation. But something goes wrong with this novel. Olivier's fanatical zeal culminates in a witch hunt: when Atta and Mimesis become too threatening, he tries to exterminate both together.

Readers of *Les Lieux-dits* experience frustration similar to Olivier's, but for very different reasons. Ricardou's text, like Atta, is intriguing and desirable. Germaine Brée calls this novel "a beautiful piece of work, impeccably constructed, a cross between a poem, a surrealistic dream and a critical meditation on the relation of language to reality."[2] As always, Ricardou encourages us to move freely between poetic fiction and explorations of linguistic conditions that make it possible. But simultaneously a "récit d'une aventure" and an "aventure d'un récit," *Les Lieux-dits* reads itself. As Atta and Olivier become aware that they are invented characters, they explicate the novel of which they are a part. The most pressing task, then. in any reading of the novel, is to find a place for the reader in this text which presents itself as closed, keeping in mind Umberto Eco's statement that "l'ouverture est la condition même de la jouissance esthétique."[3]

1

Les Lieux-dits has a plot, and this distinguishes it from the other novels, all of which have either several conflicting plots or no story at all. The story is an outrageously improbable quest, however, whose vicissitudes are determined by word-play, by permutation of letters and of geometric shapes, and by the exigencies of its theoretical and didactic purposes. Therefore, in order to present the story, it is necessary already to have discussed theories the story represents; in order to discuss mechanisms of the fiction, on the other hand, we need already to have acquired familiarity with the story. This impasse makes it necessary to follow a zigzag course in our quest for an understanding of *Les Lieux-dits*.

Atta and Olivier are both students seeking information about a certain Albert Crucis, painter and observer of nature. In the course of their respective investigations, they find each other, as both had mapped out the same itinerary for a quest through an imaginary countryside. This itinerary, deduced from Crucis' allegorical paintings, takes them and the reader through a story and a book. The novel's subtitle hints at the nature of this double journey: "Petit guide d'un voyage dans le livre." Guidebook and novel struggle for supremacy in each of eight towns, eight chapters:

BANNIERE
BEAUFORT
BELARBRE
BELCROIX
CENDRIER
CHAUMONT
HAUTBOIS
MONTEAUX

The guidebook is represented by alphabetical sequence in the leftmost column; the novel can be seen to the right in an anagram of the word "texte." Belcroix, the most important town, appears twice on the grid, horizontally and diagonally. These features of the novel are explained by Olivier (pp. 138-9) as well as by Ricardou elsewhere.[4] The two genres contained in *Les Lieux-dits* are in conflict as the story becomes a thinly veiled theoretical debate about whether reality motivates the story (as in the guidebook discourse) or the reverse (language produces the story in Ricardolian fiction).

The novel opens with the explanatory voice of a guidebook. From a bird's-eye view, an imaginary landscape, divided by the river Damier, shows its "quadrillage, l'alternance quasi régulière des bosquets et des prairies" (p.9). However, it is impossible to know whether the river took its name from the topography, or the name suggested this unusual agricultural pattern. Long ago, archives in each town were destroyed by fire, erasing history (and etymology), leaving explanation to the imagination of story-tellers.

Inhabitants of the region have long been divided by "guerres doctrinales" between those who believe things to be the origin of words (the "realists") and their opponents who see words as the source of things (the "poets"). In each chapter, place names occasion debate between the two ideologies. Where history falters, guidebook gives way to romance. A *lieu-dit* is a place whose name describes a topological feature: although there is no corresponding English word, the phenomenon is found in such names as Salt Lake City or the Grand Tetons. In the novel, however, it is the place names that have given rise to geographic and historical particularities. Brée suggests that the title be translated as "Places Deciphered,"[5] a translation that preserves the opposition of reality (*lieux*) and language (*dits*) and the conjunction of real and poetic space. The subtitle adds a voyage, that is, a story. Rhetorical and geographical space correspond in the names of the towns/chapters: each chapter refers to either book or town, but of course the two are the same.

The story begins, appropriately, in Bannière. According to the *Robert*, the expression "C'est la croix et la bannière" means "C'est beaucoup d'histoires, toute une affaire (V. Difficile)." Taking this expression literally in the context of opposition between words and things, the first chapter is dominated by cross and banner motifs. Two meanings of the French word *histoire*—history and story—correspond to the weaving of guidebook and fiction. The fiction takes literally what the guidebook intends figuratively. Thus the guidebook's "eau soyeuse," "rubans de fumée," "moirure de l'eau," and "broderies" that peasants have added to the "motif central" of legend constitute a figurative banner to correspond to a literal one in the fictional discourse. Such systematic structuring metaphors, uniting guide and fiction in each chapter, are controlled by a principal emblem, here the banner. Enclosing both types of discourse is the novel we read; final victory of novel over the guide discourse is a foregone conclusion, since both are fictional.

Ideological opposition between realists and poets is Ricardou's particular crusade, and Bannière's legend is that of the crusades. Guidebook fades into drama and toward fiction as the legend weaves an overdetermined medieval theme:

> A l'angle du parvis se tenait huit étrangers, secouant la poussière de leurs vêtures. L'un d'eux dressa et introduisit dans l'interstice qui béait entre quatre pavés la hampe d'une bannière brodée de la croix emblématique. (pp.11-12)

An orator incites the crowd, invoking a "rivalité primordiale entre les biens et les maux" (p.12). Continuing as guide, the narration describes two sites of interest in Bannière: a church and a studio, now a museum, belonging to the late painter Albert Crucis (Latin genitive for "cross").

Just as in *L'Observatoire de Cannes* a view implied a viewer, in *Les Lieux-dits* a voyage needs a traveler. Such a traveler, inevitably the reader in guidebook format, is directly addressed by the narration: "Avant de reprendre sa route, le voyageur est invité à porter son regard au sol" (p.11). Describing Crucis' tableaux, the guide discourse is imperceptibly transformed into a guide (person), a metamorphosis that brings a corresponding incorporation of the reader into the text as "monsieur." Dialogue marks the advent of the novel in the guidebook. "Monsieur," logically the reader in a guidebook discourse, is later personified by Olivier as fiction takes over. As in *L'Observatoire de Cannes*, traveling and reading are assimilated, this time in a single protagonist: Olivier.

Describing the museum, the guide remarks that a vast allegorical tableau and eight landscapes "ont trouvé asile dans une discrète salle du premier étage" (p. 15). The word "asile," here used figuratively, immediately afterwards makes a literal appearance in an interrupting incident involving an ambulance (a red cross this time) and a pyromaniac escaped from a nearby asylum. Resuming description of the allegorical painting, the narration enumerates, in a different arrangement, many elements already introduced: cross, crusades, fire, soldiers, landscape. A similar rearrangement of constituent elements produced Bannière's church, which was built from materials salvaged from a previous edifice.

The chapter ends with a return to the debate over words and things, told this time from the perspective of the "poets." According to them, the crusade story is a "pure fiction déduite du nom de la bourgade." The same causal logic occurred to a manufacturer, it seems, for a flag and banner factory was established in the town. The factory (whose trademark was, naturally, a red cross) no longer exists—it too was destroyed by fire, which began at the window frames ("croisées"). By the end of this first chapter, most of the novel's major geometric motifs have been introduced, and the reader attentive to their various disguises can continue to find them in dizzying proliferation. Its particular configuration of motifs gives each of the seven remaining chapters/towns its unique (hi)story.

In Beaufort-le-haut, situated on a hill, there is no fort. The town does resemble a fortified city, however, thanks to its crenelated hedges bordering a spiral road leading to a square at the summit. These features are the product of the town's name, according to the poets. This city's archives were also destroyed by fire, so the guide discourse spins a story involving "galleries" dug in the sides of the hill from four sides. Where the four tunnels crossed, dynamite was used to destroy the hypothetical castle.

A smaller spiral adorns the sign of a different kind of gallery—an antique shop belonging to one Monsieur Epsilon, who assumes the voice of the guide. After a futile attempt to find the lady in red by way of one of the four vertical staircases superimposed on the spiral road, Olivier tours the antique shop. Mirror inversions and reflections dominate the chapter: three seduction scenes appear on a tapestry, an etching and a mannequin display. Following the logic of duplication, a fourth version, containing all three, is the book we read. Similar displays can be seen in all the antique shops, the only type of business to be found in Beaufort. In the different exhibits, the same objects reappear according to an orderly principle:

> Tout voyageur qui visitera l'ensemble des vitrines sera donc
> en mesure d'observer, d'une part des séries de pièces similaires,
> de l'autre des objets divers ordonnés selon leur fonction dans la
> scène exposée. (p.41)

If the reader finds in this distribution of objects certain echoes of linguistic and literary categories, Olivier does not hesitate to explain this reappearance of the grid motif.

> Faut-il aujourd'hui préciser que certains controversistes,
> utilisant toute circonstance pour faire rebondir leur querelle, se
> sont plu à lire dans cette double mise en place, une parabole de
> la linguistique distinction entre le paradigme et le syntagme?
> (p.41)

Making use of his linguistic insights, Olivier is able to see in the reuse of stones from an earlier church to build a new one a "fable de l'anagramme", which he then applies to Epsilon's name, unmasking him as a spy (*l'espion*).

Belarbre transforms mirroring structures into a circle motif. Its chapter opens with discussion of the sources and meanders of the Dame and Demoiselle rivers (*eau*) and moves to the circular galleries ("0's") formed by rows of trees joined at branches and roots forming mirrored arcs from opposite sides of the road. The rivers produce multiple female images in the guide discourse: "gorge étroite," "la métamorphose de la Demoiselle en Dame s'accomplit en un lieu plus secret," etc. (pp.48-49), helping Olivier to find, at last, the woman in red.

Cycles of repetition and revenge are formed by the story as well. Olivier discovers a child incinerating black ants using an inverted round magnifying glass, a trick he learned from Atta. To punish the ant-murdering child, Olivier whips him with nettles containing, says he, formic acid:

> —Sache que maintenant tes victimes se vengent, commente
> le jeune homme, en plein effort, d'une voix saccadée. Sache que
> l'urticant principe qui pénètre ta peau et y accomplit ses ravages
> n'est rien d'autre que l'acide formique, présent dans la moindre
> fourmi. (p.56)

Another cycle of vengeance was attempted by the Belarbre city council, investigating bizarre cases of vandalism. Under the bark of trees had been discovered tiny cavities carved to accommodate cadavers of dead ants carefully wrapped in cellophane. An anonymous letter denounced the "Père La Fourmi," guardian of the town's public square and an old eccentric dedicated, like Crucis, to observing ants and recording their behavior in a diary. En route to an asylum, the old man swallowed insecticide and died.

> Sans vouloir fournir aucune inédite révélation, il murmura jusqu'au bout, sans cesse: 'Le Jardin des Oppositions, Le Jardin des Oppositions, Le Jardin des O...' C'était le titre de son mémoire, et le nom qu'il donnait au square Lenpois, dont il avait jadis été le garde. (p.61)

"Lenpois," another anagram of "L'espion" and "Epsilon," forms a three-word cycle.

The garden is also the scene where Olivier and Atta meet. Their meeting forms an *enjambement* over the chapter break. Sharing his name with a species of tree, and having the initial O, Olivier is probably a native of Belarbre, whereas the symmetry of Atta's name with its two crosses (will she double-cross Olivier?) places her more appropriately in Belcroix.

Relaxing in a café in Belcroix (the chapter), Atta enumerates her repertory of shadow figures, eight animals in alphabetical order: "Un chat, une chèvre, un chien, un cygne . . . un éléphant, un lapin, une mouche, un poisson" (p. 64). She orders a glass of tomato juice and Olivier drinks a mint beverage, while pointing out that red and green are complementary colors. The two will henceforth collaborate in their quests.

The chapter entitled "Belcroix" involves, curiously a trip to Monteaux, in Atta's red car. The chapter can be placed, however, under the sign of exchange and the cross that represents it. Atta and Olivier exchange drinks and stories. Light and shadow reverse the powers in the struggle between red and black ants, and the magnifying glass reverses size relationships. Olivier Lasius, working on research into his father's papers, is investigating the latter's admiration for Crucis. The painter (who reversed relationships between paintings and reality, the sky changing to resemble his tableau), may have been involved in some sort of revolutionary or spying activity. Olivier asks Atta if he may ride in her car, since his tires have been punctured by nails in the road. Presumably these are the nails from the cross, the stages of their journey also evoking the "stations of the cross."

The town and chapter named "Cendrier" afford an opportunity for a description in minute detail of a package of Pall Mall cigarettes. Its emblem, its slogans, colors and significance are presented in what is well known as the New Novel's "objective" style. The description also marks an intersection of many themes: bilateral (mirror) symmetry, the color red, the numbers four and eight, binary opposition (conflict) and fire. Here, Atta too recounts the motivations for her research: her great-aunt, wife of Crucis, died in a fire on the island of Malta. Atta too seeks answers to questions about Crucis. What was his real identity? What is the source of his name? Debate about names continues on more than one front. Cendrier was so named (perhaps) because it too had been destroyed by fire. On the other hand, clever merchants capitalized on the name to open an ashtray (*cendrier*) factory.

To continue their research, the pair will have to continue toward Chaumont to the "Librairie de la Cigale" temporarily lodged there after a fire. A second Monsieur Epsilon, brother of the Beaufort antique dealer, is their guide. Oppositions are underlined between the "cigale" (bookstore) and the "fourmi" (referring to Epsilon's gift as a collector of antiques). This mention of La Fontaine's fable points further to the conflict between words (found in books) and things (catalogued in antique shops). Much of the town is reflected in the bookshop window, through which one can also view seduction scenes of the same description as those in Beaufort. Having inscribed themselves in the display, Atta and Olivier are troubled by desires ignited by artistic causality. Atta would like to reenact the seduction at Monteaux, in the "Hôtel de La Fontaine."

Chaumont is the scene of much of the novel's self-reading. One of the books discussed there is the old park guardian's journal, which bears a striking resemblance to *Les Lieux-dits*. On their way to Hautbois, Atta and Olivier read aloud ("à haute voix") selections from "Le Jardin des Oppositions." Its author, the park guardian, has adopted the penname Asilus and uses the word "aujourd'hui" in place of dates to ensure anonymity. The journal tells of an encounter with a young woman in red who was projecting hand shadows on the ground. Most of the narrative concerns observations of two armies of ants and the odd dreams that seem to have been produced by feverish research. Two dreams are verbatim repetitions of the crusade episode and of the seduction scene. The object of the guardian's research, it turns out, was the perfection of an insecticide formula. Atta and Olivier interrupt their reading to admit that their first meeting was a dramatization of the scene in the journal which both had already read. "Reality" follows a script proposed by a work of "art," again, reversing the traditional relationship between words and things.

Monteaux is the title of the last chapter, but the travelers never reach their destination. Atta wants to reenact the seduction scene, but Olivier is more inclined to theorize. He points to further characteristics of the novel they inhabit: a postcard mentioned in the first chapter suggests a trip to the "Laboratoire A.C."; at the laboratory, Atta and Olivier find a sample of a mysterious insecticide, but Atta drops and breaks its container before anything more about it can be discovered. The postcard laboratory is partially obscured by the arms of a cross, which covers the three letters of the word "labora(toi)re." Olivier explains to Atta the postcard's secret meaning: "travailler (laborare) selon les directives d'Albert Crucis (A.C.) consiste (obliteration de la syllabe toi) à te faire disparaître" (pp. 156-7). He proceeds to direct Atta to a deserted clearing, order her to remove her clothing (in alphabetical order, of course), and tie her securely. Revealing his complicity with the escaped pyromaniac, he declares he will set fire to her in a revenge for the ants. The red of her dress and her "ardor" are responsible for her death. Crucis, nearby, remarks, "Tout celà, une fois de plus, aujourd'hui, est une métaphore" (p. 160).

2

Ricardou sees reading as a process of rearranging elements dispersed throughout a text according to the principle "qui se ressemble s'assemble." I have shown, for example, how geometric forms serve to assemble objects found in *L'Observatoire de Cannes*. In an essay,[6] Ricardou represents this principle by means of a diagram:

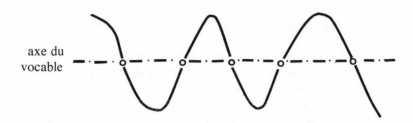

axe du
vocable

The wavy line shows the flow of reading; dots mark repetitions of words or larger units. Critical reading superimposes the dots to produce a second configuration:

These flowers of Ricardou's rhetoric are presented elsewhere as an algebraic formula: superimposition of dots becomes a "mise en facteur commun," so that a text composed of elements "abc$d$+ ... +h$d$ij" can be read as "d(abc + hij)" where d is the repeated unit.[7]

These two demonstrations of Ricardou's mathematical structuring imagination have in common the reader's selection for attention of a single repeated factor. When all, or nearly all elements are repeated, and when in addition the novel contains numerous autoreferential structures, as is the case in *Les Lieux-dits*, reading becomes vertiginous and plot summary nearly impossible. In keeping with Olivier's structuralist proclivities, I propose representing the novel's internal correspondences on a grid (see next two pages). On a vertical axis, I can arrange the chapters in the order they occur; horizontally appear eight motifs that occur in each chapter. Each motif is important both as a spatial configuration and as a theme of the novel. On my grid, "plot" reassumes its spatial meaning of location in terms of coordinates. Because of its dual function, each motif is a locus where fiction and theory intersect, or, in other words, where the story contains a reading of itself. In the squares formed by the axes, examples of each motif's appearance in each chapter are arranged so that each column corresponds to a single "flower" or to the formula "$d(\text{abc} + \text{hij})$." Reading *rows* of the grid from left to right and top to bottom presents a summary of the novel as it is read: elements are linked by contiguity (metonymically) in the successive chapters. Each of the *columns*, by contrast, yields a metaphoric reading. Variants of the cross motif, for example, propose mutual metaphors similar to triangles or the word "dentelle" in *L'Observatoire de Cannes*. Although each chapter is dominated by a single motif, all the figures appear in some form in all the chapters.

chapter	grid	cross	opposition	mirror	circle	fire	anagram	principal emblems
Bannière	Damier river and landscape	Crucis, red cross, crusades, *croisées*	allegory, crusades, good/evil, diachrony/ synchrony, poets/ realists	water reflects, banner colors inverted, Olivier's shadow	"voûte réfléchie" in water	banner factory, town history destroyed pyromaniac	rebuilt church	cross and banner
Beaufort	paradigm/ syntagm *créneaux*	4 underground galleries	poets/ realists	mirrors in antique gallery	"anneaux" of spiral, "encerclement" of town	fort exploded, red car, red dress	rearranged debris, Epsilon/ *l'espion*	spiral and mirror
Belarbre	"square" Lenpois, "grilles" of the park	Crucis, ant tombs marked on trees	red and black ants	magnifying glass, repetition, ants/ crusades, abysses	"Jardin des O…" "circulation" of tourists	killing of ants	Lenpois	circle and tree
Belcroix	"café du square"	exchange, "clous de la croix," Maltese cross shape of itinerary	male/female, history/ fable, order/ disorder	*Atta* as palindrome, "ombres chinoises"	magnifying glass	Atta's car, dress, tomato juice	Lasius	cross

chapter	grid	cross	opposition	mirror	circle	fire	anagram	principal emblem
Cendrier	multiples of eight	Crucis Maltese cross itinerary	2 lions on blason history/fable	ashtrays, cigarette package are *mises-en-abyme*	oval blason "formule elliptique" "circon-stance"	cigarettes and matches bookstore burned	Crucis, circus postcard and painting	Pall Mall package (literal emblem)
Chaumont	chess, "quadruple rang de huit perles"	death of Crucis "croix de par Dieu" alphabet	books/antiques, cigale/fourmi, guide/novel, blue/red	"Réflexion" repetition in display	Jardin des O... *eaux*	Crucis' death Chau(d)mont	Asilus Epsilon	mirror and book
Hautbois	"nuit tissue de cauchemars"	crusade nightmare	humans/ants, fate/free will, novel/auto-biography, "Jardin des Oppositions"	humans/ants Jardin des O... as *mises-en-abyme*	bicycle	killing of ants	Asilus, Lasius	ant
Monteaux	8 languages x 8 spots on body, iron asylum grill	Atta crossed out	novel *vs* itself	metaphor	*-eaux* of chapter title	figurative and literal flames kill Atta	folie, fiole	cross and fire

My grid closely resembles the one proposed by Claude Lévi-Strauss in his "structural study of myths," where he analyzes the Oedipus story into constituent units. Here is how he explains his rearrangement of the story's "mythemes":

> Si nous avons à *raconter* le mythe, nous ne tiendrons pas compte de cette disposition en colonnes, et nous lirions les lignes de gauche à droite et de haut en bas. Mais dès qu'il s'agit de *comprendre* le mythe, une moitié de l'ordre diachronique (de haut en bas) perd sa valeur fonctionnelle et la 'lecture' se fait de gauche à droite, une colonne après l'autre, en traitant chaque colonne comme un tout.[8]

What makes *Les Lieux-dits* a more difficult story to tell is the impossibility of recounting the horizontal dimension alone. A zigzag plot summary is unavoidable, because in *Les Lieux-dits* the metonymic axis *tells the story of the columns*. In his "Ouverture" to *Le Cru et le cuit*, Lévi-Strauss calls his book the "mythe de la mythologie."[9] *Les Lieux-dits* could be called the "metaphor of metaphorics," as Crucis' final remark suggests.

Crusading against arbitrary and capricious figurative language, Ricardou's structuring metaphors take responsibility for literal meanings of what may have been introduced figuratively, and for the entire semantic field of a word first used in a restricted sense. As a result, almost every image is overdetermined by this systematic method for restoring the "initiative to words." Rather than expressing a preexisting "quelque chose à dire," then, structuring metaphor exploits the story potential of description. A great deal of word play is one consequence of these procedures. In other words, the novel is articulated on elaborate networks of puns. In Chaumont, for example, where the book emblem dominates, Epsilon announces to visitors at his bookstores, "Quant à vos travaux, je crois pouvoir leur être utile à plus d'un titre" (p.99). In Hautbois, literal and figurative meanings coincide in a "fourmillement intense" (pp.119-120). Like so many aspects of this novel, this procedure is explained during Atta's and Olivier's discussion of "Le Jardin des oppositions," a *mise-en-abyme* of the larger narrative:

> Suivant une décision irrévocable, la prose de tout chapitre se trouve infléchie par le nom qui en forme l'enseigne. Sous le signe de Balarbre par exemple il est facile d'établir l'excessive fréquence de toute une botanique, non seulement au sens propre, mais dans maintes tournures figurées. Echangeant de plus, entre leurs domaines respectifs, les résultats de ces étranges aptitudes, les huit noms figurent donc ce conseil suprême par lequel le langage dicte ses conditions. (p.113)

This manner of writing where content comes to resemble form, Ricardou calls, after Raymond Roussel, a poetic technique. Rhyme, for example, requires pairing of words which in turn motivates a rapprochement of two elements of fiction. Such rapprochement results, not from any relationship between signifieds, but rather from similarity of signifiers. The challenge of rhyme is to construct a fiction which justifies the juxtaposition of two sounds. All rhyming follows this principle, but the more restricted the choice of words, the more difficult the challenge becomes: Mallarmé's "Sonnet en -yx" (one of Ricardou's favorite intertexts) and the Renaissance "rhétoriqueurs" come to mind. Roussel systematically applied the same rules to the novel, and was widely misunderstood. He habitually began work on a novel by inventing two ambiguous rhyming sentences. "Les deux phrases trouvées," Roussel explains in *Comment j'ai écrit certains de mes livres,*

> il s'agissait d'écrire un conte pouvant commencer par la première et finir par la seconde.
>   Or c'était dans la résolution de ce problème que je puisais tous mes matériaux.[10]

Ricardou too, like his persona Olivier, espouses the ideology whereby words are at the origin of things. His novels, like Roussel's, strive to accomplish certain rhymes, such as that of the words *femme* and *flamme* which dictate the manner of Atta's execution. From figurative to literal and back again, *Les Lieux-dits* is constructed following what Ricardou calls "la fonction créatrice du calembour."[11]

The first prologue to Ricardou's *Problèmes du nouveau roman* constitutes a manifesto of his position. This deceptively short article, entitled "Naissance d'une déesse" addresses itself to the origin of the myth of Aphrodite. As in *Les Lieux-dits*, there are two points of view. The majority of writers on the subject (Hesiod, Plato, and Mallarmé are cited) fall prey to a "demon de l'étymologie." As their reasoning would have it, Aphrodite's birth from the waves is the origin of her name (*aphros* is Greek for "foam"). One dictionary, however, states that the etymology of the word is unknown, and Ricardou takes advantage of this to expose his opposing view. According to him, the myth evolved to account for the name and its similarity (a sort of rhyme) with the Greek word for "foam." "C'est une parturition roussellienne qui a mis au monde Aphrodite," he declares. Aphrodite is thus for Ricardou a "mythe crypté de la création poétique."[12]

3

Les Lieux-dits is a "mythe crypté—or parable—of reading. As personifications of the two attitudes Ricardou discusses in his article, Atta and Olivier are diametrically opposed types of readers. By means of a series of superimposed allegorical quest stories, their positions become more distinguishable as the novel progresses. At the beginning, their adventures are compatible. Both are students engaged in a quest for knowledge: both seek information about Crucis, who figures in both family histories. They are not sure what they are seeking, however, and in fact are in search of a quest:

—Ton voyage serait-il dicté par quelque objectif précis?

—Oui et non. Je cherche, mais ne sais encore quoi. A vrai dire, ajoute Olivier, c'est tout un roman. (p.73)

Their research is an excuse for a story; the quest itself is more important than its object. The novel proceeds by elaborating and subverting two familiar quest models: the spiritual or religious journey and the detective story.

In the course of intellectual pursuits, a detective (Olivier) witnesses a somewhat ludicrous crime: the killing of ants. He embarks on a hunt for clues in the case. A murder weapon (the phial of insecticide) is at last unearthed, but one of the criminals (Atta) distracts the detective and cleverly destroys the evidence, thus betraying her guilt. Our not-so-loyal hero proceeds to take the law into his own hands by plotting to execute the criminal. The detective plot is appropriately interlaced with seduction and betrayal. That Atta finds Olivier irresistible helps cast him to the James Bond role—the sexy detective who resists women who throw themselves at him, and who is far more dedicated to solving mysteries and deciphering enigmas.

Typical mystery novels usually proceed from result to cause. A murder is discovered, and the detective must discover its source (the act, criminal, motive, weapon, etc.). The trajectory is linear from question to answer. In *Les Lieux-dits*, it is the linearity of the detective quest model that is at stake. With its emphasis on plot and character, suspense, its "referentiality," its goal-directed story, the detective novel prototype is an obvious target. Again, Ricardou can be understood as pursuing and elaborating on research begun by the older New Novelists, especially Robbe-Grillet. Ricardou has pointed to Robbe-Grillet's *Les Gommes* (1953), for example, as an "Oedipe inverse":

> Dans *Oedipe-Roi*, tout est consommé: les actes se sont déjà accomplis; dans *Les Gommes*, rien n'est arrivé: les actes vont se produire. Dans *Oedipe-Roi* il y a un rapport extrinsèque entre les actes et l'enquête; dans *Les Gommes* le rapport est intrinsèque: c'est l'enquête, en quelque manière, qui provoque les actes, induit Wallas à accomplir le meurtre sur lequel il enquête. En d'autres termes, l'activité d'Oedipe est une **opération aléthéique: elle** *dévoile* **ce qui a eu lieu; l'activité de** Wallas une opération productrice: elle *engendre* ce qui n'était pas. Avec Oedipe, on passe d'une erreur (Oedipe est innocent) à une vérité (il est coupable); avec Wallas, d'une fiction (Dupont fait semblant d'avoir été tué) à une réalité (Dupont a été réellement tué).[13]

Butor's *L'Emploi du temps* (1957) offers a similar inversion, where Revel (the "hero") inadvertently becomes accomplice to crimes he wants to prevent.

Instead of inverting detective myths, *Les Lieux-dits* erases them. Olivier is no heroic detective. He and Atta are both spies for opposing camps, both unsavory individuals. Whereas *Les Gommes* and *L'Emploi du temps* contest the mystery novel at the level of the story, *Les Lieux-dits* operates at the level of the signifier. By means of a clever pun (for once left undesignated as such), the mystery and its explanation neutralize each other as acid and base chemicals produce water. The crime (killing of ants) and the "solution" found at the end of the novel coincide in one word: insecticide.

This circularity is one way *Les Lieux-dits* subverts the linear quest. "Real" logic involves cause and effect, means and goals, sign and referent. By giving priority to the word, *Les Lieux-dits* subordinates story to rhyme and other poetic structures. The quest has as its goal language itself. Two-dimensional motifs are another alternative to the story "line" and to corresponding one-dimensional reading by travelers who are impatient to reach a destination and fail to appreciate the terrain being "crossed."

It is not its linearity but its themes of transcendence that make the second type of quest a target for subversion in *Les Lieux-dits*. Complicated allusions link Ricardou's novel to the religious or spiritual journey. Not the least of such allusions are the crusade themes; even Olivier's name comes from the most famous crusade epic, *La Chanson de Roland*. As it turns out, however, certain insoluble contradictions prevent the novel from being as successful at undermining this second quest model.

According to Joseph Campbell, the quest hero's journey is divided into three stages:

> The standard path of the mythological adventure of the hero is a magnification of the formula represented in the rites of passage: separation—initiation—return: which might be named the nuclear unit of the monomyth.
>
> A hero ventures forth from the world of common day into a region of supernatural wonder: fabulous forces are there encountered and a decisive victory is won: the hero comes back from this mysterious adventure with the power to bestow boons on his fellow man.[14]

Olivier embarks on his double quest upon seeing the paintings of Crucis. He first seeks the lady in red. She could be called "la Belle Inconnue," a composite of two medieval types: the mysterious young knight and the unattainable Lady. Having found Atta, Olivier continues to seek answers to his questions: Who is Crucis? Who was the guardian, and why did he kill the ants? (The guardian's real name, Gallois, is a further link with Chrétien's "Perceval le Gallois ou le Conte du Graal.") Unmasking Atta as a spy and executing her constitute Olivier's ritual initiation and prove the success of his venture.

Olivier is hardly the ideal crusader or quest hero, however. We learn at the end of the novel that he is an escaped lunatic and pyromaniac. Although his motives appear more pure than Atta's, he turns out to be quite diabolical. Françoise Calin and William Calin, comparing protagonists in medieval romance with modern quest heroes, remark about the latter that "their adventure is indeed a 'journey to the end of the night.' However, modern heroes do not cross the return threshold."[15] *Les Lieux-dits* ends as Atta goes up in flames overdetermined by the red of her dress and the rhyme *femme/flamme*. Although Olivier declares himself, in humble epic style, to be "seulement un servile auxiliaire" (p.160), he is never reintegrated into a society of any kind. Looking closer we see why. Whereas Perceval, Olivier and Roland, Lancelot and others were servants of God and state and carried out the will of these sovereign powers, Olivier is the "auxiliaire" of language. His function is to materialize what words initiate, to complete structuring metaphors and rhymes and to allegorize a theoretical stance. As a pyromaniac, it is his task to accomplish the journey from rhetorical "ardeur" of crusaders to the literal fires throughout the book. His quest is for rhyme as Roussel defined it. The "region of supernatural wonder" visited by Olivier in his quest is the special circumscribed space I have already defined as the world of *ludere*. Each of the religious symbols in the novel serves Olivier's ludic quest.

The insecticide Olivier and Atta seek is explicitly associated with the Grail. In the last chapter, the two find this insecticide, an emerald phial of liquid, an "elixir" (p.145). Apparently the old guardian, here finally identified as Monsieur Gallois, had entrusted his discovery to the laboratory. Explaining reasons for deferring the visit to Belcroix, Olivier draws a parallel between their journey and the quest for the grail:

> Quelque jour, écrit Chrétien de Troyes, Perceval assiste à un
> culte énigmatique, mais, en son ingénuité, it ne découvre pas
> que cette cérémonie se rapporte à l'objet même de sa quête; ce
> n'est que plus tard, après s'être instruit au cours de diverses
> aventures qu'il pourra atteindre le Graal, sa coupe d'émeraude
> et son précieux liquide. (p.141)

Chrétien's Perceval did not read the signs correctly when he first saw the
grail, and so was unable to recognize its importance. Neither would Olivier
and Atta have profited from a premature visit to Belcroix, where the
insecticide is kept. Chrétien's grail is made of gold, set with precious stones,
but their color is not specified. In Wolfram von Eschenbach's *Parzifal*,
however, the grail originates as the emerald that fell from Lucifer's forehead
when he fell from heaven. The emerald passed to Adam and into Christian
mythology.[16]

Its emerald color further links the insecticide with the "emerald
tablet," origin of the alchemist's quest. Several elements of the emerald
tablet's multivalent symbolism are relevant to *Les Lieux-dits*. Alchemy
too is a quest for knowledge, and the emerald tablet contains guidelines for
that search. The second of its twelve statements points to analogies of
microcosm and macrocosm, heaven and earth:

> Ce qui est en bas est comme ce qui est en haut, et ce qui est en
> haut est comme ce qui est en bas, pour faire les miracles d'une
> seule chose.[17]

This is the principle of the mirror, or *mise-en-abyme*, that can be recognized
in the first sentence of *Les Lieux-dits*:

> A peine franchie, sous les nuées, cette sombre ligne de faîte, tout
> le pays, en contrebas, dispense des reflets. (p. 9)

Discussing this sentence, Ricardou assimilates the "ligne" to the horizon
and also to the first line of any text, which marks the frontier between visible
and *lisible*, text and world, or text and blank paper above.[18]

Quest for the grail or emerald tablet is only one of many elements of
Les Lieux-dits built on religious symbols. Albert Crucis acts as a kind of
god. In the beginning, his paintings provide a predetermined itinerary. He is

the absent but omniscient ancestor whose clues the protagonists read and whose identity they hope to discover. At the end, it is he who summarizes the ultimate meaning of the novel's microcosm in a sweeping *deus ex machina* final revelation. Crucis is the origin and term of the quest. Atta and Olivier are its alpha and omega. More important than these isolated allusions, however, two spatial motifs—the grid and the cross—give the novel the shape of an ironic spiritual quest. By means of these two motifs, transcendent and referential meanings are translated into the spatial terms of a game, and the text is transformed into a "meditation on the relation of language to reality" (Brée).

The grid is first and most obviously a gameboard. New Novelists' choice of games, especially chess, as structuring devices derives perhaps from Saussure's famous comparison of language and chess.[19] Chess, like language, is a signifying system composed of signs whose value is defined by position (selection and combination) in a structure. In *Les Lieux-dits*, repetition of games reveals that strategy rather than outcome is the primary attraction. Players advance according to rules as inviolable as they are arbitrary. "Sportsmanship" consists of making best use of available moves within those rules.

Alphabetical constraint is one such rule that "generates" episodes by means of the grid shape of the gameboard. Paradigmatic and syntagmatic choices regulate Atta's and Olivier's game of *ombres chinoises*. Similarly, Olivier's father's diary tells of an outrageous *ars amoris*, presenting eight erogenous zones listed alphabetically in eight languages. Each list prescribes a different amorous itinerary over the body: since alphabetical order differs from language to language, the list of body parts multiplied by number of languages produces a grid on which many stories or itineraries can be played. Olivier admits that, according to the diary, "c'est au cours d'une des plus complètes cérémonies que ma personne aurait été conçue" (p.151). Olivier apparently inherited his father's alphabetical mania, but he uses it for more sinister purposes. Before killing Atta, and following an implied grid analogous to the others, he then forces her to remove her clothing—in alphabetical order. Both kinds of itinerary over the body propose a sort of modern "Carte du Tendre" pointing to the preciosity of the whole novel, and reaffirming the assimilation of landscape, text and woman's body and of *voyeur*, voyager and reader.

The grid is also, inescapably, the emblem of structuralism. As a novel that reads itself, and as a parable, *Les Lieux-dits* demonstrates a structuralist model of reading. Perceiving antitheses, organizing the world according to paradigm and syntagm, grouping components (Lévi-Strauss's mythemes) in terms of their function, Olivier methodically if somewhat overzealously personifies that model. By seeing opposition as a category in itself, Olivier perceives the meaning of his universe and the novel's. The various forms that Olivier points out and their repeated manifestations throughout the novel fill in a grid of mutual metaphors. It is the grid itself which is the meaning of the novel.

Emphasis on structured configurations of signifiers in *Les Lieux-dits* is confirmed by systematic erasure of origins. In *L'Observatoire de Cannes*, a pocketknife, detached from any scriptor, is inscribed in a "text" of graffiti which offer in turn a model for reading the novel. In *Les Lieux-dits*, just as histories of each town were destroyed, traces of the author as origin are obliterated. This is accomplished first by the intervention of Crucis as the artist; the "course au trésor" of *L'Observatoire de Cannes* is analogous to the search for Crucis, his identity, his secret. Secondly, the author's name on the cover of *Les Lieux-dits* is inscribed in the wordplay within the novel. The words *Jean* and *Ricardou*, containing four and eight letters respectively, participate in the novel's numerical and anagrammatic structures.

The importance of numbers and letters is made explicit as part of a description of the emblem on a package of Pall Mall cigarettes:

> Avant de quitter cet emblème, certain voyageur desirera peut-être que lui soient prodiguées d'ultimes précisions sur la symbolique mise en oeuvre. On a sans doute déjà noté que les quatre inscriptions sont faites, chacune, de quatre mots: pall mall famous cigarettes, wherever particular people congregate, *in hoc signo vinces, per aspera ad astra.* Il faut non moins reconnaître que le blason, en ses quatre quartiers, agence huit signes: trois lions et une tour, une tour et trois lions.

Focusing next on a detail of the cigarette package—"deux personnages, proches de se battre"—the description relates numerical structures to the chessboard/book as an arena where two forces (Atta and Olivier and the modes of reading they represent) come into direct conflict:

> Ainsi l'ensemble, signale-t-il une sanglante opposition, imminente, sous le constant signe du huit. Le sous-multiple quatre désigne en outre l'idée de carré; il y a donc tout lieu de croire que la bataille exploite le huit au carré, ou soixante-quatre. (pp. 84-85)

Such a description serves to show *en abyme* how the novel's many motifs are interconnected.[20] Ricardou's name participates as well in a reservoir of crusade images and lexicon, thanks to letters it shares with *Villehardouin* and *ardeur*. By establishing a series of phonetic and fictional screens, the text represses the author as origin, permitting reading of the name as just another verbal form with variable content.

Word grids have been used since antiquity for magic purposes and also in Christian mythology. Thought to be of special protection to persecuted Christians, the palindromes of one particular magic square present five words when read in any of four directions. Rearranged, the same letters form the words "Pater Noster" in the form of a cross with an *alpha* or *omega* (or Atta and Olivier) at the end of each arm.[21]

```
                                    A
                                    —
                                    P
                                    A
                                    T
        S A T O R                   E
        A R E P O                   R
        T E N E T         A/PATERNOSTER/O
        O P E R A                   O
        R O T A S                   S
                                    T
                                    E
                                    R
                                    —
                                    O
```

As can be seen in the magic square above, the cross is a variant of the grid. As a symbol for multiplication (8x8, for example), it transforms axes into two-dimensional space, and suggests the intersections of words that structure *Les Lieux-dits*. In an article, Ricardou mentions what he calls "coëfficients de surdétermination."[22] This scientific-sounding term is an attempt to measure the degree to which a given element is justified or motivated by multiple anchors in the text. The higher the coefficient, the less arbitrary the element seems. Itself an emblem of overdetermination, the cross is the most overdetermined of the motifs in *Les Lieux-dits*.

Boyscouts learn to rub sticks together to produce fire. Fire appears in *Les Lieux-dits* wherever lines meet. Bright but contagious, fire is an apt image of proliferating overdetermination itself. Quite logically, then, literal fires break out at intersections—of window frames, tunnels, etc. An ashtray factory in Cendrier is destroyed by (red) fire escaped from the "prison géometrique" of its logos, a red cross. Fire and cross are further joined in the crusades. Soldiers met to share crusading ardor. When Olivier's and Atta's paths cross, their ardor is of a different order. This specific figure is a classical one, and love and war are ancient poetic themes. Figurative and literal fires in *Les Lieux-dits* bring to mind another famous literary pyromaniac, Pyrrhus, who perhaps also acquired his name through a "parturition roussellienne" resulting from his lament that, because of his unhappy love for Andromaque, he was "Brûlé de plus de feux que je n'en allumai."[23] That Ricardou should turn the same ambiguities to comic and theoretical purposes makes the figure no less poetic.

Cross and fire are both heavily associated with Atta, whose palindromic name bears two crosses, and whose dress, car, nailpolish and tomato juice are red. Atta disappears in flames escaped from her dress. Her death by fire is "inevitable" within the novel's logic. Perhaps the fact that she is somewhat "louche" (literally "cross-eyed", figuratively "shady or suspicious") determines her pose, which Olivier corrects as he binds her hands: "Ne tends pas les bras ainsi, tu ressembles à une crucifiée." (p. 153).

Before murdering Atta, Olivier explains that her death results from a postcard imperative (a picture of Crucis' laboratory where the syllable *toi* in the word "laboratoire" is obscured by the arms of a cross). In this instance, the cross appears as a "crossing out" or censorship. Another crossing out occurs in the old guardian's journal. Rereading his "Le Jardin des Oppositions," he removed each date, substituting the word "aujourd'hui." Similar erasures (by fire) obscure histories of the towns, forcing travelers to free ambiguous relationships between words and things without the help of diachrony (etymology or history). In all three cases, crosses can be seen to censor the referent, encouraging a corresponding increase in importance of the literal dimension. If Atta can be "crossed out" she can be no other than an "être de lettres." Towns too have no origin other than verbal.

The laboratory is the scene of another cross: the "X" that represents an unknown quantity in a chemical or algebraic formula. As such, it is symbolic of the quest itself, or the question a researcher seeks to answer, and which can be formulated on a graph or grid. Before Atta's appearance she was called the "inconnue." The chemical "solution" sought in *Les Lieux-dits* and found in the laboratory is, again, the insecticide. Words, too, behave like chemical compounds. As we saw in *L'Observatoire de Cannes*, elements of words can be detached and reassembled to form other "virtual" compounds. In *Les Lieux-dits* the particles "ard-" and "croix" with their variants, for example, are found in many contexts. Anagrams, another form of word intersection involving rearrangements of letters, link several words by showing two or more signifieds intersecting in one set of signifiers, or letters. Several series of anagrams are quite obvious in *Les Lieux-dits*: Lasius and Asilus; folie and fiole; Lenpois, l'espion and Epsilon. (In fact, the Greek letter epsilon is used as a symbol in formulating mathematical series.)

More complex examples are to be found in the "fables de l'anagramme." A postcard, clue to secrets of Crucis' laboratory and directive for Atta's execution, portrays a rearrangement of elements constituting Crucis' allegorical painting. Similarly, stones take the place of letters in an anagrammatic rebuilding of Bannière's church from stones of a previous edifice. Such fables qualify as part of the practice of anagram, as is made clear by the following definition:

> Dans sa généralité, l'anagramme peut être définie comme une transformation opérée sur les éléments d'un ensemble ordonné. Prenons pour exemple d'ensemble un mot, pour exemple d'éléments ses lettres.[24]

Rearrangement of letters is just one of many possible manifestations of a broad conception of anagram in Ricardou's fiction. Use of anagrams undermines referentiality by deconstructing the word and by establishing intersections and series only possible at the level of the signifier. Even the morpheme, smallest unit of semantic meaning, succumbs in the fragmentation and rearrangement of graphic units. In this way, letters can be seen in their materiality as geometric entities devoid of content. Such entities can be assembled and given meaning by the text.[25]

The cross motif is thus, appropriately, an intersection of spatial and verbal games. The painter, Crucis, is at the center of these configurations. Atta's and Olivier's (that is to say the novel's) entire journey traces the outline of a Maltese cross on a map, making each chapter one of the "stations of the cross" ("étapes du chemin de la croix," or Delacroix, i.e. Crucis). Crucis shares with his namesake, Eugène Delacroix, an interest in scenes from the crusades, along with a particular fondness for the color red. (See especially Delacroix' "L'Entrée des Croisés à Constantinople," a painting that figures in Ricardou's *La Prise de Constantinople*). More importantly, however, Crucis is simply an artist figure within the fiction. And although the novel claims to be generated from its own internal configurations, there is no question that Crucis is the creator of his paintings in a very traditional and authorial sense. He even signs them in a singular manner: instead of a dot, he puts a tiny cross over the letter -i-, thereby declaring, in Olivier's thinking, "c'est mon nom que je dessine" (p.27). His strange signature points to another artist figure, the author of the novel we are reading, who similarly inscribes his name within his work. Ricardou's name in turn contributes to the book's crosswords, sharing five letters with Villehardouin, chronicler of other crusades, and famous for his descriptions of the fires that destroyed Constantinople—those same fires figured in Delacroix' painting.[26] At the end of the novel's quest, a celestial guide voice, assumed by Crucis, speaks Ricardou's theoretical discourse. Where the reader is traveler, the artist, however hidden, is the guide who points to the "metaphor" (or parable) demonstrated by the novel we have just read. Banished from the plot, the quest paradigm returns at the level of theory.

If the transcendent author—subverted by anagrammatic play—returns to the novel by means of an artist figure, the manichean opposition between two types of readers becomes equally problematic. Olivier advocates reading literal dimensions exclusively, it will be remembered, while Atta has a retrograde referential streak. If Olivier is a *persona* for the active reader, capitalizing, so to speak, on the verbal condition of language, Atta remains a passive victim of her refusal to decipher signs. Unaware of the logic—or even the direction—of textual causality, she thinks she is free to fall in love with Olivier. She is blind to the determinism of the signfier that makes Olivier a madman. She fails to read the rebus which calls for her death. Olivier shows about as much self-knowledge as a cipher ever could: he is aware of his own anagrammatic identity and that of others. He knows what Atta refuses to see—that she is a two-dimensional signifier, and can be erased. He breaks her down into semantic (the color red, her ardor) and graphic (alphabetical ordering) components and effectively anagrammatizes her out of existence. Atta never gives up her fatal delusions of personhood and so succumbs in the victory of the signifier over the referential illusion.

Or does she? Rather than resolving once and for all the conflict between "Poets" and "Realists," between two views of language, the contradictory denouement in fact reproblematizes that opposition and reveals Olivier's duplicity. Olivier's murder of Atta derives its *form* from the graphic and rhetorical devices he describes. But he *justifies* his act by his hatred of her referential heresy! She thus becomes a martyr to mimesis, probably going directly to that lost linguistic paradise so regretted by Socrates. Far from being eliminated, her illusions are confirmed by her death. Olivier, on the other hand, must be seen as a philistine. Slipping easily from graphic to semantic operations, he kills her *because* . . . His referential intentionally belies his disbelief in motivation and his insistence on the primacy of textual surfaces. Furthermore, the same is true of the novel as a whole, which contradicts its own position by aiming to represent a theory by means of a transparent fiction.

A look at Atta and Olivier's respective readings of one scene will clarify their differences and demonstrate what is at stake besides theory. The scene in question is a kaleidoscope of reflecting and transparent surfaces, Ricardou's standard figures for the text in his fictional staging of problems of referentiality. Mirrors and repetition are thus devices which demand close examination.

In an article entitled "La Population des miroirs,"[27] Ricardou elaborates a theory to subdivide the problem of reflection into two domains: *redoublement* and *dédoublement*. A text characterized by *redoublement* mirrors the real world, thus using language referentially, in accordance with the "idéologie dominante de l'expression." A text that exploits techniques of *dédoublement* on the other hand, emphasizes the opacity of language. Structured repetition produces a text that represents (i.e. reflects) only itself. Signifiers refer to each other within a frame.

Recardou's use of mirrors points to conventions that regulate repetition in the novel. If an event occurs more than once, traditional novels usually describe the first and merely name subsequent occurrences. The following quotation from a Sherlock Holmes novel demonstrates traditional handling of repetition. After more than forty pages of action, Doctor Watson returns home to relate his adventure to his wife. Relaxing after dinner, he recounts:

I took a pull at my brandy, made a great show of lighting my
pipe, and then related the entire catastrophe.
'Poor Holmes!' She cried at the end.[28]

Between these two paragraphs, Ricardou would undoubtedly have included
an entire repeated story-within-a-story, making readers realize that events
and recounted events have the same textual status.

Ricardou's use of repetition forbids us to assume that anything exists
beyond or behind the text. In Belarbre, for example, Olivier surprises a
child absorbed in killing ants. A complete account of the event appears on
pages fifty to fifty-two. Then Olivier asks the child to explain his actions,
and the child replies with a description of Atta engaged in the same activity
(pp. 53 and 54). The two renditions are of equal length and are almost
verbatim repetitions. Small differences between versions prevent repeated
passages from being completely superimposed, however, which would
reduce the total text. Paradoxically, the most "realistic" rendition (repetition
of events corresponding to repetition of text) is also the most "literal."
Repetition in *Les Lieux-dits* is felt *as repetition*, and the text is the only
event. Furthermore, since Atta's behavior precedes the child's but the
accounts are reversed, the word "repetition" includes both French
meanings of the term (rehearsal and repetition, before and after). The only
order is the order of words: Ricardou's novel, like the structuralist paradigm
on which it is built, admits no events *in illo tempore* to be reenacted later.

In *Les Lieux-dits*, repetition takes the forms of *redoublement* and
dédoublement both. Within gradually expanding frames, initially
independent sequences are engulfed by larger units, producing imbricated
repetitions that resemble the optical illusion of depth. In the scene we want
to examine, then, Epsilon the bookseller shows Atta and Olivier a painting
by Crucis. Pictured on the canvas is an antique shop, as Epsilon explains:

Jouant sans doute sur l'ambiguïté du vocable, cette oeuvre se
nomme: Réflexion. Bien que nulle enseigne spiralée sur la vitre
ne nous en avertisse, nous sommes devant la boutique d'un
antiquaire; et celui-ci, au lieu d'offrir en vrac la somme de ses
objets, les a réunis en une scène unique par laquelle de part et
d'autre dans le temps tout un récit s'esquisse. (p.100)

A "scene" presents objects endowed with simultaneity. A "récit" unfolds
in time. The distance between the two is the space between things and
words, between reflection and repetition.

The *récit* that follows is a description of Crucis' painting. In order to present in hierarchical arrangement the dizzying series of *mises-en-abyme* that structures this description, one must indulge in endless subordination or proliferating series of parentheses: an etching of a seduction scene appears next to a tapestry showing a seduction scene which forms part of a mannequin display of a seduction scene. At each shift of the description, units that seemed autonomous become part of larger units. Atta and Olivier and then the reader are finally engulfed by carefully framed scenes. The reader can easily forget that all these seductions are pictured in a painting (of a display of antiques) that is itself in a book(store). Atta has a tendency to forget too. Her punishment thus has didactic implications.

The first scene described is an 18th century etching representing a "scène galante" in which "un homme et une femme luttent à demi, étroitement enlacés." The woman apparently wants to prevent the man from bolting the bedroom door. The room's décor includes an unmade bed, a mirror that reflects the entire scene, and an ambiguous framed print on the wall (pp.100-101).[29] Next to the etching can be seen an Aubusson tapestry in which an elegant and noble lady and her respectful suitor display a calm dignity that contrasts sharply with the disorder portrayed in the etching. This second scene also depicts a seduction, however, and repeats features of the first: a couple, a bedroom, ambiguous amorous behavior. The noble lady wears a quadruple string of eight pearls, suggesting that the tapestry is exactly half of a chessboard paradigm. Articulated by reference to a mirror, the two scenes form inverted images, as in a diptych. Correspondences between the two scenes encourage the reader/viewer to seek *dédoublement* within a grid rather than representation of external reality.

The description goes on to encompass other objects in the display: a bow and arrow, a heart-shaped tea table with a porcelain vase on which figures yet another galant scene, and a mannequin, who appears troubled by all these suggestive objects. The viewer's imagination and the mechanisms of description animate the scene, attributing to the lady an understandable desire to escape:

> S'étant approchée du miroir bleuâtre, elle y découvre non la délivrance obscurément entrevue, mais le dédoublement des inquiétants symboles, et son propre visage empourpré. Comme ses jambes se dérobent, elle se laisse choir sur un siège regardant l'homme qui, lentement, s'avance. (p.103)

Imagined motives are interpreted as actions, as the viewer is encouraged to
forget the level of reality being described. As each paragraph ends, we think
we have rejoined the primary narration. The phrase "dans le magasin
même" that begins the description of the mannequin display refers to the
painted antique shop, however, and not to the bookstore where Atta, Olivier
and Epsilon examine the painting.

It is significant that our mannequin lady, looking to her mirror for
"délivrance" (escape outside the dilemmas of her texts) finds only
"dédoublement." The lady's "trouble" circulates from frame to frame,
however, eventually contaminating Olivier and Atta. One final paragraph
further incorporates Atta and Olivier into the scene of desire:

> En deçà de la vitrine, sur le trottoir, vus de dos, debout, deux
> jeunes gens se tiennent par la main. La femme, brune, porte une
> robe rouge; l'homme, blond, est vêtu de bleu. En se répercutant
> de face sur la paroi de verre, leurs silhouettes viennent inscrire à
> l'intérieur, semble-t-il, de nouvelles figurations. Mais peut-être
> les deux jeunes gens se bornent-ils à s'admirer, l'un près de
> l'autre, en l'ample miroir improvisé. Outre ces personnages, se
> reflètent la façade ombreuse de l'église et, tout en haut, amassées
> dans le ciel visible, d'épaisses sédimentations de blancheur.
> —Etes-vous certain, malgré la signature et l'abondance des
> nuages, de l'authenticité de la toile? dit Olivier. (p.104)

Although Atta, too, wears red and Olivier's shirt is also blue, the "deux
jeunes gens" mentioned above are part of the painting. Only with Olivier's
question are we finally returned to the bookstore and the novel's
protagonists.

Hesitation before this ambiguous passage is inscribed in the
description itself. What do the blond man and brunette woman see as they
peer in/at the painted window? Through a transparent pane, they might see
the shop's interior and become part of its display. If the window is not totally
transparent, however, they would see themselves mirrored on the glass.
Hesitation between opacity and transparence causes a breakdown in the
distinction between self and other, repetition and difference, the written
world of the novel's protagonists and the written rendition of the painting.
Outside the tableau Atta is seduced by the same illusions. Mediated by
painted doubles, Atta and Olivier are inscribed in proliferating scenes of

seduction. Their response to this situation defines their status as models for two types of reading, or so the novel claims. As it turns out, however, Olivier fails to practice what he preaches, and the responsible reader must detect fundamental contradictions in his position and understand their serious implications.

Atta is a fairly straightforward version of the Ricardolian realist or romantic. Identifying with her referential illusions, she urges Olivier to short-circuit their planned itinerary and head directly for a hotel to reenact the stories she has witnessed. She sees everywhere images of her mimetic desires. The phial of insecticide, object of their joint search, she interprets as a love potion or a phallic symbol. As soon as the precious container—she calls it an "objet équivoque"—is finally in her hands, she drops and breaks it. The laboratory director reassures her, saying that "ce flacon n'avait nulle autre valeur que symbolique," and, as if we had not understood, Atta explains: "mon esprit n'a pu s'empêcher de voir en cet objet, instantanément, un symbole masculin." Atta's fantasy leaves her vulnerable to an alternative scenario; the ardor of her desire is displaced and she is burned. She fails to recognize the literal dimension of language until it is too late. "Mon erreur," she finally admits bitterly to Olivier, "est d'avoir eu recours à une métaphore. Votre folie n'était nullement au sens figuré: avec horreur, je vois se découvrir en vous, indiscutablement, le pyromane évadé de l'asile" (p. 155). If she had read the anagram in Olivier's last name, she would have learned his identity much sooner.

Olivier, on the other hand, claims to be an anti-referential reader. He perceives the painting's opacity, its difference. His philosophy echoes that advocated by Ricardou, who declares, for example: "Nous le savons; lire, c'est explorer les relations spécifiques par lesquelles sont liés les éléments d'un texte."[30] This short definition encompasses two aspects of Olivier's strategy: he looks for structure, and he executes the directives of words. Rather than tracing a causal link between crime and perpetrator, between a quest and its objects, Olivier reads necessity in and of inter-linking series of words. His strategy depends on a linguistic determinism that is the opposite of a referential illusion, or what Ricardou calls the "euphorie de récit." He resolves the "équivoque" of Atta's fantasy by reducing its symbol to simple literality, a "poussiéreuse verrerie." But if the bottle is a symbolic phallus, its destruction, however accidental (Freud and Ricardou claim nothing is accidental) poses a formidable threat to Olivier's world view. Furthermore, it is not only reference but also eroticism he finds threatening. In response, he suppresses Atta by invoking the intentionality of words in a way that sounds less like a theory than an alibi.

The use of linguistic and thematic generators and of closed geometric figures makes *Les Lieux-dits* a static configuration. Anagrammatic permutation too, produces rearrangements of the same givens, revealing hidden identities (Epsilon is a spy, Olivier a maniac) but transforming nothing. Similarly, religious and occult symbolism, refusing any transcendent meaning, is limited to the restricted space of a ritual game. Far from revealing the potential creativity and liberating virtues of non-logocentric reading, *Les Lieux-dits* demonstrates the dangers inherent in a rigidly formalist viewpoint that refuses desire as it erases history. Lévi-Strauss defines the strategies of structural analysis in a way that hints at the problem in *Les Lieux-dits*. When studying a corpus of myths, he explains, "il s'agit toujours de dresser un inventaire des enceintes mentales, de réduire des données apparemment arbitraires à un ordre, de rejoindre un niveau où une nécessité se révèle immanente aux illusions de la liberté."[31] It is because of Atta's illusions of liberty, her tendency to forget that she is a character in a novel not her own, that Olivier finds himself justified in killing her.

Olivier's mode of reading, explicitly rejecting a religious viewpoint, nevertheless contains the traps of any totalizing system. His dogmatic belief, confirmed by the novel's overdetermined geometry, produces a critical gridlock that immobilizes the circulation of meaning, producing an effect of entrapment by means of some very dangerous "enceintes mentales." Olivier, as it turns out, does believe in a transcendent truth after all; he even subscribes to an orthodoxy that justifies murder. Subversion of the linear quest model is possible in this novel only because Olivier knows from the beginning how the novel will end. Atta constitutes the obstacle that allows a story to develop, but most of all she provides occasions for Olivier's discourse to unfold. When she becomes a threat to the system, she must be erased. The novel does indeed reflect itself, but that reflection transcends the work to make general theoretical statements about what art is, and what is more, what art should be. *Les Lieux-dits* more than any of Ricardou's other fiction so far is not art for art's sake but art for theory's sake.

In a far-reaching critique of structuralism, Anthony Wilden points out some implications of perceiving structure as a closed system, a conception he finds in Piaget's psychology, Lévi-Straussian anthropology and the sociology of Talcott Parsons, among others. In the work of these thinkers, Wilden argues, order ceases simply to mean "organization", but comes instead to imply a normative pattern. Wilden's warning applies as well to

Olivier's structuralism, which "makes order a synonym for LAW AND ORDER." Wilden goes on to impute a similarity between this kind of normative structural analysis and the socio-economic theories of J. Edgar Hoover. In all these cases, he says, global perceptions of order leave no room for "noise" in the system. As a result, "Deviations, disturbances, contradictions, conflicts are therefore necessarily and consequently the work of OUTSIDE AGITATORS."[32] Such is the role of Atta in *Les Lieux-dits* and one of the reasons she is eliminated.

I am arguing, then, that the claustrophobic effect of *Les Lieux-dits* is a signal that this novel, while claiming to subvert representation, in fact actually does represent what amounts to a totalitarian ideology. By dramatizing the antics of two fictional reader-personae, Ricardou would teach us to distinguish between two modes of reading. Indeed, the novel would like its readers to feel that we too are characters inscribed in the fictions as "voyageurs issus de quelque conflit formel" (p.115). And if Atta can forget, at her own peril, the level of reality she sees before her, tactics of description, illusion and ideological smokescreening make it likely that the reader too will be "framed." Ricardou's shifting frames produce what Genette calls metalepsis, an intrusion of extratextual reality into a story, or the reverse, a text's aggression on the world outside. The tricks of metalepsis, he explains,

> manifestent par l'intensité de leurs effets l'importance de la limite qu'ils s'ingénient à franchir au mépris de la vraisemblance, et *qui est précisément la narration (ou la représentation) elle-même*; frontière mouvante mais sacrée entre deux mondes: celui où l'on raconte, celui que l'on raconte. . . Le plus troublant de la métalepse est bien dans cette hypothèse inacceptable et insistante, que l'extradiégétique est peut-être toujours déjà diégétique, et que le narrateur et ses narrataires, c'est à dire vous et moi, appartenons peut-être encore à quelque récit.[33]

It begins to look as if there is no space where the reader can enjoy freedom of movement in this text that threatens to enclose us.

It does, however, seem unreasonable to suppose that Olivier's didactic self-analysis is the only alternative to a realistic or logocentric strategy of reading. Olivier does, after all, fail to represent anti-representation. It is in fact possible to reject both Olivier's totalizing system and his (and Ricardou's) manichean hypothesis by realizing that *Les Lieux-dits* does portray competing and viable points of view even if Olivier is unaware of them. Olivier is after all a villain, and we are free to refuse to become characters in his novel. "A la limite, un livre qui ne résiste pas ne mérite guère lecture," Ricardou believes. "Or certains textes, dont l'ensemble forme sans doute ce qu'on appelle littérature, paraissent offrir une résistance toujours renaissante."[34] It is at the level of a series of metaleptic frames that compete for control that the novel, does, in fact, insolubly resist reduction to its own theoretical pronouncements.

In this light, the discussion of Crucis' tableau in the Chaumont bookstore ends with a sentence worthy of further attention: "Outre ces personnages, se reflètent la façade ombreuse de l'église et, tout en haut, amassées dans le ciel visible, d'épaisses sédimentations de blancheur" (p.104). The long description begins with the painting's title—"Réflexion"—and ends with clouds. The phrase "sédimentations de blancheur" serves, in a sense, as Crucis' signature, locating the frame of his painting within an imbricated narrative. The entire novel is framed in parallel manner. Its first sentence evokes reflection: "A peine franchie, sous les nuées, cette sombre ligne de faite, tout le pays, en contrebas, dispense des reflets." Its last sentence, after Crucis' farewell, marks a reappearance of clouds: "Et son regard, en l'extrême profondeur fictive, contemple les massives sédimentations de blancheurs" (p. 160).

The frame of Crucis' tableau enlarges to engulf progressively more text in an expanding *mise-en-abyme*. Given parallel structure of painting and novel, the suspicion arises that the entire novel is no more than a description of a painting, with imagination producing story from description; the novel is framed by Crucis exactly as is the tableau. Early on, Olivier's appearance is literally "foreshadowed" by his shadow projected on a painting: "Obéissant à l'injonction du guide, le jeune visiteur s'approche du tableau: il est bientôt gêné par l'ombre que ses cheveux blonds, en léger désordre, projettent sur l'allégorie. Il se recule un peu" (p.17). Naturally Olivier resists entering the frame of someone else's image; he has his own story to write.

It is impossible, however, to consider Crucis's painting as a *mise-en-abyme* which would reveal the larger fiction to be a description of a painting. If the entire novel is engulfed by this painting, at least two other similar objects compete for control of the text. One of these is the package of Pall Mall cigarettes, whose description also begins with a reflection of the novel's opening sentence: "A peine offert, sous les nuées, entre les doigts du voyageur, le paquet de cigarettes, en contrebas, dispense ses reflets" (p.82). Elements of the novel are found on the package: heraldry suggests crusades; color schemes, number symmetry and the central emblem propose, in miniature, an interior reduplication of all the novel's major motifs.

As a third text within the text, the old park guardian's journal also threatens, amoeba-like, to engulf the whole book. Reading the journal aloud in "Hautbois," Olivier and Atta discover a repetition of their initial encounter. Interrupting their reading, they are forced to admit that their own meeting followed the journal's script which both had already read. They also find partial repetition of the seduction scenes and a comparison between crusades and fighting armies of ants.

The word "aujourd'hui" serves to identify sections of the journal as it is read in "Hautbois." However, this word escapes the journal's frame to wander through the novel, disconcerting the reader. Olivier points out that

> Le voyageur attentif remarquera dès lors la retorse tactique selon laquelle, par un usage immodéré du mot aujourd'hui, *Le Jardin des Oppositions* s'efforce de s'accaparer rétrospectivement des pages antécédentes, maintes fois attaquées, au préalable, pour cela, par d'intempestifs identiques adverbes. (p.135)

Incongruous appearances of the word cause us to suspect that, rather than being contained in the novel, the journal is actually the larger frame.

Bellicose vocabulary in the quotation above is not gratuitous. Crucis' tableau, the Pall Mall package and the guardian's journal vie for control of the novel. Each is given full attention in one chapter, "Chaumont," "Cendrier," and "Hautbois" respectively. However, each mirrors aspects of the novel found outside that chapter. Hence each can be seen as perhaps enclosed in, perhaps enclosing the novel as a whole. As with the graffiti in *L'Observatoire de Cannes*, it is tempting to see each case as source of the many motifs that structure the novel, but their coexistence prevents any such reduction. Because of multiple *mise-en-abyme*, no single explanation of the novel is satisfactory.

Intently pursuing his own manichean plots, Olivier remains oblivious to these competing frames, and so he can be captured and made part of a story we read. *Les Lieux-dits* talks about a break with representation, but it does not, in effect, accomplish this break, in spite of its metafictional narrative level. It does, however, at least dramatize in an entertaining way some of the difficulties inherent in mimetic modes of reading and some of the dangers of an excessively formalized anti-representational discourse. And despite the fact that it explicitly reduces possible modes of reading to a schematized binary conflict, it does offer some possibilities for multidimensional readings.

Campbell's composite hero is aided by a guide figure, often a child. The guide discourse in *Les Lieux-dits* passes from character to character or to the narration itself. The novel's subtitle prepared us for a narrative that is part guidebook, part novel discourse. Quite often the voyager mentioned by the text refers to the rhetoric of the guidebook addressing its reader. The reader, much more than Olivier or any of the characters, fulfills Campbell's definition of the questing hero. Leaving the "monde quotidien" (Ricardou's term) when we open the cover, we are isolated from society as we plunge into a magical mystery tour in a fantastic ludic country. We are initiated into a language which *does* rule events, and we witness Roussellian quests for rhyme, symmetry, overdetermination and metaphor. On the last page we are reintegrated into our everyday social world by Crucis' farewell. Our guide is the book itself. In this light, the whole novel is a parable that tells of the adventure of reading. The reader's frustration, mentioned at the beginning of this chapter, can be found in the poverty of the quest proposed for us. We are more spectators than heroes, and our heroic potential is constantly underestimated. But as incompatible *mises-en-abyme* compete to incorporate extra-textual reality into the novel, the reader has a chance, albeit limited, to become heroic by resisting the orthodoxy espoused by Olivier and Ricardou and by reading the scene of these contradictions as a fiction in its own right.

CHAPTER III

Metamorphoses of a Superbook: *La Prise/Prose de Constantinople*

> Once upon a time, Chuang Chou
> dreamed that he was a butterfly, a
> butterfly fluttering about enjoying
> itself. It did not know that it was
> Chuang Chou. Suddenly he awoke
> with a start and he was Chuang
> Chou again. But he did not know
> whether he was Chuang Chou who
> had dreamed that he was a butterfly,
> or whether he was a butterfly
> dreaming that he was Chuang Chou.
> Between Chuang Chou and the
> butterfly there must be some
> distinction. This is what is called
> the transformation of things.
>
> —Chuang Tzu

La Prise/Prose de Constantinople takes into account the fact that while fictional characters may be "êtres de lettres," readers are not. Although published four years before *Les Lieux-dits*, it is more successful in dealing with the questions all Ricardou's fiction poses about the text's relation to other texts and to the world. For this reason, it will be more rewarding to study it here *after* consideration of the later novel.

The greater satisfaction of reading *La Prise/Prose* derives, I think, from its less rigid, dogmatic posture and its consequent openness to its own contradictions. This novel not only exploits its points of departure (puzzles, material givens of the cover design, generative wordplay), but also explores the enigmas of its own evolution and takes responsibility for meanings produced. Its parables can thus never be reduced to their didactic meaning alone. What is left—the inexhaustible excess—might be a definition of good literature.

This, Ricardou's second novel, published in 1965, renders problematic even the enunciation of its title. Two conflicting titles resembling Roussel's metagrams bring into question the traditional format of the book as object. Between *La Prise de Constantinople* on the front cover (suggesting the "Realists" of *Les Lieux-dits*) and *La Prose de Constantinople* on the back (the "Poets"), the novel is a world in constant flux. Absence of pagination and complex networks of repetition further defy traditional prose linearity.[1] The two titles, interacting with other oppositions, proliferate to unfold a novel of cosmic proportions: past, present and future, the ages of life, inner consciousness and outer space, prose and poetry are all included in this novel which sees itself as an entire library or Superbook. Parable blends into myth.

Where *Les Lieux-dits* trapped its readers in two-dimensional closed figures, *La Prise/Prose* invites us to wander in open-ended three-dimensional space. It is helpful in comparing the two novels to see *Les Lieux-dits* as manifesting certain formal characteristics of classicism: it proposes harmony, balance, and crystalline purity of structure while seeking to teach an ideology ("instruire") and to entertain ("plaire"). *La Prise/Prose*, on the other hand, corresponds more closely to the tension and movement of baroque forms. Imbrie Buffum suggests (appropriately for Ricardou) eight interrelated features of the baroque, all of which can be used to describe *La Prise/Prose*. Ideology or "moral purpose", "emphasis and exaggeration", and "organic unity" characterize to some degree all of Ricardou's novels. An "O de surprise" recurrent in *La Prise/Prose* points to the use of "contrast and surprise," another of Buffum's categories. "Horror and morbidity" are the effects of Ricardou's "scriptural striptease" which, while ostensibly playful, suggests sadistic aggression against female figures. "Theatricality and illusion" are especially apparent in the middle section of *La Prise/Prose*, where a pantomime is repeatedly acted out by eight characters. Each presentation of the mime transforms the previous one, so that the whole section demonstrates principles of "movement and metamorphosis" which regulate the entire novel. Ricardou's microscopic focus on changes in water, sand, and hair could be described by Buffum when he states that "stability itself is an illusion; actually it is an extremely slow form of change."

Especially relevant to *La Prise/Prose* is "incarnation," which Buffum describes as "the baroque tendency to express intangible ideas in concrete form." He explains that "Instead of abstractions, we have images which appeal to the senses. Through the creative activity of the baroque artist, ideas take on physical being.''[2] Ricardou's theories, highly abstract in his critical articles, take on concrete form in his fictions. Spatial configurations also acquire more tangible reality. Well-known myths evoked in *La Prise/Prose* present dramatic and visible parables of ideological stands. The biblical idea of incarnation of the Word is quite literally present in the opening pages of *La Prise/Prose*, as we shall see. Whereas in *Les Lieux-dits* religious symbolism is schematic and superficial, in *La Prise/Prose* closer ties link theological ideas with conceptions of writing.

Ricardou claims to have generated *La Prise/Prose* from jokes, a rebus, mathematical calculations and geometric correspondences. His own comments about his novel and his explanatory sketches,[3] though interesting and helpful, represent curious oversimplifications, an attempt, perhaps, to tame a text that became too wild, or an effort to divert his own or our attention from the novel's more disturbingly protean aspects. Like *Les Lieux-dits*, *La Prise/Prose* is organized by a series of mutually inclusive frames, each of which seems at times to provide a key to the others. Like all of Ricardou's novels, it stages a dramatization of its own mechanisms. Between its entrance and its exit, however, *La Prise/Prose* can be seen not as a grid but as a labyrinth, in which the reader despairs of finding Ariadne's thread ("Jamais nous ne retrouverons le fil secret du texte" II, 3:6). Each of five interwoven stories seems to offer a "fil secret," but their convergence leaves us entangled. The result is Ricardou's most dynamic work of fiction. The novel's ludic dimension, more than a *mise-en-scène* of theory, remains open to the risks of its own desire and the unpredictability of its generative word-play.

The novel emerges as an interweaving of three tales, a history, and an autobiography. Each of these five fictions proposes a quest for a desired but inaccessible object. The hero wants to capture his object—this is the "prise"—but he must also cover a certain route, the "prose." Along the way, each hero adopts literal and figurative postures ("poses"): the stance of a crusader or space explorer, the role of an artist, a vacationer or a fairy-tale prince. Throughout the novel, the fictions interrupt each other so that each can be read as a digression from the others. Within the field of influence of a mysterious rock, for example, space explorers are invaded by a collective memory of a summer vacation. Each time an element appears in one context, it evokes and enriches the others, and textual mechanisms introduced in one story can be used to read the others, so that the novel's complexity increases exponentially as reading progresses.

1. Three tales

Each of the three tales includes eight characters. The three stories are united by the name Isabelle, which represents both the goal and the quest route. Most obviously, "Isabelle" provides an acrostic for each list of characters: *I*sa, *S*erge, *A*lice, *B*laise, *E*dith, *L*aurent, *L*éonie, *E*dmond, for example. This and other similarities suggest that the stories are transformations of each other. In some ways, the three sets of characters can be collapsed into one, and then further reduced to two figures—a subject and an object of desire and of discourse.

In a first story, children act out a fairy tale called "La Princesse Interdite." Two children play roles appropriate to their names. Sylvain, as the "Prince Charmé" must cross "l'hallucinante sylve du domaine d'Hessel" (I, 4:2) in order to reach the forbidden Princess Belle, played by Isabelle. Edouard directs the play, which is eventually to include a "Princesse Apocryphe," a "Fillette Fallacieuse," and a villain, Basile, three obstacles to the Prince's quest. While Edouard, Isabelle and Sylvain prepare their roles, five other children perfect a singular décor on a grass-covered "rond-point" which serves as a stage. Aligning small stones, they inscribe in giant script the word "Belle" on the grass. As he cuts his way through thick vegetation to reach the Princess, the Prince will follow the circuitous route determined by the name of his beloved:

> Sans doute inspiré par quelque singulier livre de la bibliothèque, Edouard a donc apporté un raffinement inédit à l'histoire de la Princesse Interdite. Si le Prince choisit, comme il est probable, toutes les boucles, il devra parcourir, en sens inverse, l'intégralité du nom de celle qu'il désire, affrontant ainsi les pièges et les oubliettes qui s'y trouvent agencés. (I, 4:2-3)

Here, attainment of the goal is deferred by the indirect itinerary of the name itself, as well as by obstacles, traps and villains which function like the series of photographs in *L'Observatoire de Cannes*, each interposing a screen or veil which hides the "jeune baigneuse" from view.

Edouard has added one further complication to the drama. At the threshold of the Princess' door, the Prince will be required to undergo a final delay: he must read a book in which are recounted his own adventures! Like

Zeno's arrow, he will never reach his goal, for at the end of his story *en abyme* this second Prince will read his own story, and so on indefinitely. The hero of the tale is thus doubly a reader—a self-reading and a reading of the name of his lady provide his quest route.

The "capital" element of this tale is the letter B of the princess' name, which forms a vestibule to her chamber. It is here that the Prince will be drawn into successive readings of his own story in an infinite deferral of satisfaction. The "murs symboliques" indicated by rows of stones are literal walls of symbols as well, in that the Prince cannot reach beyond language in his quest. An insurmountable barrier between sign and referent similarly condemns the novel as a whole to repeated self-readings. But rather than taking this as a didactic stance, *La Prise/Prose* shows how a quest *in* language can only be a quest *of* language and dramatizes this limitation as a frustration.

A second tale proposes eight commandos on a space odyssey. Led by Edgar Word, members of a "Légion Solaire" fight their way through copious vegetation on the planet Venus. Choice of this planet is over-determined by its metagram *Venise*, city of departure for the fourth crusade, by star imagery beginning with the Editions de Minuit insignia, and by the veiled but pervasive presence of the goddess of love. The object of these explorers' quest is a forbidden city (a "Cité Interdite" instead of a Princess this time) named Silab Lee. Toward the end of the novel, one of the explorers will be required to read his own adventure in a manual called "La Prise de Constantinople," where "Constantinople" is a code word for "Constellation." Here again, language is the object of a quest, "Silab Lee" being a homophone of "syllabe les" or "les syllables."

Language, however, is also a formidable obstacle to the commandos' quest. A mysterious rock called "*La Borne*" throws in the commandos' path obstacles analogous to loops in the cursive script of the word "Belle" written in stones. In any linear novel or goal-directed quest, progress is slowed by anything resembling a digression. Under the nefarious influence of the *Borne*, the Légion Solaire involuntarily indulges in memories, hypotheses and explications which divert attention from goals at hand. In particular, the pace of their adventure is slowed by the intrusion of description, which has the capacity to dilate uncontrollably, as an object of fascination comes into progressively closer hypnotic focus.

Digressions, provoked by the *Borne*, are kept in control by a textual *borne* or limit: the command "Arrêtez!" stanches digressive flow and forces return to another point of departure. Description of a Légion Solaire uniform, for example, could continue indefinitely, especially if the shirt covers the curvaceous attractions of Lou, whose red hair and freckles associate her with Isabelle:

> La rectitude des cinq segments que l'écusson propose—les côtés du triangle et du L—est métamorphosée en incurvations diverses par les volumes sous-jacents de la poitrine. Projeté en cet espace courbe, le triangle tend à s'effiler. Si l'attention s'arrête à de nouvelles minuties . . .
> —Arrête? Ah oui, arrête . . . (I, 7:2)

Desire and description run parallel in the example above as elsewhere, so that limits imposed on description are equivalent to restraints imposed on desire. Such restraints do not imply a puritan morality, however, but simply signal an inherent necessity of language.

A third tale introduces eight more characters into the total *dramatis personae*. While Serge teaches Alice how to skip stones, the rest of a group of vacationing adolescents swims and dives. The order and description of their dives follows a strictly regular pattern:

> Blaise et ses camarades poursuivent imperturbablement le cycle de leur plongeons. La régularité de leurs évolutions est si précise que, d'ici, les nageurs paraissent composer une horlogerie au fonctionnement très rigoureux . . .
> Une observation périlleusement prolongée révèle une loi moins lisible du phénomène. Il semble que chacun s'inspire du saut de son prédécesseur, mais, soit qu'intervient des modifications de détail s'accroissant d'un plongeon à l'autre, soit qu'un contre-sens provoque une mutuation brusque, la succession des figures proposées trahit une métamorphose continue. (I, 4:2-3)

This cycle introduces an important mechanism that regulates repetition following a model.

This principle of "duplication intégrant une constante d'irrégularité" is deployed at length in the novel's second or middle section. In those eight chapters, eight adults play a ritualistic and somewhat sinister parlor game in the library of the château d'Hessel. Although they seem to have aged during the course of the afternoon, these are the same characters who played on the beach, diving and skipping stones. The game begins with Isa and Serge, who present a short mimodrama for Alice. Then Alice takes Serge's role, while Serge, joined by Blaise, watches. The game continues until each of seven players (or actors) has imitated the model proposed by a predecessor.

Isa, the constant in the formula, remains on stage as the object of the pantomimed action. Proposing a model for subsequent actors, Serge first lights a cigarette, extinguishing his match with a circular motion of the arm. Muttering something obscure, he selects a book at random, reads a few pages aloud, then replaces the book and closes the glass-doored bookcase. Finally, before summoning the next actor, he falls at Isa's feet, caressing her hair while pretending to readjust her pose. These ambiguous activities lend themselves to the prodigious metamorphoses of description. With each successive enactment of the drama, the gestures change slightly and/or the description evolves. By the end, the cigarette has become a major conflagration in which a soldier burns to cinders. Double meanings of key words allow Isa's body to be transformed into a landscape: her long liquid red hair swirling over her breasts (*la gorge*) becomes a cataract tumbling over a precipice into "*une gorge.*" Serge's kneeling pose is subsequently seen as that of a soldier, a supplicant, a medieval hero, a bather throwing stones and a character in a painting.

Each description is further colored by the passage selected to be read aloud. The middle section of *La Prise/Prose* serves as an elaborate parable of intertextuality, showing how a given text is adopted, transformed and integrated into a new context by means of closely documented shifts in meaning. The pantomimes take place in a library, and the novel itself becomes a sort of encyclopedia of related subtexts. Some of the passages thus transformed refer to other layers of the novel: fairy story, crusades, and a space voyage become books read by the eight characters as they present their cyclical drama. Other readings include two from an apocryphal Villehardouin, whose account of the burning of Constantinople demonstrates the processes by which another text is "captured", as Ricardou might put it, within a novel.

2. Ricardou's Intertextual Crusade

The fourth crusade in fact figures as a fourth fiction in *La Prise/Prose*. Not itself a parable of textual processes, the crusade story unfolds according to mechanisms of verbal expansion, transformation and especially intertextuality, as demonstrated in the three tales. Intertextuality is one of several possible answers explored in this novel to the question of origin: the text emerges through transformations of previous writing.

The fourth of eight crusades set out in 1203, hoping to conquer Jerusalem. Crusaders from all Europe assembled in Venice, recruited by impassioned speeches of preachers and soldiers. Besides evoking Villehardouin's chronicle, the opening paragraph of a subtext read in part II of the novel "embroiders" the same themes found in "Bannière," the first chapter of *Les Lieux-dits*.

> Elu pape en 1198, Innocent III considère comme un devoir de reconquérir les Saints Lieux. 'Tous les Princes, répète-t-il, à quelque conte qu'ils appartiennent, sont les vassaux du Christ et doivent libérer son domaine.' Par tous les pays catholiques, il envoie prêcher la Croisade. Chaque prêcheur brodera, selon l'inspiration qui lui sera envoyée du ciel, sur un modèle commun. (II, 2:4)

The crusaders never reached their goal, however. Instead of going directly to Jerusalem, they were persuaded to attack Constantinople. After the death of their leader Boniface of Montferrat, the crusaders followed a certain Baud*ouin* de Flandre, who adds his name to an already established network of phonetic correspondences that includes Ric*ardou*, Villeh*ardou*in, and Ed*ouard*. Actual histories supply these and other overdetermined elements in Ricardou's story. The numbers four and eight, for example, and the fact that the crusaders fail to attain their goal, correspond to his preoccupations. The rest, he redesigns freely, following processes of regulated variance. Several recurrent refrains from *La Prise/Prose* are present: "se déplacer vers l'ouest," "interdit," "si elle se laisse astreindre à une étude perilleusement excessive." Even Venus ("Vénusiens" as a misspelling of Venetians) appears in Ricardou's account. Of especial importance is his addition of a storm which follows the burning of Constantinople recounted by the real Villehardouin[4] and which contributes to Ricardou's fire and water themes. These crusaders, it must be noticed, after all, are ruled by stories (*contes*), not feudal *comtes*.

Following suggestions that the novel has a secret center where everything converges, we find in the middle of part II a description of Delacroix' painting "Entrée des croisés à Constantinople." This huge masterpiece depicting the arrival of crusaders in a burning Constantinople was exhibited with that title in the Paris Salon of 1841, but at the Exposition Universelle six years earlier, the same painting was exhibited under the title "Prise de Constantinople par les croisés." According to some, Delacroix himself served as model for the central figure, Count Baudouin of Flanders. Such an inscription of himself strangely corresponds to the presence of Ricardou's name in *La Prise/Prose* and to the novel's impersonal but autobiographical tone.[5] The painting as a whole makes contributions on many levels to Ricardou's novel, which, seen from this angle, becomes a fiction (prose) constructed with reference to Delacroix' painting (a *prise*).

Eugène Delacroix, *Prise de Constantinople par les croisés*. detail
(the Louvre, Paris)

A detail from the Delacroix painting plays a more obscure role in transformations within the novel. Referring to the lower right hand corner of the painting, Ricardou's description, appearing in one of the subtexts of Part II, is quite precise.

> Au premier plan, à droite, très jeune, une femme est tombée à genou, au sol, auprès de sa soeur blessée, ou de son amie.
>
> Elle soulève délicatement la tête abandonnée et se penche vers ce visage, guettant intensément le souffle, les infimes métamorphoses de la physionomie. Dans l'affolement et la fuite éperdue, les hurlements, les cris—et peut-être touchée un instant, déjà, prématurément, par la main d'un obscur soudard—, son vêtement s'est défait.
>
> Le dos est nu, en sa courbure, jusqu'à la taille.
>
> La nuque ploie. La chevelure rousse s'effondre en une longue cascade verticale dont l'extrémité va effleurer, presque, le bras droit de la jeune mourante couchée en chien de fusil par terre, dans son manteau bleu.
>
> De plus profonds parentés, semble-t-il, isolent les deux femmes de l'agitation périphérique, les accordent en l'intimité de cette mort où l'une, simplement, précède de peu l'autre. (II, 4:4)

A descriptive eye focuses on this pathetic scene, seeing it as a center from which death radiates, pervading the entire tableau. Adding imagination to description, the text has already begun to elaborate a story, with movement and chronology, from the immobile scene.

Elements from this description supposedly chosen at random are integrated into surrounding pantomimes and radiate through the entire novel as well. A part of each pantomime involves readjusting a zipper at the back of Isa's strapless blouse. The blouse is progressively unzipped until Isa falls to her knees to prevent it from falling off: her bare back, cascading red hair and kneeling posture recreate the tableau. A zipper, with its metalic teeth becomes an instrument of torture when its frame of reference is removed. Her kneeling position itself transforms Isa, erstwhile patient and princess into a victim. As the pantomime continues, the actor's gestures are interpreted according to fiction latent in the description: "Laurent, déjà debout, brandit à deux mains, ainsi qu'une lourde épée dont la lame horizontale, argentée, surplombe . . . mais il est interrompu" (II, 6:11). The sound of a little girl crying effects a return from Constantinople to a library, eight vacationers and their bizarre game. The text thus interrupts this audience "qui s'est laissée fasciner," suggesting that excessive imagination is responsible when one falls prey to a referential illusion. The crying "fille" is no doubt "fallacieuse," since nothing more is heard from her. She serves to reestablish frames, thus redefining for the characters the crucial separation of fiction from "reality."

Obsessive repeated descriptions of a red "chevelure" occur throughout *La Prise/Prose*, and especially in Part II. Each repetition of the parlor game gives increased attention to Isa's hair, which the regulated modulations of description transform into a waterfall. The point of departure is a precise rendition of what happens to Isa's long red hair when she bends her head: "Rousse, la chevelure s'effondre, verticale, en cascades diverses, en remous imprévus" (II, 2:9). The term "cascades" must be taken more literally in the next version: "Liquide, la chevelure, s'effondre selon des cascades que les rochers épars diversifient en courants imprévus, en tourbillons" (II, 3:10). The hair is completely replaced by its liquid metaphor during its next two appearances:

> la cataracte rousse s'effondre en chutes diversifiées par les tourbillons, des courants imprévus, jusqu'à humecter amplement le cou et les épaules. (II, 4:8)

> l'eau boueuse, rousse, s'effondre selon des chutes que plusieurs rochers subdivisent en cascades annexes, en tourbillons accélérés, jusau'à mouiller amplement le dos, le cou et les épaules. (II, 5:13)

As her hair proves more and more menacing, Isa finds herself increasingly in danger of being swept away in the cataract and the description. In the first enactment, "La figure se penche, déjà atteinte, de chaque côté, par la double vague des cheveux" (II, 2:9). But soon she is forced to notice what is happening; her face is "attentif aux pages fictives." (II, 3:10). In chapter four, Isa's neck and shoulders are covered, and in chapter five she becomes "la nageuse (qui) doit être remontée à la surface par une violente poussée ascendante" (II, 5:13). By chapter six, it may be too late to save her: "Aussi faut-il, par une poussée violente ascentionnelle, remonter d'urgence le corps vers la surface" (II, 6:11).

The words "rousse," "s'effondre", "gorge" reappear in each description, but their meaning changes depending on context. Near the last transformation, only these words and the constant position of the description of Isa's hair in the chapter remind us that it is hair that is being described. Thus, from chapter to chapter, duplication of description is regulated by a "constante d'irrégularité." The last description abandons polyvalence, and the description returns to the parlor game:

> Branches, fragments d'écorces, brindilles et aiguilles viennent se joindre au corps abandonné—qu'un ultime sursaut, cependant, inattendu, cambre soudain: au moment où, d'un geste précis, le bustier a été dégrafé, les deux mains d'Isa se sont crispées sur sa poitrine, essayant de retenir le vêtement que, selon une nécessaire lenteur, peu à peu on arrache. (II, 7:16)

In the process of the "game" Isa has become a swimmer helplessly submerged in swirling water. The detail from Delacroix' painting and the storm from the false Villehardouin's history visit their destruction on Isa, the victimized Princess, who represents Constantinople, the Cité Interdite.

The burning of Constantinople is similarly enacted at Isa's expense by means of the same sort of minuscule transformations. One ambiguous gesture in the pantomime involves lighting a cigarette (Lucky Strike this time in accordance with this novel's emblematic letters L and S). At first harmless, this manoeuvre becomes threatening when Edith accidentally ignites Isa's hair: "Un infime déplacement de la cigarette, cependant, met en contact l'extrémité incandescente avec la chevelure qui se met à grésiler" (II, 5:3). The word "déplacement" refers to Edith's hand movement, but also to gestures in her pantomime compared to those already presented. By means of tiny displacements in pantomime and description, Isa's hair is transformed into a waterfall in one part of the drama, and is set on fire in another. Actual characteristics of her hair (flowing and red) assimilate it to fire and water and, by similarity, to the city of Constantinople. The incident caused by Edith's cigarette is already sinister as the word "grésiler" evokes horrible deaths of crusaders recounted in one of the subtexts. In the next section, Isa is more seriously victimized:

> Un claquement retentit à l'extrémité qui rougoie. Aussitôt la
> flamme est portée contre la silhouette pétrifiée. Les flammèches,
> les crépitements se multiplient. Un cri s'élève.
> —Non, non, Ed, pas moi . . .
> Déjà, les soubresauts ultimes ravivent, au bout des
> membres, les flammes amenuisées. De brèves ellipses de la
> main, bruissantes dans la pénombre, réussissent à éteindre le
> petit brasier. (II, 6:2-3)

The "silhouette pétrifiée," actually that of a cigarette, as we know from
previous descriptions of the mimed gesture, nevertheless contributes to
transforming Isa into a victim. In the next section, burning match, cigarette
and hair are condensed into a single terrifying description:

> Frappée à la tête, l'allumette rougeoie. La flamme
> enveloppe le segment, y fait des ravages, incendiant d'un seul
> coup chaque protubérance ligneuse. Un cri même, va jusqu'à
> s'élever:
>
> —Non, non, Ed, pas moi . . .
> mais il est couvert par les crépitements, à l'extrémité des
> membres, des ultimes combustions. Léonie dépose alors dans le
> cendrier, avec des précautions subtiles, la silhouette aux
> contours fumant. (II, 7:2)

A cry that is almost raised and is covered by crackling of the flames is not a
cry at all. Ambiguity similar to that uniting sea foam, lace, eyelashes and
teeth in *L'Observatoire de Cannes* here suggests death by fire. Themes
from Delacroix' painting (fire combined with romantic sado-eroticism)
threaten Isa in a progression of descriptions which unites the same two
kinds of fire. Conjunction of two kinds of "ardeur" was more comically
lethal to Atta.

Intertextuality thus brings Delacroix and Villehardouin into a
constellation of meanings harmonized by Ricardou in *La Prise/Prose*. It is
not unlikely that reverberations from a third text contribute to
transformations in Isa's hair. Mallarmé's "La Chevelure"[6] constructs a
similar juxtaposition of flames and hair. Given the presence of Mallarmé
elsewhere in *La Prise/Prose*, it should not surprise us to find Ricardou

giving attention to the Mallarméan theme of the "chevelure," especially
since the theme intersects with Delacroix' painting. Flame materialized by
the sonnet is in no way literal in origin. In the first quatrain, the brilliance of
a woman's hair is evoked through allusion to desire and to flames:

> La chevelure vol d'une flamme à l'extrême
> Occident de désirs

Like Isa's hair, the "chevelure" reflects external correspondences. Isa's
hair, rather than reflecting colors of a setting sun, braids together reflections
from Mallarmé and Delacroix. In both cases, ambiguity of flame (desire
and fire) comes from within the text and the perceiving consciousness
("L'ignition du feu toujours intérieur").

Ricardou's text plays with some of the same ambiguities and
conjunctions as Mallarmé's sonnet. The poem describes hair as a "vive
nue" (cloud) which joins a series of celestial bodies such as the sun and an
"astre." But the word "nue" also connects with the word "nudité"

> Mais sans or soupirer que cette vive nue (line 5)
> Une nudité de héros tendre diffame . . . (line 9)

Similarly, Ricardou's clouds ("nues") continuously changing shape and
dividing as they float "vers l'ouest" correspond to several stripteases
("mises à nu"). Isa's hair floats "vers l'ouest" as well. In Mallarmé's poem
(and in numerous of his other texts) the word "fulgurante" is an adjective:

> Rien qu'à simplifier avec gloire la femme
> Accomplit par son chef fulgurante l'exploit
> De semer de rubis le doute qu'elle écorche
> Ainsi qu'une joyeuse et tutélaire torche.

Lightning (éclair) is part of the storm in part II of La Prise/Prose, and
Ricardou adopts Mallarmé's word in this context, but using it as a noun.
Space explorers carry weapons called "fulgurants" as well: Ed. Word
incinerates each of his companions with a single blast. Cigarettes with
which actors describe orbits in the dark are also called "fulgurants."

What is significant here is the way in which intertextual threads
intersect and are transformed in La Prise/Prose. The three threads
examined here in connection with a crusade fiction come from three

historical periods and three genres—history, painting and poetry—which are integrated into a single "byzantine" prose. Gross differences in scale, however (Mallarmé renders in one line what Ricardou develops over eighty pages), should not obscure similarities in procedure or theme. Since description involves presenting in successive time what has been offered to the eye in near simultaneity, there is no reason why a painted or versified *chevelure* should not be the "reality" with reference to which an elaborate fiction can be created. Each intertext pushes back reality and the problem of the words' origin by means of an interposed intertextual chain.

Transformation of an intertextual "chevelure" in *La Prise/Prose* is just one, albeit a major, "duplication intégrant une constante d'irrégularité." The name "Isabelle" undergoes similar evolutions. Split into eight letters, it designates three series of eight characters. By means of an echo effect, it can be repeated and prolonged:

> des appels s'élèvent de la plage, dirait-on, selon une superposition vite contradictoire de voix masculines et féminines. Impossible de déterminer l'origine de cette confusion. C'est peut-être une profé, ration simultanée de phrases différentes qui a jailli, se divisant puis retombant en variations infinitésimales; ou presque rien, au contraire, d'abord: une phrase unique mais dont chaque version s'est décalée d'une ou deux syllabes vers l'occident. Divers assemblages sonores,
> —Saisa, Isaïs, Saïs, Isis, Isa . . .
> paraissent se distinguer pourtant de ce réseau d'allitérations. (I, 2:9)

Here a voice resembles triangles rotated to obtain the various chapter-heading motifs, including a six-pointed star, composed of triangles which are "superposés" but also "décalés," in other words a "superposition vite contradictoire." Included in the rotation of these "variations infinitésimales" (or "révolutions minuscules") is the name to which the novel is dedicated (Isis) and a name also found in an exergue found at the novel's end, a quotation from Novalis' *Les Disciples de Saïs*:

> Le chanteur fut bientôt parmi nous, et, une béatitude indicible peinte sur le visage, nous apportait une humble petite pierre d'une forme singulière. Le Maître la prit dans sa main, embrassa longuement son disciple, puis il nous regarda, les yeux mouillés de larmes, et mit cette petite pierre en un endroit vacant, parmi les autres pierres, là tout juste où, comme des rayons, plusieurs lignes se rencontraient.

Another exergue at the head of the novel presents another image of intersection: "Une telle figure est le lieu de convergence de toutes ses parties et doit être son propre support."

Here a stone and variations of a word (Isa, Saïs) evoke the rest of the woman's name (Belle) written in stones. This name is, if not *the*, certainly *a* place where lines intersect. Like the stones of Bannière's church, letters of Isabelle's name provide another more complex "fable de l'anagramme." In *Les Lieux-dits*, anagrams often formed closed circuits, producing always more of the same: the brothers Epsilon (or *l'espion*) are indistinguishable. Stones from Bannière's church were used to build another church so that the second edifice *replaced* the first. Combined with mirror images and static superimposable metaphors and oppositions, such minimally productive anagrams yielded a novel that lacked movement. Lebensztejn calls this kind of rudimentary anagram a "jeu de société":

> L'anagramme classique est confectionnée en renversant le mot de départ, puis en cherchant empiriquement des redistributions particulières: associations, correspondances. Cette méthode manque de rigueur et de fécondité: on reste dans le champ sémantique du mot de départ auquel on associe par le déplacement de ses lettres un attribut cocasse. Par exemple Salvador Dali est cupide puisque son nom le dit: Avida Dollars. Mais par là même Salvador Dali reste Salvador Dali. De même la Révolution française porte en elle sa propre fin puisque un véto corse la finira. De telles anagrammes ne disent sur ce qu'elles déforment que la vérité: on retombe sur ses pieds. Comme si ces anagrammes, jeu de société destiné à dire la même chose autrement (avec esprit), avaient pour fin de réduire le pouvoir formidable des anagrammes, qui est de tout transformer en autre chose. Jeu tout-puissant dont l'objet est l'univers des signes.[7]

Anagram as used in *La Prise/Prose* establishes intersections, but not perfect correspondences among words. It fragments the word in order to transform it into something *different* which does not replace the first word, but rather adds to it. This type of practice produces a snowball effect; like a pearl, anagram builds an accumulated richness around a central grain of sand, or a stone, producing always something new. The name "Isabelle" is such a stone. We have seen it broken into no less than twenty-four chapters. We have seen it written in stones to form a path to be followed. It also appears in such anagrams as Bel Asile, Doctor Baseille, the forbidden city Silab Lee, and a multitude of bees (*abeilles*). Systematically, each time the text offers one of these words we are reminded of something which is present but unsaid (perhaps "interdit"). The graphic name becomes a hidden refrain resembling the names found by Saussure to be hidden in Latin poetry.

Saussure's anagrams were less graphic than phonetic, and such anagrams also occur in *La Prise/Prose*. Isabelle is one obsession in *La Prise/Prose*, and the Book is another. The two intersect in the letters S and L, which come to emblematize the myth of a Superbook. Appearing as "singulier Livre," "Liber Sanctus," "Livre Saint," and "Son Livre," reappearance of the letters constitutes an unchanging circle. However, the letters also appear in "Lucky Strike," "Silab Lee," the "Légion Solaire," and so on. As phonetic anagrams closely resembling Roussel's "à peu près," the two privileged letters also reappear as the Château d'Hessel and the Ile des Sels.

These anagrammatic games hide the presence of another hidden name: combining red hair with letters representing the Book, we can read the name "Roussel" through a variety of operations similar to chemical reactions. As a simple fusion reaction: Rousse + L, or Roux + Sel ⟶ Roussel. As a more complex displacement reaction: Rousse + Hessel ⟶ Roussel + S. Other evidence of Roussel's presence can be found in the book's format which moves from "Prise" to "Prose" ("Les deux phrases trouvées, il s'agissait d'écrire un conte pouvant commencer par la première et finir par la seconde"), and also in the very presence of Constantinople, a small model of that city being described in *Locus Solus*.[8] The author of *Locus Solus* reappears in recurrent "taches de *rouss*eur, groupées en archip*els*" (my underlining).

Secret acknowledgement of this important predecessor is the most revealing intertextual layer of *La Prise/Prose de Constantinople*. Working from two almost identical sentences, Roussel constructed his stories as a means of getting from one to the other. For example, *Impressions d'Afrique*, Roussel claims, traces an itinerary from "Les lettres du blanc sur les bandes du vieux pilliard" to another sentence which differs only by the substitution of "billard" for "pillard."[9] Ricardou's external intertextuality (Villehardouin, Delacroix, Mallarmé) and his internal intertextuality (minuscule displacements in repeated descriptions) systematically reenact and go beyond Roussel's *procédé*. *La Prise/Prose* moves from "prise" to "prose" through the transformation of hair into a cataract, of breasts into a precipice. The parlor game in part II, and the pervasive functioning of anagram, point to that process as both ludic and dangerous.

3. Je(u)

One of the books chosen "at random" during the parlor drama evokes a hospital, in which most of the novel's third section is set. If any of the fictions dominates the others, it is the story of "je," a patient who undergoes shock treatment and psychoanalysis in a psychiatric hospital called Bel Asile. When he is not being led through the hospital's labyrinthine corridors, this patient is absorbed in observing his room, deciphering his environment, and remembering his childhood. The narrative layer in which he appears is more diffuse, less coherent than the others, adding to the novel as a whole a psychological dimension whose subject is decentered.

Within boundaries of this hospital decor, the novel's other fictions are enclosed as memories of childhood games and favorite books. Memory does not extend beyond the frame of *La Prise/Prose*, however; the patient at the novel's end "remembers" (with the reader) building sand castles in the first chapter while his adored red-haired cousin Isabelle sat nearby. Like Proust's *A La Recherche du temps perdu* and Robbe-Grillet's *L'Année dernière à Marienbad* (1961), the text thus creates its own memories, which are entirely intratextual. Narrator and reader share a common past, which is the time of reading. As a dream produces condensed images, memory produces an Isa who is a composite of Forbidden Princess, nurse, childhood friend, and so on.

Identification of *Je* with any of the named characters remains similarly ambiguous. In Part I, it is Edouard who builds sand castles while Isa reads nearby. The "je" Part III can be identified with Edouard and his avatars. But the remembered scene also includes a third party, another unidentified "je" similar to the observing eye in *L'Observatoire de Cannes*. The narrator of Part III remembers being both *Je* and Edouard, or perhaps they are the same person, one a child, the other an older version of the same. A child wishing to be older (old enough for Isa) and an adult remembering childhood are reflected in a composite and floating subject.

Many complex threads tie the story of *Je* to the novel's other fictions. First, the book his remembered Isa reads at the beach in Part I was entitled "La Princesse Interdite." In the novel's opening chapter, a narrator observes Isa closely in order to sketch her while she reads. He scrutinizes with particularly close attention the cover illustration of her book, whose details reappear in other contexts throughout *La Prise/Prose*: a carpet similar to the one described here appears in the library of section II; in that library, a "fauteuil profond" like the one on the book jacket is occupied by another Isabelle, whose dress, like that worn by the pictured princess, is printed with a bee design ("Abeilles" being another anagram of Isabelle). In addition, the book jacket princess has another familiar feature, described in familiar terms: "L'abondante vague des cheveux, que la figure sépare, est une autre fois scindée, perpendiculairement, par la crête des épaules en partie submergées" (I, 3:5).

The paper princess is, in her turn, reading a book:

> Les yeux sont abaissés, et les paupières, ainsi offertes sous la pure ligne des sourcils, découvrent les hachures convexes, entrecroisés de leur maquillage. Il n'est donc pas permis de déterminer l'exacte direction du regard vers le livre que les mains tiennent ouvert sur les genoux, ni même de localiser la petite page rectangulaire sur laquelle il est fixé, ni à plus forte raison sur la phrase capable de susciter une pareille fascination. On peut tout au plus supposer qu'il s'agit d'une page paire puisque l'autre est consacrée, semble-t-il, à une illustration qu'il faudrait observer de plus près. (I, 3:5)

Reference to "lignes" and "hachures" signal the level of reality being described: Isa reads a book about a princess reading a book. Ricardou's readers recognize such structured repetitions. This passage could be continued in an endless series of dizzying *mises-en-abyme* or imbricated parentheses.

A detail of the book's illustration in fact confirms what we suspected-- the princess on Isa's book is reading a tiny copy of "La Princesse Interdite." The cover illustration on this "abyme minuscule" depicts the Château d'Hessel portrayed elsewhere as part of eight children's dramatic presentation. Here, however, it is the princess who reads the story of her own adventures. The suggestion is, of course, that Isa is reading her own story as well. And as we read this novel about a character reading a novel about a princess reading a novel about a princess, an obvious implication is that perhaps we too are part of a novel being read by someone. As readers, we too read the story of our own adventure, since *La Prise/Prose* is in part the story of the adventure of reading. The text finally escapes the danger of digressing into endless *mises-en-abyme*, however. Instead, descriptive attention is diverted --by a recurring "déplacement de l'oeil"-- and we return to a larger frame of "reality."

Complementing the fairy tale milieu of "La Princesse Interdite," another book remembered by *Je* in his hospital bed explores future time and is called "La Cité Interdite." Another series of *mises-en-abyme* structures description of the book's cover:

> Sous le titre courant, 'La Cité interdite', le texte imprime une ombre semblable, plus petite, sur le rectangle blanc du papier. Pour lire, il faut s'approcher de plus près:
> membres de la petite troupe, désormais sur le qui-vive ne laissent plus aucune observation excessive les détourner de leur lente marche. (I, 6:4)

Here again an "abyme" of progressively more minute description is avoided by a "déplacement de l'oeil." The first sentence of the text-within-a-text demonstrates the vacillation between description (simultaneity and immobility) and narration (successivity, here materialized by a "lente marche").

During the reading from this book, we are introduced to the *Borne* (itself producing phenomena similar to the above-mentioned "excessive observation"). The passage ends with a change of focus to a finger, which marks a page in a closed book:

> C'est la sensation, soudain, que la main droite--l'index étant demeuré inséré dans une fente de l'écorce--est devenue parfaite-ment insensible, et glacée. Ainsi, de proche en proche, se recompose le spectacle: d'abord le livre, dans la main d'Edouard. (I, 7:8)

The finger in question belongs to the child Edouard, but the book is no longer "La Cité interdite" but rather "La Princesse interdite" from which Edouard directs his playmates in their little drama.

The two books remembered by the patient in Part III are thus not clearly distinct one from the other. Rather, they flow together like two sides of a moebius strip, in a dreamlike memory. Furthermore, they also overlap with a book which contains them both: *La Prise/Prose de Constantinople.* The cover of "La Cité interdite" bears the insignia of the Editions de Minuit:

Plus bas encore, sur le fond nocturne, se détache également issu d'une diffuse association d'orange et de jaune, le symbole de l'éditeur. C'est une étoile linéaire à cinq branches, pointée vers le haut, et dont le tracé détermine une étoile interne, noire, plus petite. La branche inférieure droite donne naissance à un *m* cursif. L'emblème doit donc se lire: 'Mystère dans les étoiles'. (I, 6:2)

Assimilated by *mises-en-abyme* and their similar format, the three books have even more in common. As I have shown, the fairy tale and the science fiction novel are quests. Both also involve a hero who must read the story of his own adventures. Reading one's own adventures is a theme that pertains to *La Prise/Prose* as a whole as well. *Je* attempts to remember his own life in an autobiographical quest that dominates the novel's third section. The inner space he seeks is a composite of Venusian outer space and the desired object of the novel's other fictions. *Je* sees the hospital as a labyrinth. Endless gray corridors prevent him from knowing where he is. As he wanders, led by the nurse, passages of other fictions interwoven with the narration function as memories, interludes of reading, or as delirious vagaries of a confused mind making associations from one reality to another. In "La Princesse interdite," the Prince fights a duel with his double at the door of the Princess' chamber. *Je* finds, at the center of his labyrinth, a similar mirror, which is his own mind.

Even as it adds a psychological dimension to the novel as a whole, this psychiatric patient's self-reading does not permit the reader to hypothesize the presence of a centered speaking subject. *Je*, already a composite of a diffuse narrative consciousness and the character Edouard, acquires yet another identity in the novel's last paragraph:

Certaine lecture consciencieuse suffit maintenant pour que l'irradiation de toute la figure élabore qui JE SUIS, et par un phénomène réflexif point trop imprévu, en un éclair, me LE LIVRE. (III, 8:18)

Thanks to ambiguity in the first person singular of the verbs *suivre* and *être*, this sentence has two simultaneous meanings, both applicable to *La Prise/Prose*:

--"I follow the book." The hospitalized narrator follows traces of books he has read in quest of his present and former selves. He attempts, by winding threads of his past, to escape from the labyrinthine hospital. Furthermore, he may have a third book in mind--the one we read--where he reads the story of his own adventure.

--"I am the book." *Je* is a metaphor for what Don Rice has called an "exploded subject." Like a human consciousness, the book proposes composite memories through condensation and also produces multiple images of a single (composite) idea. Isabelle, the idealized child-woman, fragmented by description, assimilated to a moving landscape, is also present in the many identical red-haired girls, many of them named Isa. Desire sees its object everywhere, and so "excessive observation" produces a plethora of doubles for Isa. *Je* is a condensation of child, adolescent and adult, of narrator and quest hero. These facets of *Je* appear in Edouard and his transformations. Rice suggests an equivalence of a whole series of characters:

> Who then is the narrator? Through the complex *glissements* to which Ricardou subjects the identity of the *je*, it is possible to determine that the narrator is Edmond who, by a series of linguistic operations, adopts various other identities. Moreover, the analysis of these displacements--phonetic, semantic, and graphic--lead eventually to the 'subject' mentioned previously-- i.e. EDMOND EDMOT* ED. WORD EDOUARD J*E*AN RIC*A*RDOU.[10]

It would be tempting to call *La Prise/Prose* Ricardou's autobiography except for a calculated ambiguity whereby there is no self that precedes the text. *Je follows* the text, and so, if Ricardou is to be associated with *Je* and Edouard we can only say he is their result, not their source.

One of the *nouvelles* of *Révolutions minuscules* is called "Auto-biographie." The life (*bio*) therein recounted (*graphie*) is not the history of a subject. There is a narrator, "je," but the personal pronoun echoes the day ("jeudi") on which the story unfolds and thus suggests that the narrator is a formal game (*jeu*), no more and no less. In fact, "Autobiographie" recounts the elaboration of a story, and that story bears striking resemblance to *La Prise/Prose*:

> [. . .] c'est une byzantine histoire, peu à peu, qui s'inscrivait en moi. Récit invraisemblable en lequel se trouvait prise, inverse Asie, une Isa nécessaire. Autant qu'il m'en souvienne, l'itinéraire

où les fragments épars se rassemblaient ressemblait fort, en dépit d'un luxe de détails souvent alternatifs, à celui de la quatrième Croisade. Venise, les Lieux Saints, Constantinople et ses tours s'y trouvaient naturellement impliqués avec même, au bord du Nil, les colosses mutilés de Memnon. Evidemment des crimes guerriers avaient lieu, innombrables. Et plus d'une jeune fille, interminablement, se voyait astreinte, certes sous l'influence d'un très singulier livre, à subir mainte mise à genoux.[11]

Rather than seeking to identify a coherent preexisting personal subject who tells the story of his own life, the sentence "Je suis le livre" points to a book which tells its own story, creating rather than reflecting the identity of a human subject. As a novel that elucidates its own mechanisms, that traces the stages of its own unfolding, *La Prise/Prose* can certainly be called an autobiography. Its childhood is its beginning, starting with the opening word "Rien." Near its end it remembers itself and attempts to perceive its own overall functioning. In this light, *Je* (the book) a hero in quest of itself is required to read the story of its own adventure, "l'aventure d'un récit." Meditating on its own construction, the text reviews and reinterprets some of its episodes, and realizes that the novel has had no characters at all:

Libérée de ces propositions fallacieuses, peu à peu, inversement, se reconstitue ma mémoire véritable. Pour obscure qu'elle demeure encore, une certitude, même, commence à s'accréditer, m'assurant non sans surprise que le véhicule dont je tenais les commandes était une fusée individuelle. C'est donc seul, en vérité que j'ai franchi les byzantines végétations de la planète. Et si, à un moment déterminé, semble-t-il, du bord de quelque marge lointaine, ma solitude s'est trouvée submergée par le sentiment, derrière moi, d'une présence diffuse, et si, me tournant alors, j'ai pu constater que les pièges inédits disposés dans l'espace n'avaient pas retardé le commando qui m'avait suivi jusque-là, c'est que les processus de duplication avaient déjà fonctionné, allant jusqu'à construire, à mon image, selon de simples variantes de proche en proche accrues, plusieurs personnages apocryphes.

If *Je*'s therapy results in his learning to read himself as an allegorical figure, he also recognizes in Isabelle a figment of his prolix imaginings:

> Fallait-il que je fusse victime d'une hypnose exceptionnelle
> pour que, à défaut des ressemblances de physionomie, ne me
> parût point étrange l'identité de toutes ces chevelures rousses.

And the obstacles and traps in all the novel's quest routes are similarly to be found in the corridors of the mind:

> Ainsi est-ce donc des faux semblants que j'ai entretenus, si
> prolixement parfois, de l'irréalité de nos hallucinations ter-
> restres—élaborant de cette manière, en chaque cas, pour mon
> personnel usage, des pièges plus subtils. (III, 8:10-11)

La Prise/Prose tells of its own quest for itself, split into components which are a subject (*Je*, who is far more naive than Ricardou, surely) and a desired object, represented by the name "Isabelle."

In the context of *La Prise/Prose* as a curious autobiography, Ricardou's predilection for incorporating linguistic theories in concrete form into his fiction suggests the relevance of Emile Benveniste's remarks on the nature of the first person pronoun. Benveniste points out that a given noun evokes a relatively constant representation in the mind; in other words, a fixed convention, however arbitrary, ties a noun to its referent. No such connection exists between the pronoun "je" and a reality exterior to language. "Je" can only be understood as referring to the statement in which it is uttered.

> *Je* ne peut être défini qu'en termes de 'locution,' non en termes
> d'objets, comme l'est un signe nominal. *Je* signifie 'la personne
> qui énonce la présente instance de discours contenant *je*. [...] Il
> faut donc souligner ce point: *je* ne peut être identifié que par
> l'instance de discours qui le contient et par là seulement.'[12]

The relevance of Benveniste's argument to Ricardou's theory and fiction is multiple. Benveniste remarks that words like "ici" and "maintenant" function much like "je" in that they too reflect only the "instance de discours" which contain them.

Since "je," "maintenant," "ici," and other words have no fixed referents, Benveniste calls them "signes vides," signs which are unique but mobile (the single pronoun "je" can refer to anyone). *La Prise/Prose* ends with the lightly crypted message "Je suis le livre." The empty but mobile "je" floats through the text, attaching itself to Edouard, Ed. Word, Isabelle, a narrative eye and the book as a whole. It (the pronoun) is thus a sort of "figuration du vide," a phrase which reappears numerous times throughout the novel. As I will show shortly, this phrase itself and the repeated passage in which it occurs is also a "signe vide" analogous to "je." Each time it is proffered, the passage acquires a new meaning which refers to its context. In a sense, all characters in *La Prise/Prose* are "figurations du vide"; proper nouns in the novel refer only to the contexts in which they are found. Hélène Prigogine, speaking about the "situation du personnage dans le roman contemporain," contends that "Le personnage, centre de toute la littérature romanesque, est passé d'un état *significatif à un état de signifiant à signifiés interchangeables* ou disparaît dans une affabulation impersonnelle."[13] Although characters do not disappear entirely in *La Prise/Prose*, they are forms with variable content much like geometric figures found in all Ricardou's fiction. The three tales propose three stages in life: childhood (in "La Princesse interdite"), adolescence (at the beach), and adulthood (space explorers). These stages of an individual life find parallels at a cosmological scale: the novel includes mythical past and future and an ordinary present time. As aspects of a consciousness, these stages of memory can be compared to Freud's three-part division of the self into Id, Ego, and Superego or to R. D. Laing's classification of Child, Adult and Parent "voices" that interact within the psyche.[14] In *La Prise/Prose*, each of the characters is "impersonal" while their sum is highly personal and can be seen as aspects of a single consciousness.

As such a consciousness, the patient in part III best unites all the novel's fictions. In this sense, although the process of narration begins with the first word of the novel, the fictions are not completely united until the last word: "livre." Such symmetry suggests that the novel could (hypothetically at least) be read backwards. Evidence for such a hypothesis can be found in the twin titles, in the recurrent phrase "en un sens puis dans l'autre" and in repeated references to a hypothetical center where reading in both directions would intersect. The pronoun "je" can be described by the novel's first epigraph as the place in the novel which is "le lieu de convergence de toutes ses parties." The figure returns in the second epigraph "en un endroit vacant [...] là tout juste où, comme des rayons, plusieurs lignes se rencontraient." As an empty sign, however, *Je* gives the novel an empty center.

4. Mythic Dimensions: A Cosmos in a Book

Instead of celebrating the trials and tribulations of an ego, the novel's ambiguous last sentence is a signal that *La Prise/Prose* aspires to the status of a mythical Superbook. The letters S and L, prominent in the anagrammatic permutations of Isabelle, Bel Asile, Silab Lee, and the Légion Solaire, contain all geometry in their curves and angles, thus serving as an emblem for the Book which would contain all books in one volume.

One of the descriptions of Delacroix' painting gives brief attention to a small coffer which lies open on the tiles in the lower left-hand corner of the canvas. It is suggested that this coffer has "les exactes dimensions d'un livre fermé" (II, 4:7). As story-telling evolves from the description, the box that *resembled* a closed book changes to *contain* a mysterious black volume. Pillaging Constantinople, soldiers find this mysterious book, which is engraved with the letters S and L. Suspecting that the letters signify "Sanctus Liber," the soldiers hasten to inform their leader, who reads portions from it aloud. From selections he reads, its similarities with *La Prise/Prose* become apparent: fictions, names and repeated refrains from the novel we read are mentioned, in abyme, during the Doge's reading. It is clear that we are to believe that the *Sanctus Liber* in question is the volume we hold in our hands, and that its superiority over ordinary books results from a superposition of many works, including esoteric medieval "grimoires."

In connection with Le Basile, villain of "La Princesse interdite," we read that the name might be a reference to "Basile Valentin, alchimiste du

Moyen Age, déchiffreur d'archaïques grimoires." *La Prise/Prose* bears significant resemblances to several well-known Grimoires. The *Grimorum Verum* (1517), for example, is a textbook of black magic that gives instructions for invoking devils. Like *La Prise/Prose*, it is divided into three parts. In the first, various devils are introduced; the second part describes ritual secrets, and the third offers keys for reading the work itself. These divisions correspond to the three sections of Ricardou's novel, the first introducing fictions and sets of characters, the second proposing a mysterious ritual or game, and the third offering interpretations of the whole book.

Secret books of the Kabala offer more similarities. As handbooks of Hebrew occultism, the *Sepher Yesirah* (Book of Creation), for example, and the *Bahir* are based on ancient oral traditions. The *Bahir*, probably written in the 13th century, contains mention of the crusades and their secret meanings. Most interesting is the use of words, codes and permutations of letters to reveal or hide secret knowledge: anagrams, palindromes, magic squares and approaches to reading and writing that involve encoding and deciphering are shared by these grimoires and *La Prise/Prose*.[15]

Kabalistic science was used by medieval alchemists who hoped to find secret formulae, this time for transformation of base metals into gold and of physical substances into spiritual essences. Origins of some of these books are completely fabulous. The books, like the philosopher's stone, the grail, the fountain of youth, are often less important as objects than as pretexts for quests.

It is in the light of Mallarmé's "Livre," however, that the myth of the Book as it appears in *La Prise/Prose* takes on its fullest meaning. Mallarmé saw his masterwork as a Grimoire and compared its secrets to those of alchemy. Although he made notations for his Book all his life, Mallarmé never wrote (or performed) it, so it is mainly thanks to Jacques Scherer's editing and deciphering that Mallarmé's notes are accessible.[16]

Echoes from a Mallarméan "marge lointaine" pervade Ricardou's novel. In addition to the theme of the *chevelure*, Mallarmé's presence is suggested by the many stars and constellations of *La Prise/Prose*, and perhaps even by its dedication "à Isis, donc" on the first page, and "Donc, à Isis" on the last. ("Donc" is the French word for Igitur, Mallarmé's hero who descended into a cellar to read a mysterious grimoire.) Mallarmé is most explicitly invoked in connection with the *Borne*, whose capacity to produce syntactic aberrations and whose mysterious inscription ("CA.ME BLOC ICI BAS CHU D'UN DE.ASTRE OBSCUR'-I, 7:4) sends the reader to two lines from "Tombeau d'Edgar Poë": "Calme Bloc ici bas chu d'un désastre obscur/Que ce granit du moins montre à jamais sa borne."[17]

In short, *La Prise/Prose* bears overwhelming echoes of Mallarmé's themes and vocabulary, and it is worthwhile to hypothesize that Ricardou has attempted to write the Masterwork that Mallarmé planned. Close comparison of the two sheds light on concerns shared by other New Novelists as well. Part II especially resembles the setting and dynamics of Mallarmé's Work, which was to involve systematic repetition and reading from loose sheets ("feuillets") read aloud before an audience.

Mallarmé imagined a book whose overall format is strikingly visible in *La Prise/Prose*. The Work would be reversible, so that it could theoretically begin at either end ("répéter en sens inverse").[18] His description could be applied to Ricardou's novel which accomplishes reversibility symbolically with its double title:

> 2 feuilles
>   le titre
> au verso
>   de l'une--qui devient recto
>   --au recto de
>   l'autre--qui
>   devient verso[19]

In fact the Book would present itself by doubling[20] all its elements. Its worth would emerge from its confrontation with itself and from its internal correspondences: "équation sous un dieu Janus, se prouvant."[21]

Composed of unbound pages, the Work would be read aloud to an audience by an "opérateur," Mallarmé himself, who would assume possession, not because he was its author, but because he materialized it in ceremonial reading. The numbers three and eight reappear in Mallarmé's notes. At one point he imagines eight genres, each given three volumes,[22] numbers to be found in *La Prise/Prose* in its three eight-part sections and in its three stories with eight characters each. The same numbers appear in Mallarmé's audience, which was to number twenty-four people, seated on eight sofas ("8 places triples".)[23] Significantly, the operator would be a twenty-fifth person ("moi 1/25e")[24] who would supply unity to the whole performance. Similarly, Mallarmé saw himself as a double of the book: "m'identifier au livre" and "c'est moi qui reliant et résumant le tout. . . ."[25] Beyond three sets of eight characters, *La Prise/Prose* offers a twenty-fifth major character, *Je*, who unifies the others in a single consciousness and/or in a single book ("JE SUIS LE LIVRE").

Reading of the Book would be regulated by a strict ritual and would take place in a setting carefully chosen for its symbolic value. Conceived as a theatrical performance, reading would take place in a library similar to that found in Part II of *La Prise/Prose*. A "canapé bleu" in the library of the Château d'Hessel seats three people (II, 4:9), and Ricardou devotes much attention to a lamp which follows Mallarmé's recommendation for a "lampe électrique unique."[26] Ricardou's lamp is a source of patterns on the rug, in a semi repetition of the novel's first page: "Bientôt, ellipse au dessin parfait, la lumière du lampadaire se détache sur la pénombre qu'elle adoucit" (II, 1:2). As a metaphor for reading, Part II emphasizes contrast of light and dark which allows the drama to take place. The same contrast opens *La Prise/Prose* and recurs at intervals throughout.

For each performance of his Work, Mallarmé would select sheets at random from drawers in a lacquered chest. In this way, controlled chance (Ricardou's "duplication intégrant une constante d'irrégularité") would play a role in producing each version of the performance. In *La Prise/Prose* a bookcase supplies books which performers integrate into their pantomime. Although the characters choose books at random, their appearance in the novel is far from arbitrary: Ricardou has significantly reduced the role of chance.

The principle of regulated irregularity is the most significant similarity between Mallarmé's Masterwork and *La Prise/Prose*. Mallarmé's Work would actually be a large number of books superimposed in one. Mobility of the performances (or Book, the two are the same as all genres are integrated here) comes from permutation of a small number of basic elements. Polyvalent words and phrases would be chosen deliberately in order to produce as many meanings as possible from the various combinations. The pantomimes of *La Prise/Prose* are transformed both by the actors themselves and by the descriptions, which are repeated with changes. The Book, giving maximum initiative to words, would contain its own variants.

This kind of systematic principle regulating repetition was also part of Valéry's ideal novel:

> Peut-être serait-il intéressant de faire une fois une oeuvre qui montrerait à chacun de ses noeuds, la diversité qui peut s'y présenter à l'esprit et parmi laquelle il choisit la suite unique qui sera donnée dans le texte. Ce serait la substituer à l'illusion d'une détermination unique et imitatrice du réel, celle du *possible à chaque instant*, qui me semble plus véritable.[27]

Valéry's statement resembles Freud's contention that in dreams "either/or" must be read as "both," a principle I have used to account for Ricardou's composite characters. Mallarmé too saw the ideal book as containing its own variants. His recurrent fan images suggest, among other things, expansion of what was superimposed, in a play (theater but also game) between fiction and language: "Le livre, expansion totale de la lettre, doit d'elle tirer, directement, une mobilité et spacieux, par correspondances, instituer un jeu, on ne sait, qui confirme la fiction."[28]

Part II of *La Prise/Prose* offers an example of what Mallarmé and Valéry had in mind. Each pantomime is a variant of the others, but their sum produces a story not contained in any one of them; this story results from regular though minutely transformed repetitions. In spite of their vast differences, Mallarmé, Valéry and Ricardou betray a quest for totality that assumes a common form. Ricardou and others have been able to pursue their predecessor's ideals by developing the longer and looser form of the novel in a way that better includes poetic structures.

Potential for near-infinite mobility of the Book is due in part to its fragmentation. Mallarmé's Masterwork would be divided into constituent parts ("feuillets") which could be rearranged according to systematic (and anagrammatic) principles. Marc Saporta follows this road to mobility in his *Composition n° I*, whose pages can be shuffled at will and the book read a number of ways.[29] Queneau uses a similar principle with verses of ten sonnets in *Cent mille milliards de poèmes*.[30] Robbe-Grillet's films and novels move backwards and forwards in "retakes" of similar scenes. In *La Prise/Prose*, each tale in split into many mobile fragments. The various fictions interrupt and disarticulate each other, producing discontinuous discourse riddled with holes.

Fragmentation is central to a second myth present in the novel--that of
Isis and Osiris. As chief god in the Egyptian pantheon, Osiris presided over
natural cycles such as those of the sun (with which he is identified), tides and
vegetation. Isis, goddess of curing and of spinning and weaving, was his sister
and spouse. Together, the pair represented the primal couple, children of
Earth and Sky. Murdered by his jealous brother, Set, Osiris was placed in a
sealed coffer and cast into the Nile, but Isis recovered his body after a long
quest and buried her husband. Set then stole the corpse, chopped it into
fourteen pieces, and threw the fragments into the river. Isis gathered
together the dismembered body, all but the phallus which had been
devoured by a crab, and reassembled it. Osiris then retired to rule the
underworld as god of death and rebirth.

References to Egypt can be found throughout *La Prise/Prose*, mainly
in the tale of Venusian explorers. Berthold *Toth* can be seen as an allusion to
Toth (Thot), god of learning, inventor of writing, arithmetic and astronomy.
The name Annie *Nahaut* is homophonous with *naos*, the inner sanctuary of
an Egyptian or Greek temple. (An Egyptian *naos* usually took the form
of a stone block with a carved niche in which was placed a statue of a high
divinity, often Osiris.) Homophony of Karnac, an ancient stone temple on
the Nile, and Carnac, an ancient stone temple in Brittany, allows themes of
ancient and personal history to intersect as the space commandos try to
decipher the *Borne*, a third ritual stone. (Photos of Carnac and Karnac also
appear in the hospital room in Part III.) Pyramids appear as stacks of open
books when Edouard (Part I) and *je* (Part III) pursue their respective
research into book after book, continuously opening new parentheses as
their attention becomes progressively concentrated. Books already consulted
are left open and piled in "pyramides" which come to represent the novel's
many "lectures emboîtées."

Two passages evoke the god Osiris who, in this incarnation, is
broken into not fourteen but eight fragments. The first passage is itself an
interruption which breaks the text, as it is a digression in discussion of the
Borne:

> --C'est au pied de la cheville, donc (mais il me faudrait ici
> ouvrir des parenthèses dans les parenthèses), dans le dé même
> du piédestal (lorsqu'Isis interrompt les larmes--versées, vous
> connaissez la légende, sur les huit fragments de son époux
> qu'elle va assembler enfin pour une vie de gloire--et que le Nil
> décroît) qu'apparaît le bloc rocheux tout à fait comparable. . .
> .(I, 6:7)

This parenthetical reference to Isis is the only explicit mention of the goddess to whom the novel is dedicated. To discover who Isis may be, we will first be required to find Osiris as he is scattered in the text. A second passage offers clues. Immediately following description of blue-green eyes (especially the "iris," which connects Osiris, Isa and Isis), we read this:

> Tenir ici, encore, cependant. Accréditer ces yeux, ce visage. Tracer des raccourcis dans le texte et s'y risquer. Reconstruire ainsi le corps en son ensemble et, l'entourant, cet improbable espace où, peut-être, je respire. (I, 8:4)

This "je," appearing in Part I, is not associated with any particular character, and so is something of a mystery. There is, however, a "je" whose existence depends on the reconstruction of a fragmented body. When we learn on the last page that "JE SUIS LE LIVRE," the possibility presents itself that Osiris, like Aphrodite, is a parable, or a "mythe crypté de la création poétique." The text, like Osiris, is a body (*corpus*) which has been disarticulated in a number of ways: it is broken into three sections; more significantly, objects in the text, especially bodies, are dismembered by the process of the description's scriptural striptease. Words are broken and reassembled in anagrams.

The *Je* of the hospital fiction, like Isis, seeks to reconstruct an object of desire, Isabelle, who is split into multiple characters and scattered, her name by anagram, her body by description, throughout the flowing river of novel and memory. Parallel quests exist as well in all the other fictions, which are themselves fragmented and dispersed. But this new "Je"--the text itself ("Je suis [être] le livre")--is, like Osiris, this time, hidden, dismembered and scattered. Reading *La Prise/Prose* or any one of its stories involves a complex "lecture virtuelle" which seeks and assembles dispersed fragments. The reader can thus be compared to Isis, the seeker of fragments, to whom the novel is dedicated. Variants of the phrase "en un sens comme dans l'autre" and another phrase "le froissement d'une page qui tourne" recur repeatedly, reminding us that the reader is part of the story. Careful fitting together of broken parts is another refrain, which first appears as an "anfractuous" break separating a toy soldier's head from its body. The break has been mended by fitting "protubérences" into "encoches" as one would assemble a jigsaw puzzle. Frequent repetition of these two words in a variety of contexts serves as a shorthand reminder of this process of piecing parts together.

Death and resurrection, dismemberment and reassembly of Osiris, text and body form a series of paired but opposing movements present in *La Prise/Prose*. In an article, Ricardou speaks of opposing movements which can create a text without reverting to the ideology of expression.[31] His analysis, which makes apparent a system which sees reading/writing as a process of fragmentation and rearticulation, can be profitably applied to *La Prise/Prose*.

Forces which bring elements of a text together Ricardou calls "le cimentaire." These forces include "la mise ensemble" (selection), "la mise en ordre" (arrangement in linear series) and "la mise en unité" (integration of units to produce intersections and an organic spatial whole). Corresponding to "le cimentaire" in *La Prise/Prose* are forces of that "convergence" mentioned in the epigraphs, notably a "Force" in Part III where disparate stories are united in the consciousness of *Je*. Also "cimentaire" are allusions to the book's centripetal force, implying a secret center which one seeks by following "les mouvements circulaires de la fascination" (I, 6:6). Related images of convergence are references to "lectures emboîtées," "oubliettes," "abymes," and concentric circles or parentheses. Close focus (optical or critical) pushes away surrounding context and focus becomes "périlleusement excessive." Quest for a center occupies all the characters who read. Other images for centripetal movement of "le cimentaire" are suggested by the text. A machine has brakes which slow its movement, causing smaller rotations of parts (c.f. III, 2:6). A labyrinth also has a center. At the limits of convergence only the center remains; movement and the circle itself are eliminated.

The risk of falling into *abymes*, gorges and vortices or smaller parentheses is prevented by an opposing centrifugal movement, that of divergence. In his article, Ricardou calls such forces "le ruptif," which includes "la mise en pièces" (interruption or fragmentation), "la mise à l'ombre" (hiding by censorship or transformation of crucial information) and "la mise en autre" (repetition with variance, mutual metaphors, or anything in a text which refers us to another piece of the text.)

Many images in *La Prise/Prose* point to the functioning of "le ruptif." Concentric parentheses also suggest outward movement: a toy soldier dropped in water evokes an

O!

de surprise qui se dédouble, se multiplie en cercles concentriques
s'élargissant jusqu'à disparaître, tandis que plusieurs bulles
montées des profondeurs se soumettent bientôt, seules ou
assemblées, à la rotation générale. (III, 4:5)

Eyes dilate (III, 2:7) and machines are set in motion by acceleration
mechanisms which produce larger and larger rotations. The *Borne* produces
strange sentences characterized by dizzy proliferating movement. Instead
of moving toward the center of a labyrinth, one can attempt to escape
beyond its outer walls. Opposing the search for a center, centrifugal
movement is expressed geometrically in the recurrent refrain "le centre
autorise la suite."

Also corresponding to "le cimentaire" and "le ruptif" are textual
modes of narration and description. Excessive observation can halt the
progress of the story and arrest time. Narration is a principle of movement.
The two forces work together to produce a text and a geometric form that do
not stop moving and break down completely, and yet do not disintegrate in
an opposing manner either, spinning off in many directions. In his article,
Ricardou says that the total text, integrating forces of divergence and
convergence, can be seen as "mosaïque impossible":

Bref, le texte est atopique: il ne se situe nulle part. Tout lieu
qu'on lui assigne n'est jamais qu'une stase dans un procès de
métamorphoses incessantes.[32]

Presence of outer space fiction as a "roman d'aventures spatiales"
(III, 1:10) and constant reference to centers and circumferences enjoin us to
take seriously the question of *La Prise/Prose* as a geometric configuration,
and as an "improbable espace où, peut-être, je respire." Properties of a
circle do not adequately account for the text's preoccupation with almost
frenetic motion. Don Rice suggests that an ellipse, with its two centers,
elucidates some aspects of the novel which are otherwise obscure.[33] Even a
mobile cycle is a closed configuration, returning always to the same point by
an identical path in one direction or the other.

However, *La Prise/Prose* has a more complex and dynamic shape, I
believe. A path moving toward or away from a circle's center can be seen in
the geometry of a *spiral*, emblem of the labyrinth, path for a questing

wanderer, and baroque figure *par excellence*. A moving spiral or pinwheel presents an optical illusion; either contraction or dilation appears. Moving in the direction of ever smaller curves, a spiral converges upon a center which is infinitely deferred (cf. Zeno's paradox). Moving in an opposing, outward direction, the curves of a spiral are congruent but not superimposable, as each rotation is slightly displaced with respect to the former. An outward-moving spiral is a hungry line engulfing progressively more and different space in its repetitions in a desire for totality. Ricardou's expanding frames and his use of metalepsis can also be represented by a spiral into which everything in the reader's world is eventually enclosed. Many are the cases in *La Prise/Prose* where we read the book ("dans un sens") while the book reads another reader ("dans l'autre sens"). Because a spiral has no absolute beginning or end, every one of its points can be seen as its origin, or center, as in the refrain "le centre autorise la suite, non les extrémités." Actual spirals can be found in the novel as orbits (of stars, bees, hand gestures in the pantomime), vortices of moving water, and shells.

The presence of seashells (especially a large "coquille conique") suggests that perhaps with the spiral we confront yet another "mythe crypté de la création poétique" similar to myths of Aphrodite and Osiris. In one of his most delightful essays, Valéry attempts to account for the existence of a seashell by describing it and imagining how it might have been produced. The relevance of "L'homme et la coquille" to Ricardou's textual production is broad. Valéry begins his exploration of shells and his attempt to comprehend them by describing their form. Unsatisfied with the results of his attempt (in fact a remarkable description), Valéry states that "le langage ordinaire se prête mal à décrire les formes, et je désespère d'exprimer la grâce tourbillonnaire de celles-ci." Instead, he tries to imagine how he would set about to produce a shell, realizing in the process that it is in the nature of shells (and spirals) to be produced from a series of minute transformations that could theoretically continue forever. His expression of this troubling fact is comparable to Ricardou's definition of the text as a "mosaïque impossible." Valéry states:

> La moindre réflexion, le moindre retour sur le *comment je m'y prendrais pour façonner une coquille*, m'enseigne aussitôt que je devrais intervenir diversement, de plusieurs manières différentes, et comme à plusieurs titres, car je ne sais pas conduire à la fois, dans mon opération, la multiplicité des modifications qui doivent concourir à former l'objet que je veux. Je les assemble

> comme par une intervention étrangère; même, c'est par un
> jugement extérieur à mon application que je connaîtrai que mon
> ouvrage est 'achevé', et que l'objet est fait puisque cet objet n'est
> en soi qu'un état parmi d'autres, d'une suite de transformations
> qui pourraient se poursuivre au delà du but,- *indéfiniment.*

Going on to compare nature's production of seashells with the creation of
art objects, Valéry notes that a mollusk "emanates" its shell from within its
own substance. Perfection in art, he surmises, would require an effort to
construct something closely resembling a shell:

> Nos artistes ne tirent point de leur substance la matière de leurs
> ouvrages, et ils ne tiennent la forme qu'ils poursuivent que d'une
> application particulière de leur esprit, séparable du *tout* de leur
> être. Peut-être, ce que nous appelons la *perfection* dans l'art (et
> que tous ne recherchent pas, et que plus d'un dédaigne), n'est-
> elle que le sentiment de désirer ou de trouver, dans une oeuvre
> humaine, cette certitude dans l'exécution, cette nécessité d'origine
> intérieure, et cette liaison indissoluble et réciproque de la figure
> avec la matière que le moindre coquillage me fait voir?

Rather than *describing* a shell, then, Valéry would like to create something
different in its image. The final paragraph of his essay describes a very
Ricardolian case of visual fascination which in turn provokes the suspicion
that Valéry's meditation on shells has itself taken the form of a spiral shell:

> Comme Hamlet ramassant dans la terre grasse un crâne, et
> l'approchant de sa face vivante, se mire affreusement en
> quelque manière, et comme il entre dans une méditation sans
> issue, que borne de toutes parts un cercle de stupeur, ainsi, sous
> le regard humain, ce petit corps calcaire creux et spiral
> appelle autour de soi quantité de pensées, dont aucune ne
> s'achève. . . .[34] (Valéry's periods).

Shell motifs in *La Prise/Prose* lend support to a hypothesis that the
novel has the structure of a spiral. So compellingly conjured in the content
of the novel, properties of the spiral appear in the structure of some
strangely digressive sentences. Within the *Borne*'s field of influence, syntax
is disturbed and phrases proliferate like concentric circles emanating from a
rock dropped in water. Such sentence structure occurs in the context of "les

mouvements circulaires de la fascination" associated with descriptions of infectious laughter, of a seductive mouth, and most frequently of eyes.

Close examination of an example will show in what particular it resembles a spiral:

> Des ombres grises, luisantes, métalliques, apparaissent des ombres grises, luisantes, métalliques, apparaissent en divers points de la surface verdâtre de l'iris, des ombres grises, luisantes, métalliques, apparaissent en divers points de la surface verdâtre de l'iris, s'effacent, affleurent, plus loin des ombres grises, luisantes, métalliques, apparaissent en divers points de la surface verdâtre de l'iris, s'effacent, affleurent plus loin selon un cycle si lent autour des ombres grises, luisantes, métalliques, qui apparaissent en divers points de la surface verdâtre de l'iris, s'effacent, affleurent plus loin selon un cycle si lent autour de la pupille sombre, lumineuse, qu'il est impossible, sans relire davantage, de les suivre plus longtemps. (I, 2:4; II, 1:6; III, 2:2)

Proceeding in ever-longer segments, the sentence circles back to its point of departure. As in a spiral, each successive ring repeats the previous one but includes progressively more material. The sentence includes its own brake, which prevents it from continuing indefinitely. Its "duplication intégrant une constante d'irrégularité" can be followed by distinguishing its separate movements or rotations. A constant principle of irregularity is contained in the pivotal word "de," initially a plural indefinite article, then meaning "of," the word is subsequently transformed to complete "loin," and "autour." The total sentence is the sum (or convergence) of all its parts and gives scriptural "incarnation" to the idea of a spiral, thus fulfilling the conditions of the novel's epigraph: "Une telle figure est le lieu de convergence de toutes ses parties et doit être son propre support." (The *Larousse Encyclopédique* gives as a figurative definition of *support*: "Ce qui donne une sorte de réalité concrète: Les figures sont les supports des abstractions. Les images servent de support au rêve poétique.")

Such sentences--there are eleven in all--form but a small fraction of *La Prise/Prose*. Their importance should not be underestimated, however. They occur throughout the novel, even outside the frame of the space exploration fiction, which explains them as emanating from the *Borne*.

Associated by allusion with Mallarmé, they are the only instances in all Ricardou's fiction where representation is disrupted at the sentence level. Moreover, most of them are *mises-en-abyme*: Ed's laughter, for example, like the sentence that describes it, "se communique ... de proche en proche" following a pattern of "transformations miniatures" (I, 6:5). In the example quoted above, the eyes (whose grey shadows "apparaissent, ... affleurent plus loin selon un cycle si lent autour de la pupille sombre") belong to Isabelle, but also simultaneously to the reader, who visually traces the cycles of a spiral-shaped sentence.

The same principle can be perceived in the structure of the whole novel. As a spiral moving in ever smaller rings, the text offers multiple examples of "lectures emboîtées" or concentric parentheses, in which we read of a reader reading a reader and so on: Isabelle reads the story of "La Princesse interdite" and other sub-story protagonists read the stories of their own adventures. Infinite gyration toward an (absent) center is the mechanism of multiple imbricated *mises-en-abyme*.

As a spiral moving in ever larger rings, Ricardou's novel sets a rotation in motion with its first sentence. Repeatedly coming back upon its axis of departure, the novel opens outward (theoretically forever) accumulating more and more space between its lines. The novel's opening passage recurs throughout, with progressively enriched meaning. Each time the passage appears, its signifiers are constant, but its context provides an irregularity which unfolds completely new meanings. As the novel progresses, occurrences of the passage are not superimposable because meaning is cumulative, like the space of a spiral. The passage first appears as follows:

▽

Rien.

Sinon, peut-être, affleurant, le décalage qu'instaure telle certitude.

Le noir.

Pour obscure qu'elle soit, il semble qu'on ne puisse revenir du plus loin sans accréditer cette figuration du vide.

C'est la nuit, donc.

Et déjà, peu à peu, une clarté diffuse l'élucide.

Bientôt, cercle au dessin parfait, la lune se détache, s'élève dans la transparence au-dessus d'une sombre architecture.

Quelques pas, risqués en oblique, permettent d'échapper à sa dangereuse évocation.

Exposées à l'astre, plusieurs surfaces claires matérialisent des créneaux. L'ombre, que la forteresse projette jusqu'ici sur la pente selon une réplique approximative, est raffinée en innombrables échancrures par les accidents du sol. (I, 1:1-2)

The passage continues for several pages, emphasizing optical phenomena, especially contrasts of light and darkness and optical illusions. Having lingered over the fortress, description moves above to a cloud, which, although appearing immobile, undergoes constant metamorphosis, eventually splitting to form two clouds, the larger of which moves slowly "vers l'occident," the direction of reading.

In an article entitled "Naissance d'une fiction," Ricardou presents some of the generative devices he brought into play while writing *La Prise/Prose*. Speaking of the novel's first word, he has this to say:

Mais puisque ce livre prétend se construire sans mettre en place quelque entité préalable que ce soit, quelle base génératrice peut-elle donc être choisie? Il va de soi que rien ne convient, que ce livre doit s'établir sur rien. Congédiée d'emblée une première illusion, celle de l'*expression*, une autre s'offre donc, celle de *création*, assurant qu'un texte peut s'écrire sans base, 'ex nihilo'. Alors puisque rien ne peut être pris pour base, ce qui est pris pour base, c'est le mot rien.[35]

Ricardou usually avoids the word "creation" because of its theological overtones and its association with the notion of inspiration. He prefers a more marxian vocabulary including "work" and "production." The word "rien" is a paradox, as he suggests, because it signifies an absence but *is* a presence. Its very appearance, he goes on to point out, brings into play a host of other texts from Flaubert and Mallarmé to Sarraute which begin with that word. As he remarks later in the article, "commencer de rien c'est toujours partir de quelque chose."

A theological notion of creation, is, however, at work here. Describing the role of intertextuality as the inscription, in a text, of a "certaine constellation" of other texts, Ricardou may have had in mind another famous statement which shares its syntax ("nothing . . . but") with the beginning of *La Prise/Prose*: "Rien n'aura eu lieu excepté peut-être une constellation." The first word of *La Prise/Prose*, like the opening line of "Un coup de dés,"[36] begins a constellation (poem) which, like the universe, has no discernable reason for existence outside itself. Nothing is certain; "Rien" is a "certitude" whose black presence on white page establishes ("instaure") difference ("décalage").

The New Testament proposes a version of creation remarkably similar to Ricardou's textual cosmogony:

> In the beginning was the Word, and the Word was with God, and the Word was God; all things were made through Him, and without Him was not anything made that was made. In Him was life, and the life was the light of men. The light shines in the darkness, and the darkness has not overcome it. (*John* 1:1-5)

God and the Word are a single creative power, according to this interpretation of the Creation. Taking this statement quite literally, we can arrive at a theory of language whereby creation from the Word (or a word) produces a novel which does not reflect a preexistent reality, but which encloses its own processes of elaboration. Biblical and textual genesis meet.

A more schematic theory of creation from language in *Les Lieux-dits* emerges from a binary opposition of order and disorder. The grid is a form of constellation useful for the overschematized linguistic universe established in *Les Lieux-dits*: metaphor and metonymy; selection and distribution, etc. *La Prise/Prose* poses a knottier problem with the realization that nothing is something, and that a text always refers beyond itself, if only to other texts and to the language which makes it intelligible.

In the passage above, equivalences are established which assimilate creative power (God), language (the Word) and light. Mallarmé saw writing as a constellation of light and darkness differentiations which was an exact inversion of that found in the heavens: "Tu remarquas, on n'écrit pas, lumineusement, sur champ obscur, l'alphabet des astres, seul, ainsi s'indique ébauché ou interrompu; l'homme poursuit noir sur blanc."[37]

Ricardou's creation from the word on the novel's first page is immediately followed by another version which corrects and expands it by posing its inverse. "Noir," almost "rien" backwards, is a second way of representing the void from which creation emerges. Each word is a "figuration du vide." Already light has intervened, however, in the form of white spaces which separate clusters of black words.

A third "incarnation" or "figuration" of the void follows. The idea of "nothing" and "blackness" is materialized by the night. With the coming of light (the moon) into the darkness, sight is possible. In a visible world, light and darkness materialize a fortress. From abstractions of "nothing" a fiction evolves (or is "born") through processes of differentiation and of incarnation. Since seeing implies a viewer, the phrase "quelques pas" and the word "ici" begin to situate a narrative eye.

Sun and book move "vers l'ouest" or toward the left on a map as reading and the day progress. *Genesis* tells us that the world was created in six days. The passage which opens *La Prise/Prose* appears a total of six times in the novel:

1. I, 1   The moon appears above a toy castle on the beach.

2. I, 8:2   Sylvain, playing Prince Charming, is knocked unconscious by a stone fallen ("calme bloc . . . chu?") during a storm. He literally blacks out and "sees stars."

3. II, 1:1   A lamp throws light on the darkness of a castle's library.

4. III, 1:1   View of a Venusian landscape.

5. III, 3:1   *Je* undergoes shock therapy.

6. III, 5:5   composite.

The last occurrence begins in a library recognizable as the setting of Part II; the arrangement of books on a shelf recalls the parlor drama:

Une anomalie, pourtant: cette oblique du livre incliné dans le
parallélépipède de vide et qui le scinde en deux prismes
inverses. Mais tout rentre dans l'ordre, apparemment, quand un
nouvel éclair se ramifie selon d'invraisemblables arguties, d'une
tempe à l'autre, dans l'obscurité immédiate. (III, 5:5)

An anomaly is evident in the paragraph as well. The word "éclair" refers
simultaneously to lightning outside the chateau (see 3. above) and to a flash
of light associated with shock therapy. The passage moves from the library
to a hospital setting, as is clear in the words "d'une tempe à l'autre" (a
repetition from 5. above) and in the final transformation of the moon which
appeared in I, 1:

Bientôt, cercle parfait dessine, semble-t-il, de poussière, le
globe électrique se détache à hauteur du plafond. (III, 5:6)

Only because we have seen the passage many times before, can this
occurrence produce a scene where several of the passage's meanings are
present.

In *L'Observatoire de Cannes* and *Les Lieux-dits* we saw the progress
of the text as a voyage, the reader as a traveler. *La Prise/Prose* offers a more
ambitious project: the mythical voyage of the sun, or more scientifically, the
orbit of a reading/seeing self through six days, six rings of a spiral. The novel
comes to rest after six phases with a bright light seen to the right (east) this
time:

Pour obtenir une satisfaisante vision de la convergence des
hublots, l'oeil doit se placer sur l'axe organisateur de la coquille,
ligne idéale qui joint le centre de la lucarne supérieure à celui de
pentagone basal.
Quant à l'éclairage de l'ensemble, il sera d'autant plus intense
que cette droite se confondra avec la direction de la lumière.
Certaine lecture consciencieuse suffit maintenant pour que
l'irradiation de toute la figure élabore qui JE SUIS, et par un
phénomène reflexif point trop imprévu, en un éclair, me LE
LIVRE. (III, 8:18)

This intense light contrasts with the initial darkness, and suggests the advent of the white page below. The "figure" of the last sentence is both Valéry's spiral shell and the novel itself. The voyage from creation toward the novel's last word suggest Mallarmé's belief that "Le monde existe pour aboutir à un livre."[38] Ricardou's cosmogony in *La Prise/Prose* pays tribute to Mallarmé's statement ("dans un sens") while demonstrating that the reverse is also true; a real Masterwork demonstrates the reciprocal relationship between words and things by showing how ("dans l'autre sens") "le livre existe pour aboutir à un monde."

CHAPTER IV

Still Waters: *Révolutions minuscules*

> . . . la merveille de transposer
> un fait de nature en sa presque
> disparition vibratoire selon le
> jeu de la parole.
> > --Mallarmé

> La mer, la mer, toujours
> recommencée!
> > --Valéry

Révolutions minuscules[1] takes us into the laboratory that produced *L'Observatoire de Cannes, Les Lieux-dits* and *La Prise/Prose de Constantinople*. The volume's nine short pieces of fiction interact so intimately, it is difficult to believe that the stories first appeared independently in a variety of journals over a span of ten years (1960-1970),[2] that is, over the period during which Ricardou was writing and publishing his three novels. Each of the stories restates and reworks theories about the relation of meaning to writing. The emphasis remains on process and metamorphosis, circling around the central enigma of textual origin. Subtle modulation of visible and *lisible* controls the text's straining toward and resistance of meaning. One of the volume's epigraphs, taken from Paul Klee, sets the tone: "Parce qu'elles ne reproduisent pas seulement avec plus ou moins de vivacité des choses vues, mais parce qu'elles rendent visible ce qui a été entrevu en secret" (p. 75). Introducing the central story and separated from the previous one by blank pages, this epigraph provides no antecedent for its pronoun, and so we are free to let it refer to the volume's subtitle: "nouvelles."

The order of the stories' appearance is not chronological, however, and this is a first warning to be aware of the book's overall architecture. As they appear in *Révolutions minuscules*, the stories manifest a certain symmetry, even to the casual glance. Another Roussellian metagram at its poles (the first story, entitled "Jeu," and the "je" of "Autobiographie") recalls the last sentence of *La Prise/Prose*: writing begins with game and produces a self--"Je suis [suivre] le livre"--rather than expressing a preexisting consciousness.

Dividing the book in two, "Diptyque" places all the stories under the sign of the double. Itself divided into two parts, the central text suggests further mirror symmetries of the whole. Preceding and following "Diptyque" are two pieces which deal primarily with phenomena of transparence and reflection. Forming a second set of parentheses around the center, are the stories "Sur la pierre" and "Plage blanche," both of which present beach scenes characterized by latent violence. The remaining pair of stories-- "Incident" and "Gravitation"--portray "events" which almost fulfill traditional requirements for the word "story." The incident in question involves graffiti on a wall, a mugging, and the arrival on scene of an ambulance. "Gravitation" describes events within the field of vision of a narrator, who works crossword puzzles while observing a little girl at play. Both stories involve transformation of the written trace--on a wall, on a sidewalk, on wet paper.

The collection's unity is further enhanced by the presence of a protean substance which plays some role in each of the texts: water. Six of the stories are set by a sea or pond: "Jeu," "Sur la pierre," "Lancement d'un voilier," half of "Diptyque," "Réflexion totale" and "Plage blanche." "Gravitation" takes place after a rainstorm whose effects are still visible as reflecting puddles, erosion of chalk lines on the sidewalk, and the soggy transparence of newspaper pages. "Autobiographie" begins with raindrop patterns on a windowpane and continues with description of the shapes of oceans and seas and of a wet ink blotch on a desktop. "Incident" takes place in full sunlight on a dry day, but a sandblasting crew spews sand and water, erasing graffiti. Similarly, years of rain have worn grooves in a statue. Stones, sand, water, and sun are the natural actors in a play of surface and transformation, with a narrative eye as attentive observer. Water is an agent of evolution in all the stories. Water erodes and purifies. It modifies contours and colors. Most of all, it bears images on its surface.

Opposition of transparence and reflection can be found in all Ricardou's fiction as a parable for the tension between referential and literal dimensions of writing. In *Les Lieux-dits*, a shop window in a painting entitled "Réflexion" provides a view of displays within, while also reflecting the faces of a young couple outside. A similar window in *L'Observatoire de Cannes* reflects the face of a young bather. In *La Prise/Prose de Constantinople*, a glass door only partially obscures books from view by offering superimposed reflections of a crystal vase on a table.

A more mobile surface than glass or mirrors, water moves *Révolutions minuscules* away from binary opposition toward an emphasis on hesitation and metamorphosis, as depth and reflection interact on a single surface. Rather than excluding paradox and contradiction, the book concentrates on alternation, trying to seize the shifting of optical illusion.

1

Flanking "Diptyque," two stories present the potential polyvalence of water. The title of the first of these--"Lancement d'un voilier"--hides in its last word an anagram of "livre," thus pointing to Ricardou's omnipresent themes of writing and the book. Neither the sailboat nor the book is seen as a two-dimensional surface in this story. The boat is marked on its side by a blue line at the level of the water. Dividing the boat in two, this line "signale quel partage la surface de l'eau doit déterminer entre visible et invisible." Similarly, a metal ball thrown during a game of *boules* lands and is "enfoncée aux trois quarts dans le sable," and simultaneously an orange bobs up and down in the water, "trois quarts immergée." Reflecting these similarities, the sun moves across the sky until, at the story's end, it too is three-quarters "enfoncé" behind the line of the horizon. Most of the story is devoted to the boat, part of which, although submerged and invisible, is nevertheless described: "l'invisible," we read, "est peint en noir." In this story, three-dimensional space allows for description of depths. Water can thus appear turbulent and deep and can contain objects--"débris de bois, de liège." What is below the water's surface appears cloudy or black, is partially unknown. As a metaphor for the unconscious, these partially invisible murky depths can serve as a guide to the other stories.

On the other side of "Diptyque," "Réflexion totale" (pp. 97-109) describes the surface of a pond. When calm, the pond offers a perfect mirror image of a landscape above, with trees, clouds, and a minuscule event: a butterfly is lured into a spider's web and devoured. When disturbed, the surface is dominated by concentric ripples which distort reflection. From time to time one can also catch a glimpse of the pond's bed with its mud and grasses. Point of view is localized in a narrator, who appears briefly as a "silhouette" which "s'arrête au bord de l'eau, légère, interdite," recalling the intrusion on scene of other narrators via their shadows and reflections. Time too is displayed on the surface of the pond. Movement at the bottom is seen as a muddy "brume noire" which obscures transparence. Passing time is visible as a "soleil déclinant" which becomes "un cercle de lumière visible, auréolé d'un transparent halo." Every event is translated as a change on a sensitive image.

The pond itself produces a diptych, in that when it reflects, everything is doubled: "Surgit alors, ailes battantes, plus haut, plus bas, une piéride blanche." Although the narrator's gaze remains fixed on reflected phenomena, the pond's surface produces a fiction with reference to an external reality, as we are reminded: "Mais il suffit de rien, ou presque, d'un déplacement de l'attention plutôt que des pupilles, pour obtenir l'espace original." Transparence and reflection, the pond's surface or an "espace original" constitute alternatives of two and three-dimensional space. Depending on the tranquillity of the water and the direction of attention, the eye may observe surrounding reality, a reflection, or the textures of the pond itself.

What interests the narrator, however, is neither perfect transparence nor the "miroir absolu" reflecting water, but rather that "zone intermédiaire ou se conjuguent avec exactitude la transparence et la réflexion." In such a moment of transformation, three-dimensional space above and below water are visible on a surface text. In that moment are played out contradictions between mimesis and anti-referentiality, fiction and theory. As a metaphor for the written page, the pond is recognizable as the literal dimension of a text, while three-dimensional realities represent its referential dimensions. The total text is neither reality nor reflection, but the relationships between the two: the narrator is fascinated with that "zone indécise" where perception can encompass all dimensions at once--where mud at the pond's bottom, ripples on its surface, and reflection of the world are simultaneously grasped ("entrevus") if only for a precarious instant. A spider web wherein a butterfly is captured ("prise") offers several additional allusions: a woven web suggests a text; through its association with Ariadne, we are reminded of possible threads (readings) of labyrinthine prose.

Minute "déplacement de l'attention" with corresponding focus on infinitesimal detail is an important principle integrating the stories of *Révolutions minuscules*. Attention to details of a spider web or moving sand reveals the same kind of "fascination" present in *La Prise/Prose*. Obsessive focus here again has the effect of removing an object of attention from its context, distorting size relationships and causing unexpected analogies to emerge: a burning match can be a *mise-en-abyme* for a character's death by fire, for example, and erosion of a sand castle built too close to waves shares its description with a major landslide. Although landscapes in *Révolutions minuscules* are microcosmic, the eye's perspective is large. Tiny events assume significance precisely because everything is presented on small scale. Because attention to tiny events and objects is not usually the primary preoccupation of novelists, Ricardou has been called a "miniaturist" by one critic, a "poet" by another.[3]

2

Another effect of fascination is the disintegration and disappearance
of the object described, as was seen in *L'Observatoire de Cannes*. This
phenomenon is most evident in "Sur la pierre," first published shortly
before the 1961 novel. In that story, another diaphanous long-haired beauty
is viewed as she sunbathes on a rock:

> Elle dort, peut-être. Elle est, suivant la ligne de pente,
> allongée sur la pierre. Les deux pieds nus, l'un par-dessus
> l'autre, sont complètement immergés. Les deux mollets, élargis
> par leur appui sur les algues douces, sont périodiquement
> mouillés par le flot. La pliure des jambes, totalement ouverte,
> adhère aux ulves sèches tandis que les deux cuisses, le tissu du
> maillot, les reins, le dos, les omoplates, et, de part et d'autre du
> visage, les bras sont posés à même la pierre. Les deux coudes
> sont repliés et les mains, sous la nuque, servent de support. Les
> cheveux blonds, agglutinés en torsades mouillées, ont été
> déployés au-dessus de la tête, sur la pierre chaude, au soleil. (pp.
> 36-37)

This is a familiar kind of description, which disarticulates its object into
constituent parts. In fact "Sur la pierre" first appeared the year before
L'Observatoire de Cannes. The story's refrain, "il n'y a plus rien" can be
understood at several levels. With a brisk gesture, the bather sweeps from
the rock a nearby crab which is in the process of devouring a mussel.
However, as she removes these creatures, she herself is removed by the
progress of writing:

> Un battement de cils, un frémissement de la main ou du
> coude et il n'y a plus rien. Le plan d'eau est lisse. Une brume
> légère, blanchissant le ciel, estompe la ligne d'horizon. (p. 38)

It is as if she has disappeared below the shiny surface of the water/text. She
is not a "real" woman; definite articles, description and fragmentation
reduce her to an impersonal allegory of something else, the process of
transformation itself. There is someone watching this spectacle: the
impersonal "battement de cils" can perhaps be attributed to a narrative eye,
whose blink obliterates the entire scene. A "déplacement de l'oeil" then
moves descriptive focus to the larger perspective of the horizon.

Connotations of the sentence "Elle dort peut-être" send us to similar descriptions of another ambiguous bather in *L'Observatoire de Cannes*. Violence is displaced to the calm bather from two adjacent scenes. Another (or the same) woman in an identical bikini enters the field of vision as she rides by on water skis. Precise description of this second woman fragments her, too, and masks a blurred transition which assimilates her to the bather. A long description of the skier ends with her

> chevelure blonde [qui] flotte dans le vent. Quelques cheveux emmêlés, isolés de la masse, virevoltent puis retombent sur la pierre. Le corps visible, à l'exception de la plante de chaque pied, est uniformément bronzé. Le tissu rosé, parsemé de pois blancs, a passé au soleil.
> Si ce n'est un mince filet à l'extérieur de chaque paupière, il n'y a nulle ride sur le visage, peut-être endormi. (pp. 40-41)

Traditional novels teach us to demand that discontinuities between characters be clearly signaled. Originally, there were two women, one skiing, the other sunbathing on a rock. The two wear identical bikinis, however, and both have long flowing blond hair. But if there is only one woman, how did she get from the skis to the rock? Did she fall? Was she pushed? Is she dead or simply asleep? Two descriptions (and perhaps two women) lack clear distinction and flow together, producing a single composite image. Movement of the description in the quotation above simply does not allow us to resolve this contradiction.

As a result of this and other hints of violence, the text is endowed with a violent tone which cannot be localized in any of its signifieds. In such a context, other words and phrases lose neutrality and suggest grotesque meanings: "les deux pieds sont déformés par la réfraction"; "les lèvres sourient," not the woman herself.

In the end, "il n'y a plus rien," because the body has been completely eroded by description and water. In the last paragraph, only water remains: "La mer n'est qu'une montée silencieuse sur la pierre inclinée, suivie d'un reflux immédiat." What may be a single snapshot scene is transformed by description into a drama of indeterminate length--long enough perhaps for the total disintegration of a human body until nothing remains. Deprived of temporal anchors, the minuscule becomes macrocosmic.

A second incident is similarly displaced to the bather, but this time violence has humorous and sado-erotic overtones. Before the arrival in the text of a crab, the bathing girl is assimilated by description to the landscape. The presence of "ulves" alerts the reader to the type of game being played. The woman is clothed, but the rock is bare: "Enfin, nue, couleur de brique, la pierre...." Adjectives, minimally attached to their noun (whose appearance is deferred) float free to describe the bather, whose feet are "nus." Once assimilation of body and landscape has begun, the scene is prepared for the arrival of the crab, who begins to tear and eat the flesh of a mussel. The violence of this description includes the bather:

> Les pattes centrales posées sur les deux valves nacrées, le crabe entame sa nourriture. Les deux pinces antérieures et les mandibules découpent la chair jaune, en une série de mouvements secs et précis. La bouche ingurgite.
> Un imperceptible mouvement du coude et de la main: il n'y a plus rien sur la pierre. (p. 41)

Perhaps the girl moves her hands to protect herself from the crab. Perhaps she is chained, Prometheus-like, to the rock: We are told that "Sur chaque jambe, au sommet de chaque aire de peau bronzée parcourue par le flot, s'est fixé un bracelet de sel," and again, insistently, reminded that her "deux chevilles" are "cerclées de sel." Overtones of suggested violence are so strong that "Sur la pierre" has been translated into English under the title "Epitaph."[4]

The story itself imitates the rhythm of waves washing over a body thanks to regular repetition of three refrains (with variants) which first appear as follows:
  A. "Il n'y a plus rien sur la dalle inclinée vers l'eau"
  B. "Elle dort peut-être"
  C. "Au reflux, les filaments se posent sur la pierre et en épousent la forme"

Segments between repetitions are analogous as well, with many repeated phrases, so that the entire story consists of a set of regular rhythms following a pattern: ABC (a bather is described and a crab arrives on the rock); ABCA (the bather is described, the crab attacks and eats a mussel); ABCA (another bather--water skier--is described and the crab continues its meal); A (only the sea remains). Here again, then, water and text follow reflected movements, but this time entirely at the level of rhythm.

3

Properties of water also help elucidate the sometimes strange behavior of the written word in *Révolutions minuscules*. The example of "Gravitation" (pp. 111-139) will make this relationship clearer. The story begins by describing an urban scene after a storm. Water performs two functions as the story develops. As in the alchemical precept "as above, so below," a reflected sky (or heaven) and a lowly sidewalk are joined in the transparence and reflection of a puddle. Macro- and microcosm intersect as the puddle articulates the unlikely analogy of hopscotch and religious discourse. A series of words does double duty, bringing together a sacred universe and a smaller but analogous ludic space: "ciel," "pluie," "amulette," "cruciforme," "transept," "psalmodie," "contempler," "s'agenouiller," etc.

Intervention of another game played on another grid enlarges the reservoir of such words. Crossword puzzles include the words "lune," "terre," "salut" and other words intersecting with hopscotch: "amulette" (which a player throws before hopping) and the name of the game: "marelle" (hopscotch). A third surface--the text itself--completes series of words which join cosmic with ludic space. In this context, hops performed by a child become a ritual, and conversely, religious themes are desacralized.

A second role of water is to act as solvent wherein shapes, colors and words are transformed. Rain has erased the hopscotch court's outline, necessitating a rewriting: a little girl retraces lines on the ground with a chunk of plaster, which diminishes as the lines appear. Her task completed, the girl places in a tin box the remaining "sphérule" of plaster "aussi précieuse, soudain, qu'une amulette." The instrument of writing has itself become a ritual object. With another bit of plaster, the child completes her restoration of what has become a sacred text or grimoire:

> Sa composition en sept carrés évoque une croix de Lorraine.
> Les cases une, deux, cinq, numérotées en chiffres romains,
> figurent le pivot. Quant aux deux transversales, elles sont
> respectivement représentées par les carreaux trois et quatre, et
> six et sept, accolés deux à deux. Pour que la croix fût complète,
> il eût donc suffi d'y ajouter un huitième carreau qui en eût
> prolongé l'axe. A sa place, pour peu qu'on tourne la page
> luisante, glacée, et que la feuille rugueuse, elle, du journal, soit

abaissée, il est possible de lire le mot *ciel*. Dans son ensemble, la graphie actuelle--les pleins, les déliés--est très réussie. Elle ne laisse paraître de la première, palimpseste, que les hésitations--la boucle du c, du 1--, les repentirs. (pp. 118-19)

The hopscotch court and the sky become progressively indistinguishable, their assimilation mediated by water and a series of polyvalent words. Both "skies"--the real one above, the word below--appear in the transparence and/or reflection of a puddle.

Behind the newspaper mentioned in the quotation above sits a gentleman who, when not observing the child over the top of his paper, is absorbed by the "coin des cruciverbistes" where he fills in two crossword grids that are described with meticulous precision. The puzzles unite series of words from hopscotch and its micro-macrocosm with terms from a description of the scene itself, including even the "axis" of the crossword puzzle itself. Overdetermined by the puzzle, details of each seem less arbitrary. Thus a cat, the little girl's name ("Irène") and other details are interconnected. Whether the story was generated from the puzzles or the reverse, the two work together in a tightly constructed text. The puzzle plays a role similar to that of graffiti in *L'Observatoire de Cannes*.

Some of the puzzle's letters do not form words. A few anagrams, often suggested by crossword definitions, are present, but several combinations seem to be no more than free-floating particles:

En l'état actuel, plusieurs vocables ne paraissent pas avoir atteint leur complète maturité. Si *ulne* figure bien cet 'astre bouleversé' et *eri* cet 'envers de la colère', si, à la rigueur, *iv* et *ner* peuvent s'entendre *yves* et *nerf*, une singulière complaisance doit être requise, en revanche, pour rapprocher l'épellation *acn* du mot *océane* ou de l'expression 'Oh! c'est Anne!'. Quant à *ge* et *xu*, ils restent parfaitement injustifiés, sinon comme simples chevilles susceptibles d'assurer la continuité de l'imbrication. (p. 123)

Evolution of words and parts of words, however singular it may seem, is an idea extremely important to the book as a whole. Among other functions, such a conception of the liquidity of the word makes possible permutations of words and meanings within a controlled framework.

The newspaper itself, on which the puzzles appear, is described in a curious manner:

> Le papier grisâtre, poreux, dont la matière est piquetée par places de minuscules copeaux de bois qui n'ont pu être entraînés vers le ruisseau à présent tari, est d'une qualité trop médiocre pour que la découpure du bord soit très nette. C'est une déchirure contrôlée plutôt, une succession d'infimes dents de scie. (p. 121)

Newsprint is realistically evoked here, with its serrated edges and slubs of incompletely processed wood pulp. Something goes wrong, however. The word "bois" triggers a lapsus, and the closeup of the page dissolves into another scene of a different scale. This aberrant description of paper makes sense only in terms of another description which is its complement. Similar but larger chips of wood are carried away in a rain gutter:

> Derrière la bordure en pierres du trottoir, le ruisseau est probablement tari, car on a tourné la page, mais l'averse a dû le grossir, il y a peu, et drainer vers lui qui se précipitait jusqu'à la grille de l'égout, toute la poussière accumulée et de si nombreuses épaves--morceaux de journaux presque translucides, copeaux de bois, allumettes à demi consumées tournoyant bientôt dans le flux, papiers de bonbons, bouts de cigarettes entrouvertes perdant le tabac--que la surface du goudron est à présent parfaitement appropriée. (p. 115)

In this description, the newsprint is evoked by the anomalous phrase "car on a tourné la page."

As a result of these two intermingling superimposed descriptions paper and water merge, exchanging properties. The pavement becomes a coded surface alive with readable flotsam and jetsam. Conversely, and more significantly, paper behaves like a liquid. No longer a solid immobile substance, the page allows the tiny creatures which inhabit it—fragments of geometric shapes, words, letters, asterisks and signifiers of various sorts—to float freely, forming new and surprising configurations. It is the pervasive metaphor of paper and water which supports another more conspicuous conjunction: *page* and *plage*. Such analogies are in turn reinforced by an entire series of semantic polyvalences which appear in a variety of contexts throughout the book. Mobility of words and letters thus permits the semantic shifts that structure the story, permitting parable.

Semantic polyvalence and optical illusion converge in *Révolutions minuscules*. When *plage* and *page* are mutually metaphoric, and when we read about the former on the latter, distance between signifier and signified is reduced. Words *are* things; the visible world and the *lisible* merge in a single operation and can be manipulated simultaneously. An implication: in a scriptural world such as that of *Révolutions minuscules*, it is never certain whether there has been a story at all. Perhaps there exists only a page with its "êtres de lettres." With Ricardou's near obsession with the word "rien" and the idea of nothingness ("Rien n'aura eu lieu que le lieu"), hesitation between presence and absence becomes a major theme, its two poles signaled by the volume's dedication to Illia (or "il y a") and the phrase which opens "Sur la pierre": "Il n'y a rien."

4

The mobility of letters and sounds permits another kind of metamorphosis in "Incident" (pp. 47-59), where variations in a bird's flight, in the sound of voices and in graffiti on a wall mark stages in a story. There are actually two incidents. A young man with a newspaper--perhaps the fellow from "Gravitation"--appears on the scene, takes a stub of chalk from his pocket, and adds to accumulated graffiti. Two others attack him, rub sand in his face, and burn his newspaper. Nearby, a crew is at work cleaning dirt and graffiti from the building with a stream of compressed water and sand. A worker falls from some height and is taken off in an ambulance.

Exclamations of passersby formulate auditory ambiguities or illusions, alerting the reader to the type of operations at play:

> Quelqu'un remarque: 'un instant, il m'a semblé comme en l'air suspendu'; et un autre: 'les jeux sont faits'. A partir de l'oreille, une mince rivière pourpre trace une rayure sur la joue. Nul doute que l'édifice osseux partout ne se complique d'innombrables fissures. Quelqu'un remarque: 'les yeux sont fixes'; et un autre: 'un instant, il m'a semblé comme en clair suspendu'. (p. 58)

The minuscule malentendu that separates "en l'air" from "en clair" and "les jeux sont faits" from "les yeux sont fixes" signals the presence of a Roussellian poetic practice. Earlier, the "calcaire osseux" of the wall appeared cracked in the same terms. The sand from the cleaning operation is dispersed everywhere, "intermin*able*ment," in "irrémédi*able*s symptômes" and especially in the "indéfiniss*able*" character of what is heard and read.

The same processes apply to the whole text. The title undergoes a first evolution as it opens the story: "Ainsi dans la diversité profuse, aussitôt se déclare l'intelligible." Reminiscent of the opening lines of *La Prise/Prose,* this first sentence points out that intelligibility depends on contrast between darkness and light and differentiation of "incident" from "ainsi dans." and then "occident." "accident," and "oxydé." The series also includes "incendie," and intersects with the *page/plage* series when the newspaper is burned. Once sensitized to such procedures, the reader can follow the play of such rhymes as *rêve. grève,* and *crève* and *point/poing.* This last pair yields an implicit "poing de départ" for a bird taking flight from a statue's outstretched hand.

The raised fist is also, of course, a gesture of defiance. "Incident," first published in 1970, is the only example in all Ricardou's fiction where political themes are mentioned directly, and the story provides clues as to how an ideological project is implied elsewhere. The focus of the story is a wall with graffiti which evolve in the same ways as onlookers' voices. One such mark reads "Occident" (for *Occident Libre,* a neo-fascist group). The young man is attacked while in the process of superimposing an "A" on the "O" to produce an "accident" (first the word on the wall, then the event). He also adds the word "oxydé." Another inscription is one of the better-known wall slogans from May 1968: "Au-dessous des pavés, la plage." Like other key words, this phrase undergoes several "amendements sibyllins" to become "Au-dessous des palais, la page." Only then is the newspaper burned at the base of the building's façade. Play on the location of the two inscriptions to the right and left respectively, and opposition of black and white suggest ideological conflict.[5]

These poetic stages account for the incidents of the story, but they also in a typically Ricardolian way, recount the events of 1968, while suggesting a relationship between minuscule anagrammatic and larger political (r)evolutions. In his essays, Ricardou contends that changes in language can bring about changes in perception and ultimately in reality. The frequency of wordplay and of reflection on language in the wall slogans of May 1968 testifies to a connection perceived, in the heat of those events, between the disruption of political and linguistic codes. In the words of one such inscription, "Le langage étant le mode de relation sociale entre les individus [...], il n'est aucune raison pour ne pas le faire péter au niveau de la répression grammaticale."[6] In a country where political repression has indeed for centuries been accompanied by linguistic restrictions, the graffiti of 1968 and a story like "Incident" can be seen not only to contain political themes, but also to participate in a linguistic liberation.

At several levels in the story can be read a disappointment that such linguistic spontaneity was too-soon washed away. As the stone "journal mural" is washed clean, the newspaper is burned on the sidewalk, producing in its crumpled headlines an ominous death (*crève*) of strikes (*grève*) and dreams (*rève*). Proponents of Occident Libre get the best of the young man with chalk in hand, and a worker is injured or dies. The story ends with the observation that the flames only left small marks on the surface (of the wall, of society) but will probably leave no appreciable effect: "certaines flammes se sont inscrites, un instant le long de la façade."

Key words of "Incident" rejoin Ricardou's personal themes that appear elsewhere without political allusions. The slogan and its transformations effectuate an unlikely encounter of his sandy beaches and stones with a Parisian tradition of insurrection where paving stones are symbols of revolutionary ideals. But the addition of *pavé* to the page and beach lexical series is not surprising in the light of other lapidary "fables of anagram." Manipulation of stones instead of words not only leads to construction of new edifices (*Les Lieux-dits*) but also indicates a path to be followed toward attainment of one's goals (*La Prise/Prose*). Sand and water are here not only agents of creative permutation, but ultimately of erasure.

Révolutions minuscules is about change--imagery, graphic and symbolic, erotic and ideological. Chemical changes take place in a liquid medium or solvent, and the presence of water and blood ("une mince rivière de pourpre [...] sur la joue" intervenes between two versions of onlookers' comments) suggests the persistence of Ricardou's chemical metaphor. "Oxydé" is a middle term in a chemical, graphic and political "reaction."

An epigraph from Hölderlin opens "Incident"--"Entretemps, il se disloque"
--reminding us that in all these domains, it is through disarticulation that
transformation is possible.

5

Transparence and reflection, water, description and fragmentation
are all present in "Diptyque," (pp. 73-96) which forms a pivot for the
book's symmetries. The story unfolds under the sign of the double: its first
word is immediately multiplied ("un double..."); the prefixes *re-* (*reflet*,
réflexion, *relève*, *reprendre*, *reparti*, *réduit*) and *dé-* (*décalage*, *découvert*,
découpures, *désordonné*) as well as the words *deux* and *double* supply
constant reminders that the text is ruled by fragmentation and repetition.
Reading and seeing come to a frustrated halt when the light is extinguished
and doubling is no longer possible. The story is divided into two parts,
entitled "Comminution" and "Dans les halliers de Brocéliande." Although
the two parts seem unrelated, each is dislocated to allow meanings from the
other to circulate, so that each text is hidden but can be glimpsed under the
other.

"Comminution" is set in a room where a traveler's attention is
absorbed by a mysterious activity. On a table are placed a triangular glass
fragment and numerous small bits of paper in two piles. The papers, shaped
in regular triangle and lozenge shapes, are inscribed with words on one side
and a picture on the other, "des rectos écrits et des versos dessinés."
Assembling this puzzle with words visible, a text can be read. Having read
this text, the young man transfers each of its fragments to the piece of broken
glass. He lifts the glass hoping to view a picture which should appear on the
back, but he is disappointed:

> Lorsque le texte est reconstitué, l'experimentateur soulève
> le support transparent en prenant garde de ne pas se couper aux
> arêtes vives, et, par en dessous, non sans hâte, il cherche à
> percevoir l'image que doit proposer, correspondante, le verso
> du document.
> Loin d'apporter un éclaircissement, la gravure sous-jacente
> livre d'emblée un désordre imprévu. Aucune des formes réunies
> par la reconstitution de la prose sur l'autre versant du papier ne
> se correspondent ici. C'est à peine si un examen très scrupuleux,
> malgré l'incommodité, permet d'admettre que les mains, genoux,

épaule, chevelure diversément sectionnés et dispersés en tous points de l'espace qui sert de fond, appartiennent à un unique corps féminin. (pp. 80-81)

A short while later, he begins again. Perhaps if he composed the picture this time, a second text, a "texte secret," would be revealed on the back. The picture thus composed reveals yet another red-haired woman. Her description is familiar: liquid hair, an "immense chevelure rousse, onduleuse," flows over her shoulder and down her back almost to her ankles. She is nude except for three strategically placed jewels--an eight-pointed star and two crescent moons--that transform her into a nocturnal landscape or constellation. Only her imperceptible "hachures ombreuses" recall that she is a drawing. In addition, "Les poignets de la jeune femme sont respectivement enserrés par un solide bracelet de métal soudé à une chaine." These metal bracelets, like the salt ones worn by the bather in "Sur la pierre" are surprising; Ricardou's sado-erotic themes, usually contained in the movement of descriptive striptease and fragmentation, are rarely depicted. Perhaps these bracelets are an allusion to the ones that may have bound a young girl in Robbe-Grillet's *Le Voyeur*.

The young man in "Comminution" is a traveler whose suitcase, whose blank fascination with wallpaper motifs, and whose association with the picture described above recall Mathias, the "voyageur" of *Le Voyeur*. A Robbe-Grilletian technique materializes the young man as well: from a reflection of a suitcase to the suitcase itself, the narration proceeds to a traveler, by means of a series of logical deductions:

> La valise est restée sur le lit, couvercle rabattu. Assis à l'étroite table poussée contre le mur, le voyageur a donc interrompu son installation. (p. 76)

In similar fashion, a hotel room, a table, and then the puzzle come into view.

Transition from text to image involves some danger. The jagged glass must be manipulated with caution as the young man lifts the puzzle a second time:

> Prenant soin de ne pas se blesser aux arêtes tranchantes, le jeune homme soulève alors le triangle de verre, et, par en dessous, s'efforce de connaître le nouveau texte dérivé.
> Il est bientôt en mesure d'en déchiffrer les premiers signes abracadabrants. (p. 84)

Before he can read whatever text might be on the reverse, a gust of wind scatters paper fragments and extinguishes the light. Only the moon can be seen. The wind has destroyed the two essential conditions of reading by removing light and destroying the text. In frustration, the young man gathers the papers, tears them into even smaller fragments ("une comminution raffinée"), and again scatters them, this time with the microcosmic wind of his breath.

This puzzle is indeed a puzzle. Reading its text from one side and contemplating its illustration on the other are mutually exclusive activities. Such too is the relationship between textuality and representation in Ricardou's view. The literal dimension (or prose) disarticulates and disperses the referential real (or *prise*) in its scriptural striptease. Conversely, the fascination with the real obscures or erases (blows away) the text. The young woman in question is not real, however, but is a text herself. The real woman is beyond the grasp of the picture or its description. In this sense, we are confronted with another series of *mises-en-abyme*. Within the frame of "Comminution" (which is half of a framed diptych) is a description of a woman. Words doubly screen her from view. The text we read contains her description which veils her by fragmenting her. Her picture is similarly fragmented by another text read on the reverse only at the price of disarticulating her. The traveler is a reader, another Isis, seeking fragments of text and body. The problem is that he cannot have both. Text and body are mutually exclusive arrangements; when one is integrally visible, the other can only be glimpsed underneath.

"Diptyque" begins not with description of the traveler's room but of its slightly distorted reflection in one of its windows: the reflection is not complete, however, since a broken fragment of glass is missing (the fragment on which the traveler composes his puzzle). Where glass is missing, reflection gives way to a small view of the outside: "Par le triangle de vide se révèle, soudain proche, un fragment de la nuit." Because the glass is broken, both the outside view--"fragment de la nuit"--and the inside view--a "reflet perverti"--are visible but dislocated. The same missing fragment of glass allows perception of the puzzle's image and text, but here too, both are dislocated. The triangle of glass, itself broken, thus twice mediates fragmentation. In both cases, it is only thanks to this fragmentation itself that the totality can be glimpsed at all.

An unflawed surface would offer a perfect reflection without distortions or cracks. As we have already seen in many examples, it is fragmentation which allows a *récit* to evolve. As in "Réflexion totale," here again it is the interplay of transparence and reflection which produces difference. Distinctions of figure and ground, black and light and so on permit perception of the world, both visible and *lisible*. Awareness of these necessary conditions is responsible for Ricardou's insistent emphasis on that "zone intermédiaire" where order (structure) emerges or re-emerges from chaos.

Paragraphs read on one puzzle surface are identical to segments of the second part of "Diptyque." Thus a system of partial reflection is established between the two panels of the story. Other elements from "Comminution" reappear in "Dans les halliers de Brocéliande" in changed form: a "fragment de nue" or "bit of cloud" recalls the fragmented nude ("nue") of the puzzle. Profiles, crescents and star shapes reappear as leaves in the second half of the story. What in the first part was a woman's body reappears in the second part transformed into a landscape. Once again, geometric shapes, forms without intrinsic content, establish structure through analogy. Comparable to the broken window in Part I, a mass of foliage is pierced by an interval through which rays of sun materialize particles of pollen, and shadows move across the ground with the sun's course. It is as if perhaps the two panels are twin descriptions of a single scene, an optical illusion similar to the face and vase figure/ground illusion discussed in Chapter I.

In fact, semantic illusion is present within "Dans les halliers de Brocéliande"' an ambiguity is sustained through use of figurative language. A "tapis de mouse," for example, materializes a room or a forest, depending on whether it is "tapis" or "mousse" which is used figuratively. The same ambiguity is present in the phrase "salle de verdure" which evokes either a green forest-like room or an intimate clearing sheltered by thick greenery (a room-like forest). There is a similar ambiguity of "troncs" and "colonnes" which refer either to trees or to ornate columns adorned with sculptured leaves. Polyvalence of certain phrases thus contributes to the dreamlike condensation of two radically different spaces and events.

The first space encountered is that of a mysterious forest where "mousse" and "verdure" are literal, "tapis" and "salle" figurative. At first there is no human presence except that implied by the view itself. Then, the reader is as startled by the sudden presence of a narrator as would be a wild animal, wandering fearlessly.

> Des frémissements d'ailes, des froissements de ramures diversement fléchies par des forces locales, en remuant les feuillages supérieurs, aggravent encore la complexité de cette changeante figuration.
> Pour soigneuse que fût leur apposition, les pas ont imprimé sur le tapis de mousse les traces qui conduisent à mon affût.
> A la marque restreinte, la pointe seule, mais profonde, j'ai préféré l'empreinte complète, plus superficielle. D'instant en instant, de fait, une à une, avec lenteur, les fibres végétales rectifient leur courbure, estompent ces signes où, malgré le chatoiement interposé de l'ombre et de la lumière, la bête eût pu lire prématurément. (pp. 86-87)

Except for the last lines, this passage ends a verbatim repetition of the puzzle text from "Comminution." The narrator, betrayed by a single possessive adjective, wishes to leave no trace of his presence in this unspoiled landscape--not even a footprint. A variant of this last paragraph further localizes the narrator's position and explains again how his footprints are slowly erased:

> Pour circonspecte qu'ait été sa progression, la marche a déposé sur le tapis assidûment ouvragé des empreintes qui conduisent jusqu'ici. Parce que superficielle, j'ai choisi la marque intégrale. Une application plus étroite, elliptique, la pointe seule, eût été trop appuyé. Un à un, d'ailleurs, les brins ployés remontent vers leur ordre initial.
> Toute matérialisation du passage se trouve ainsi lentement démentie. (p. 88)

This variant moves almost imperceptibly toward the possibility of a literal *tapis*. Moreover, it is not only the narrator whose traces are erased: by means of a calculated ambiguity, a metafictional level introduced in the last sentence above proves that the text itself contains illusory "passages."

The narrator proceeds to set a net and entrap a shadowy ambiguous beast whose struggle ends in its eventual pacification and/or death.

Immediately following is another scene which repeats the first with systematic variation. This time "salle" and "tapis" are literal while "verdure" and "mousse" assume figurative value. Spaces between trees become a skylight ("lucarne") where sun rays make dust particles visible. Instead of four trees there are four carved columns of a canopy bed ("ciel de lit"). Instead of a pond ("mare ovale"), the room contains a "large miroir ovale, au centre de la salle, posé par terre." A narrator finally materializes here as well and walks across the room toward the bed. In this version, however, the beast is a human being, "trapped" in sexual frenzy.

Description of an undefined person on a bed repeats with variations an earlier description of the beast. First the beast:

> Violentes, appartenant à un ordre d'abord insaisissable, certaines convulsions animent encore, entre les quatre colonnes torsadées, la silhouette de la bête prisonnière. C'est un sursaut parfois, aussitôt contrarié, de la croupe et des membres, portant sur quelques points bien délimités du filet la tension maximum. Les mailles aranéeuses s'arrondissent en cercles, s'allongent en rectangles, s'effilent en losanges, se tordent en croissants.
>
> Bientôt, une interruption s'évide dans la continuité de l'effort.
>
> Parcourue par des surfaces de frissons, la croupe se détend. Les membres s'apaisent.
>
> Les yeux se ferment.
>
> La tête roule sur le côté.
>
> Tantôt les épaules, les hanches, par une suite d'ondulations aux courbures variées, éprouvent la solidarité du réseau dont d'importantes sections, en évolution continue, modèlent selon un lacis de hachures entrecroisées, volumes et replis, le corps tout entier. (pp. 91-92)

Now the human prey:

> Violents certains, mais participant à un ordre plus nettement perceptible, divers spasmes animent la silhouette emprisonnée. C'est un sursaut, parfois, aussitôt refréné, qui cambre l'épine dorsale--et une tension accrue des jambes, des bras.

Largement déployée dans l'espace, la chevelure recompose
ses torsades fauves sur les épaules, les seins.
Mais bientôt, au-delà de la géometrie aranéeuse, les yeux se
ferment.
La tête retombe sur l'oreiller.
Quelquefois les épaules, les hanches, le buste, par une suite
d'ondulations imprévues qui s'imposent à un système plus
concerté, incitent l'ample toile blanche à recouvrir, à remodeler
avec minutie les surfaces du corps tout entier. (p. 95)

The two scenes that comprise "Dans les halliers de Brocéliande" are
opposed by antitheses of outdoors and indoors, forest and room, beast and
human, nature and civilization. Yet they merge into a condensed image
thanks to polyvalent language and repetition with differences which
underline analogies of opposing features.

Another factor brings the two scenes together. The hunting scene in
which the beast is captured very probably appears on a tapestry within a
room in which two people meet. That there is indeed a tapestry in the room
is made explicit. In descriptions of the beast's capture, the net is described
as a "lacis de hachures," a word Ricardou's readers recognize as a signal of
pictural realities. The word "tapis" appears numerous times, and the forest
is elsewhere described as being composed of "mailles vertes entrecroisées."
The "hallier," we read, is "fixé avec une telle minutie, dans le détail, d'une
brindille à l'autre, qu'on dirait, tissu de pétioles et de feuilles, buisson lui-
même." The word "tissu," appropriate both for a tapestry and for the text
which describes it, reappears in other forms with description of birds in a
forest:

Là-haut, peu à peu calmés dans les entrelacs des feuillages,
sensibles à l'événement, les oiseaux se sont tus. En s'élargissant
de proche en proche, cette censure évidé au-dessus de la
chambre une zone silencieuse oblongue dans les pépiements
naguère entrecroisés. Pendant qu'ils s'éloignent, les chants
évoluent. Bientôt, des mélodies plus concertées tissent alentour
dans l'espace une texture sans faille, qui va s'élargissant.
Quand le silence s'est épuré, évidé, lorsqu'il a enfin déterminé
un parfait réceptacle de résonance, soudain, une singulière
proposition est émise: seul, mais au sommet de son charme, un
merle s'enchante de son cri. (p. 91)

Close examination of this passage reveals that it consists mostly of silences. Such silence or "censure," appropriate for the hushed expectancy of the scene, also suits a tapestry, as a "rire silencieux" aptly described a smiling postcard woman in *L'Observatoire de Cannes*. Narrative potential of description, combined with imagination on the part of a viewer, have often produced metalepsis, thus transgressing the limits of pictural reality. Such procedures should not surprise us here.

The room thus contains the tapestry scene, and both are animated by the same rays of sun moving across a skylight. No longer is there any contradiction between "tapis" and "mousse," or between "salle" and "verdure." "Mare" and "miroir" refer to a single tapestry object. Forest and room ambiances enhance each other in a perceiving consciousness (reader's or narrator's) and in a composite textual space. Of course "real" and tapestry scenes exist only within the larger frame of pages we read. Tapestry, used in *Les Lieux-dits*, is an especially apt *mise-en-abyme* for the written word. Scenes are composed of tiny stitches ("mailles" from Latin *macula*, blotch or stain) which, like inked letters, can be combined in a variety of patterns. Upon very close inspection, a tapestry's image dissolves, seeming to be no more than a random arrangement of marks.

The two scenes in "Dans les halliers de Brocéliande" are present simultaneously in the visible world, but must appear side by side in portions of the text. A diptych configuration necessarily characterizing written or pictured scenes can be perceived by the reader in more complex and superimposed spatial patterns, however. More complex than a diptych, the dreamlike condensations of this story might better be discribed as a palimpsest, a figure capable of suggesting psychological realities while preserving the integrity of scriptural surfaces. In order for two texts of a palimpsest to coexist, each must be visible only partially; each disarticulates the other. Underlying, unconscious texts must break through a shiny surface, fragmenting it. In "Comminution" each of two forms of mediated perception (image and text) is reduced to fragments in order to permit a glimpse of the other. At the same time, any search for meaning in each is arrested by the other's presence.

This palimpsestic bivalence reveals an ambivalence. Hunter and hunted are equally dangerous and equally fearful. The ferocity of the beast explains the narrator/hunter's careful approach, and his avoidance of making a sound or leaving a trace. *Je* must remain hidden and protected.

Yet it always turns out that the prey is taken (*prise*) either explicity--if only visually--or simply by the aggressions of description and scriptural striptease (*prose*). The rhetoric of the hunt applied to a sexual encounter sheds some light on the violent and apprehensive eroticism that pervades Ricardou's fiction. The danger to the hunter is materialized in "Comminution" by the jagged glass that separates transparence from reflection and image from text: although it is the pictured woman who is repeatedly dismembered, it is apparently the man who risks being cut in the process of transformation.

In Arthurian legend, the magician Merlin performed his wonders in Broceliande forest. Ricardou's "charmes" are simply trees in which birds perch, but the two puzzles in "Comminution" are characterized as a magic "texte secret," and transformation from one to the other requires the intervention of "signes abracadabrants." For the man who assembles the puzzle, such magic has a double function: to conjur occult messages and also to protect from their power.

6

Gide used a palimpsest as metaphor for Michel's quest for himself in *L'Immoraliste*. Like "Diptyque," Gide's novel presents humans as creatures in whom layers of civilization mask animal aspects of nature. Michel travels to Africa with a desire to erase his erudition, to get below layers of culture which prevent joy. He begins to cut through thinking to rediscover feeling. Here is how he describes his quest:

> Et je me comparais aux palimpsestes; je goûtais la joie du savant, qui, sous les écritures plus récentes, découvre sur un même papier un texte très ancien infiniment plus précieux. Quel était-il, ce texte occulte? Pour le lire, ne fallait-il pas tout d'abord effacer les textes récents?[7]

In the end, Michel is unable to reveal a "texte occulte," even though the surface text has been stripped away, and in a sense, this is his double loss. "Dans les halliers de Brocéliande" does not attempt to valorize animal nature at the expense of the socialized "savant," but rather demonstrates a coexistence of two texts, one of which usually remains carefully hidden. Beneath the surface of culture, in an ornate and richly decorated room, nature can be "entrevue en secret." Awareness of prehistoric origins of such knowledge is suggested by a remark set off from the rest of "Comminution": "Telle vérification se prolonge--jusqu'à une réflexion lointaine."

The word *palimpsest* is derived from the Greek *psen* (scrape or rub) or *psammos*, sand (an erasing agent frequently found on Ricardou's "p(1)ages") and the suffix *palin* meaning "back," or "again," as when an original surface *re*-emerges. The same suffix occurs in *palindrome*, where words or letters can be read forward or backward as in the name *Atta*, in magic squares and in mirror configurations. A third figure is exploited in the first "nouvelle" of *Révolutions minuscules*. Meaning "another song or ode," the term *palinode* labels a retraction of something already said. All three figures involve doubling of some kind: of two texts superimposed, of a statement and its mirror image, or of a statement and its retraction.

"Jeu," (pp. 11-31) the inaugural story of *Révolutions minuscules*, is actually the volume's most recently written piece.[8] The story features a narrator (*je*) contemplating a painting: a copy of Piero di Cosimo's *La Mort de Procris* (see figure). The scene is a many-layered palimpsest. Human and animal coexist on its surface in the faun Cephalus, who killed his beloved Procris by accident, thinking she was a deer. "A l'origine, s'il y en eût une," we are told, "se dresse un tableau impeccable. Je ne le décrirai pas." Despite his denial, however, he does describe the painting.

As soon as the description is launched, the painting begins to evolve. Its transformation, made possible by the narrator's fascination, is mediated by the mobile reflection of his room on its shiny surface: "Ce qui m'attirait vers lui, il me semble, n'était alors, insaisissable, que la lente évanescence d'un voile si brillant." A literal veil can be read in the painting itself as a V-shaped drape inscribed across Procris' body. I will come back to this veil.

Conjunction of two images on the painting's surface assimilates Piero di Cosimo's mythical marine decor with the intimacy of the narrator's room. The resulting composite setting evokes reveries of various orders, as the narrator lets his gaze wander through "l'espace inépuisable de la toile par des chemins quelquefois imprévus." An erotic fantasy about a bikini-clad woman named Illia is interwoven with Roussellian word-play on the painter's name. These fantasies are accompanied as always by a meditation on the fantasies themselves and on the text-producing process. Desire, stoked by reverie, sends the narrator to a deserted beach in quest of elements for a (re)production of his painting in the form of a drama. Using stones, he inscribes the words *proscrit* and *corps pris* on the sand (anagrams of *Procris* which are rearrangements of her name, as the story is a productive redistribution of the painting). It finally becomes impossible for him to deny, however, that the scene he constructed was only a text, or a dream:

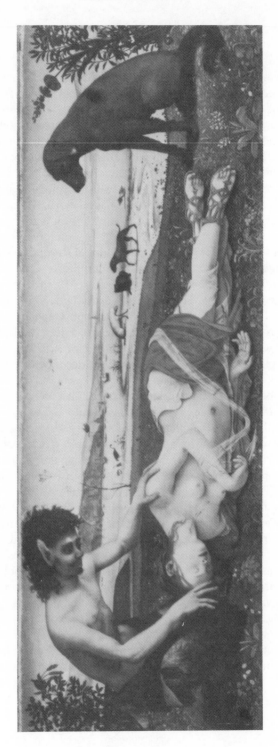

Piero di Cosimo, *The Death of Procris*
(The National Gallery, London)

Cependant, peu à peu de péripéties inlassablement contées et du recours, de phrase en phrase, à maint sortilège rhétorique, force lui est d'admettre qu'il n'y a personne à saisir, personne à supplier. Alors, sombre et la chevelure éparse, elle s'enfuit en tous sens sur la page, parmi les coquilles, au risque de se perdre, à la poursuite de quelque nouveau jeu. (p. 31)

This final statement echoes the story's opening sentence:

Je ne conterai guère, en l'extrême détail de leurs péripéties, toutes les phases qui m'ont ouvert l'accès de cette plage où, à presque l'atteindre, me voici, parmi les coquilles, proche de l'objectif. (p. 13)

The tiny slips which separate the first sentence from the last bring into focus a complicity: given that "coquilles" (shells) are also typographical errors of the type *ph(r)ase, p(1)age, je(u)*, the entire text stands as a *mise-en-abyme* of the creative process. In the story's opening statement, the narrator wanders simultaneously among seashells and typographical errors. The final sentence can be interpreted as the narrator's disappointment to find that his adventure (*prise*) was only an optical illusion, or prose.

The story poses some puzzling contradictions nevertheless. The most evident are those implied by its many palinodes. Fifteen times in the nineteen pages of "Jeu," the narrator denies the very act of narration by which he is materialized. The story begins on a paradoxical note: "Je ne conterai guère," the narrator protests, but he proceeds to recount his bizarre story. Almost every paragraph ends with a similar disclaimer: "Je ne le décrirai pas", "Je ne formulerai aucun autre détail", "Dans cette voie, on le devine, nul encouragement qui m'incite à poursuivre," etc. On other occasions the narrator states his incomprehension of his own obsession with the painting. What, one may well ask, is this narrator denying? Why does he protest so much?

The overwhelming force of such a litany of negations--perhaps "incantations secrètes"--does not succeed in arresting the narration, however. After each denial, the narrator continues on the rebound, as attention is displaced from the central female form to the less troubling seascape in the background and goes on to describe the painting which haunts him:

Je n'en proposerai aucun détail.

Seul, en effet celui dont la mémoire ne peut se défaire des îles basses au loin, du long bras de mer calme, des minces échassiers, du chenil sur la plage, des brefs cailloux épars, ni surtout de la proche pelouse où, demi-nue, la gorge blessée, accompagnée de l'ultime sollicitude d'un chien brun et d'un faune, est étendue une jeune mourante, seul celui-là, existât-il jamais, saurait admettre les excès de mon trouble. (p. 14)

Such excess energy, signaling quantitative differences between desire and satisfaction, quite precisely defines the libidinal energy expended in writing. The climax of narration is also a sexual climax, after which the image disappears.

The erotic nature of his obsession, especially with Procris' nudity and with the bleeding wound in her neck, is masked by polyvalent vocabulary and *double entendre*. Although in the painting Procris is seen as "demi-nue", expression of a minuscule progression toward total nudity becomes coyly euphemistic. This progression is accomplished through the mediation of the young bather whose image is superimposed on Procris'. In a new description which is the negative of an earlier one, the word *nul* does double duty; it incorporates the absent word *nu(e)*; it also points to the imposition of negation and denial. If, as Freud tells us about the dream-work, censorship is a "failure of translation" from image to words,[9] it is in this same gap that fantasy, hiding behind wordplay, suppresses the painting.

Censorship is reinforced by another linguistic subterfuge, which occurs twice. Here is the second occurrence:

Longtemps je me suis demandé si l'insistante inclinaison qui me portait vers cette plage caillouteuse, vers la blessure ouverte au cou de la jeune femme, ne venait point...de la fascinante rencontre d'une rêverie excessive avec les syllabes *Piero di Cosimo*. (pp. 27-8)

Word order, verbal tense and vocabulary lead us unerringly to Proust's liminary sentence: "Longtemps je me suis couché de bonne heure." Mediated by allusion to a well-known statement, the word "couché" is suppressed, but with an erasure that calls attention to itself. The surrogate word "demandé" further underlines displacement of libidinal energy to intellectual activity: reading, writing, "la longue patience de mes recherches."

In the presence of such furtive erotic play, the work of censorship is paradoxical. The narrator clearly attempts to arrest or censor the narration, but is unable to do so because of an "excès" of energy. Palinode, denial that fails, partial nudity, repressed content that calls attention to itself are counterbalanced by the work of anagram and metagram, which move in an opposing direction. Repetition with minuscule slippages reveals a progression from innocuous "crithmes" (marine plants) to "crimes," suggesting a sado-erotic attitude toward Illia, who thus becomes a "victime." In other words, she becomes Procris. The middle term between "crithmes" and "crimes" is "rhythmes," suggesting the latent force of poetic description.

Undertaking to describe Procris in detail, *Je* sees her portrait as fraught with contradictions. The tableau is described in terms of "antinomie," "aporie," "rapport inverse," and "conflit de vertus contradictoires" which betray pervasive conflict both in the posture of the woman and in the narrator's response to her. He sees the painting as an "énigme" which drives him to despair and then to exaltation:

> Combien de fois, soudain vaincu par un désespoir minuscule, ai-je songé, devant cette aporie, à moi-même me détruire! Combien de fois, l'instant après, ai-je été habité par un très impérieux goût de vivre! (p. 16)

Phrases like "contraires toujours réunis" and "équilibre réussi" later extend hopes of compromise of the life and death oppositions he finds in the painting. Repeated palinode acts as a tease, inciting him (and us) to solve the puzzle.

Comparing his description to the painting by Piero di Cosimo, several problems become apparent. Although in the painting Procris lies dead with eyes closed, a spear wound in her throat, the narrator imagines her as standing to face him, even walking! Beginning with intellectual consideration of details, fantasy takes over, as she becomes animated, ready to embrace him. Description (the scriptural striptease) seems to have rotated the entire painting, a ninety-degree turn ("torsion du buste") on the pivot of her navel ("la position indubitablement centrale du nombril").

Procris' pose brings other contradictions which the narrator fails to remark. Describing the position of the arms, he uses his own left and right as points of reference as he faces the uprighted tableau. As a result, what he describes as her "jambe gauche" is actually her right leg, and so on. In the next paragraph, introduced by the phrase "un rapport inverse," a reversal of perspective surreptitiously takes place. What is described as "le bras droit" is indeed Procris' right arm. Her head is indeed turned to the right, her left hand raised in a "geste de défense."

What can this abrupt change of perspective signify? Description materializes an image which corresponds in part to Piero's Procris. Parts of her body would offer a mirror image to the painting, however. The woman's position and the narrator's fascination are strikingly similar in many details to the puzzle image of "Diptyque." In "Jeu", a painting undergoes similar fragmentation operated by description and imagination. In a circulation of signifiers among a series of "texts" Procris is assimilated with a very different woman; her image hides a companion tableau.

Examination of another description, that of Illia in her bikini, gives us a clue as to whom this latent image might portray. We have seen the word *nue* censored in various ways. The bather's final disrobing is described with reference to her absent clothing: "...nuls plis imperceptibles n'étoilaient du pubis jusqu'à l'élastique l'aboli triangle du slip." This ribbed triangle recalls those similar shapes given so much attention in *L'Observatoire de Cannes*, where an "ulve" poses itself on the "V renversé" of a bather's pubis to evoke, like a rebus, a word which is never mentioned. The missing triangle of Illia's bikini can be found in Procris' anatomical geometry, which includes a number of V's, both veiled and not (her elbow, for instance) and in the story's "coquilles" which it resembles. Both words and body are again fragmented here, permitting us to join together two particles--unmentioned but indicated throughout--to form "V nu" or "Vénus."

Although the narrator states that "L'on sait qu'il n'est pas de peintre contemporain qui se plaise davantage à tromper l'oeil par les manoeuvres d'habiles minuties," we cannot take this remark entirely seriously. The negative of his remark alerts us to palinodic possibilities already so thoroughly exploited by this shifty narrator. Contemporary of Piero de Cosimo, but in Erwin Panofsky's estimation the "antipode" of the painter of *La Mort de Procris*,[10] Botticelli created a painting which is compellingly conjured by "maint sortilège rhétorique" and the "innombrables incantations secrètes" of "Jeu." Presenting an almost perfect mirror to Procris' pose, Botticelli's *Naissance de Vénus* (see figure) emerges as the hidden panel of a diptych.

Sandro Botticelli, *The Birth of Venus* (detail)
(Uffizi Gallery, Florence. Photo Roger-Viollet, Paris)

The myth of Venus, assimilated in most accounts to the story of Aphrodite, proposes features related to Procris' tragic story. It was Venus who enticed Procris' husband Cephalus to infidelity. One evening, resting from the hunt, Cephalus thought he heard an animal in the bushes. Throwing his magic spear, he inadvertently killed his jealous wife, who had been watching from a hiding place. Venus was, then, indirectly responsible for Procris' death according to the myth.

7

Once Venus emerges from beneath the veil of "Jeu," it becomes clear that she has been there all along. Ricardou's many narrators find her seashell on the sandy beaches, and the reader finds it in the typography as well. Mirroring surfaces, while demonstrating the doctrine of the self-reflecting text, serve as metonymic reminders of her attribute and astrological symbol. The only explicit reference to Venus is to the planet, the setting for the space exploration in *La Prise/Prose de Constantinople*. The bright "star" is first seen at the very beginning of that novel, as clouds move across the sky "vers l'ouest, où Vénus est inscrite." As a goddess, she is hidden in the novels and short stories in each scene where a bathing beauty emerges miraculously from the waves, dry and diaphanous. That all these women are variants of a single image is suggested in *La Prise/Prose* by the narrator, who finally sees all his redheads as avatars of Isabelle. Incorporating a Latinized Greek root (*iso*) so dear to Ricardou in his theories, Isabelle's very name lends itself to translation into "the *same* beautiful woman." Venus too, from the *Hottentot Venus* to the *Venus de Milo*, has come to mean Woman in general, a mysterious standard of beauty, the impersonal abstract Other, One who represents All.

Sharing the attendance of fabulous creatures, red cloth, or blood, and especially a marine setting and cascading red hair, Venus and Procris merge in "Jeu" to constitute the apotheosis of all the golden goddesses. Unlike Gide's Michel, therefore, we need not sacrifice a surface text in order to read an occult or didactic one, for it is the overdeterminations and contradictions resulting from coexisting images which inscribe the fiction's psychic decor on its surface.

But Procris and the hidden Venus are not variants of each other, and neither alone embodies the sinister mixture of proliferation and destruction that characterizes the mysterious female presence in Ricardou's fiction. In the vibration between opposing poles of birth (of Venus) and death (of Procris), presence ("il y a" or Illia) and absence ("il n'y a personne à saisir"), a statement and its retraction, a painting is broken into constituent parts and fades away under the rhetoric of a taboo. Venus is inscribed as a rearrangement of these pieces "sur tout autres rivages," as a pictural anagram suggested by word-play in the text. The result of such anagrammatic permutation is the metaphoric linking of Procris and Venus in a composite female image both irresistible and dangerous, representing both creation and destruction. Her image proliferates everywhere in Ricardou's fiction. All his narrators, ambivalent Pygmalions, bring her to life and then erase her again and again.

Linguists and literary critics alike have pointed to this kind of metaphoric structure as characterizing a distinctly poetic discourse. In a well-known monograph, Roman Jakobson applies a bipolar conception of language in order to develop a typology of aphasic disturbances. Selection and combination, he begins, are operative in the production of all utterances. Aphasic speech can be recognized as a severe impairment of one or the other function, resulting in a disequilibrium that makes speech unintelligible. But even in normal speech, he cautions, dominance of one function can be detected: "In manipulating these two kinds of connections (similarity and contiguity) in both their aspects (positional and semantic)-- selecting, combining, and ranking them--an individual exhibits his personal style, his verbal predilections and preferences." Jakobson goes on to imply that predominance of one of the two functions over the other is also a factor in genre distinctions, and he suggests that the difference between poetry and "the so-called 'realistic' trend" reflects a predominance of metaphor or metonymy respectively.[11]

Mallarmé's Masterwork, then, because of its metaphoric structure, belongs in the domain of poetry. So, thinks Gérard Genette, do certain New Novels. In an article on Robbe-Grillet, Genette contends that

> L'art de la poésie repose essentiellement sur le jeu de la
> métaphore... l'art du récit, et donc spécialement l'art du roman,
> repose sur le jeu des métonymies, la description, et la narration
> suivant l'ordre des contiguïtés spatiales et temporelles: si l'on
> adopte cette classification commode, on observe que l'art de
> Robbe-Grillet consiste à disposer dans l'ordre métonymique de

la narration et de la description romanesques un matériel de nature métaphorique, puisque résultant d'analogies entre éléments différents ou de transformations d'éléments identiques.

Preference of metaphor, Genette continues, determines the nature of repetition:

> Après une scène d'un roman de Robbe-Grillet, le lecteur attend légitimement selon l'ordre classique du récit, une autre scène contiguë dans le temps ou l'espace; ce que lui offre Robbe-Grillet, c'est la même scène légèrement modifiée, ou une autre scène analogue. Autrement dit, il étale horizontalement, dans la continuité spatio temporelle, la relation verticale qui unit les diverses variantes d'un thème, il dispose en série les termes d'un choix.[12]

Genette's observation describes Ricardou's novels perfectly, as is clear in my grid illustrating *Les Lieux-dits*, where the "story" of metaphors (in the columns) is recounted metonymically in the rows. It also describes Ricardou's female images which, although existing in metaphorical relationship, appear in obsessive succession.

Aphrodite was born in the foam which received the severed genitals of Uranus, as "Naissance d'une déesse" does not fail to point out. An obsession with fragmented female bodies in the context of danger and violence can be interpreted as projection of a fear that the self might become so fragmented. Ricardou's male characters lose their heads, their minds, fall off scaffolding and off cliffs into gorges, almost tumble from observatory balconies, risk being cut by glass, always in tentative pursuit of a fleeting female image (an accumulation of scenarios which recalls Truffaut's *L'Homme qui aimait les femmes*). These various narrators have in common their reduction to a simple rhetorical eye, an empty locus through which fantasms pass. Almost unreadable, these narrators contrast sharply with the fertility and oppressive plenitude of the female characters.

If metonymy is the axis of quest or desire, metaphor, when projected onto the metonymic axis, functions as a series of screens, maintaining an object forever inaccessible. Ferocious proliferation of words performs an "incantation secrète" or a "sortilège rhétorique," warding off direct contact with dangerous realities. It appears, then, that the narrators' fascination serves as a screen against terror: terror that the woman, once imaginary, is alive; terror of the bleeding wound, which bewitches but repels. The "incantations secrètes" and "sortilèges rhétoriques" serve less to materialize her presence than to protect from her power. Frenetic attempts to transform her image into something less threatening are at the origin (if ever there was one) of each text's functioning: turn her into another character, turn her into a landscape which can be mastered by a voyage (from Venice to Constantinople, for instance). Ricardou's poetic is characterized by what Dorothy Dinnerstein, borrowing from Freud's term to redefine it, calls civilization's most profound discontent, a pervasive and "ambivalent response to otherness"--the imagined and then feared otherness of Woman, whose links with maternity and mortality are interconnected.[13]

Gaston Bachelard has suggested that water's purity and softness can be felt as a "femme dissoute." He also remarks that in the myth-oriented imagination, water is intimately connected with both birth and death.[14] Certainly not universally applicable, as Dinnerstein's book makes clear, Bachelard's fantasy nevertheless describes rather accurately the dilemma of Ricardou's narrators. The *Je* of *La Prise/Prose* suffers from a full-blown approach-avoidance posture vis-à-vis Isabelle. The narrator of "Jeu" is torn between an urge to destroy himself and a desire to live. He identifies with the faun in the myth (and in Piero's painting), who killed Procris because of his excessive love for her. For both these narrators, the female image represents both a fascination and a danger. They see, through an alluring veil, the threat of their own violence, projected onto her.

Looking at the entire *oeuvre*, it can be seen that Venus is in many ways a patroness of Ricardou's scriptural practice: she provides the coherence of his personal poetic and a clue to the relationship of his fiction to his theoretical writings. With her various avatars, she is a constant around which principles of irregularity, transformation and intertextuality revolve. In her Greek incarnation, it must be remembered, she is a "mythe crypté de la création poétique." Her name produced her story, as *V* and *nul* give birth to a subliminal Venus in "Jeu." Finally, the goddess presides over births. She represents the energy necessary for (pro)creation.

But it is equally clear that each time the omnipresent Woman becomes too troubling, she is distanced by some strategy. In the fictions, she becomes an optical illusion or a figment of the typographical imagination. Then her presence is rationalized by theory, where all realities are metaphors for a text. In each case, when we expect the story to move on, a goal to be reached, or an interpretation to elucidate, we are presented with a repetition of the same on a different plane. The narrator in "Jeu" remains "proche de l'objectif" but never attains it. Similarly, the narrator in *La Prise/Prose*, in his role as Prince Charming in a version of *Sleeping Beauty*, must follow the path traced by loops in the name *Belle* written with stones. At the princess' door, he must indefinitely postpone his quest in order to read, from the beginning, the story of the adventure in which he is engaged.

Since 1971 Ricardou professes to be in a protracted period of emphasis on criticism and theory,[15] and given the quantity of articles he has produced in the last decade, this indeed seems to be the case.[16] It is also possible, however, that the central contradictions of his fiction can have no resolution within fiction. One story in *Révolutions minuscules* suggests that Ricardou's strategy of unanchored signifiers fails to hold the obsessions at bay, producing in turn an effect similar to Valéry's period of silence and the Mallarméan thematic of the blank page. "Plage blanche" (pp. 141-55) betrays a nostalgia for a white page, devoid of signs.

The story's opening paragraph puts into play the usual generative differentiation of light and dark, absence and presence. The scene is a beach, where encounters of water, stones and sand invite inscription and transformation. Venus appears too, metonymically in seashells washed up on shore, and also as a woman emerging from the waves, "bouche ouverte, haletante, cheveux liquides sur l'épaule." But if in all Ricardou's other stories, a narrator is encouraged to project his fantasies, in "Plage blanche," both the blank p(1)age and the idealized female image strongly resist the imposition of his text.

Instead of opening the way for the productive creativity of language, the story paradoxically and repeatedly dramatizes a rejection of textuality. Clean at first, the beach is soon sullied by tracks, which immediately accede to value as signs: "empreintes," "inscrites," "graphisme." Light, however, rather than providing difference and *lisibilité*, "simplifies." Blank surfaces are repeatedly cluttered with accumulating debris: matches, bits of paper, and even a parenthesis risk signifying. "Lacunes, mouvement: peu à peu la figure d'un texte." Each time a text threatens to emerge, the white surface is forcefully reinstated. A workman appears with a rake to smooth the sand, erasing irregularities susceptible to interpretation, leaving only a "surface vierge." In this story, water washes and purifies, removing traces. The rhythm of inscription and erasure is that of the waves and of the sea, which offers an undifferentiated, unreflecting surface: "Douce, continue, la grande image de la mer."

The lovely long-haired bather too, this time and this time only, refuses--"Elle crie non, non, non."--to become the object of a fantasy. Her refusal necessitates the most corporeal male presence in Ricardou's fiction: "Or bientôt il la rattrape, musclé, violent, et l'immerge entièrement pendant quelques battements de coeur." Pushing her under the water, where, as another story remarked, "l'invisible est peint en noir," he accomplishes a violent and explicit repression of the troubling female image back into the unconscious of the text. Venus is again materialized and erased, as the episode closes with an interrogative disclaimer: "Ou peut-être est-ce un texte qui rêve?"

If the text dreams, its dream is to reconcile the incompatible. The many narrators' approach-avoidance posture vis-à-vis Isabelle and her avatars offers a striking parallel to the whole *oeuvre*'s palinodic strategy towards meaning. Because of their efforts to decenter representation and avoid fixed points of reference, the Ricardolian fictions hover on the edge of a mimetic abyss. Even the ideal image, object of fear and desire, quest and discourse, stands for something else. With their many palimpsests, screens and veils and their descriptions that fragment and tease, all Ricardou's texts become three-dimensional spaces where layer upon layer of signifiers refer to one another. But at the same time, Ricardou does indeed have something to tell us. The difficulty is that what he has to say is that the writer should not have anything to say. What he calls the "quelque chose à dire" and the "quelque chose à faire" are at war, and the result is an image that repeatedly swims to the surface only to be resubmerged.

That that image should be an erotic one sheds light on another layer of the Ricardolian poetic myth. Aphrodite's emergence from the waves, Ricardou argues in "Naissance d'une déesse," is more accurately under-stood as a birth from words. That this reinterpreted goddess is emblematic of the self-engendered text is made explicit by the parallel title of another article--"Naissance d'une fiction"--where the generating mechanisms of *La Prise/Prose* are discussed. A vocabulary of birth, generation, reproduction pervades Ricardou's writing, and betrays an anxiety about the origins of the text, about the viability of purely textual genesis, and even about the origins of what he calls the "scriptor."

The initial design of *La Prise/Prose*, Ricardou declares in a 1978 essay, was the challenge to "écrire un livre en évitant la présence de la reproduction."[17] The conscious intention here is to oppose "reproduction" to the textual "production" he advocates. But the materiality of his own lexical choice justifies, I believe, a companion meaning. After all, Ricardou in this essay eschews his habitual critical terminology (he could have used "mimesis," "representation," "referentiality," or "expression") in favor of a biological term for the ideological position he seeks to overturn. A substitution of scriptural for sexual generation is a theme in many of the stories and gives fictional scope and resonance to his theoretical texts. Olivier's "conception" from permutations on a grid might be an ideal model for the writer's fantasy that he too might deny being "of woman born" and instead claim to issue immaculately from the language of his own choosing.[18]

All Ricardou's fictions are what Steven Kellman calls "self-begetting," but not in the usual sense that they portray a character's decision to write the novel we are reading.[19] Rather, each story recounts its own generative processes, by means of multiple *mises-en-abyme* and self-reflective interludes. Rather than being cyclical, with the novel's end preparing its beginning, Ricardou's novels seek to produce themselves from the inside after the manner of a spiral or of Valéry's seashell, emanated from its own substance following a "nécessité d'origine intérieure" (see chapter III).

It is in this light that Ricardou's valorization of the word "rien" must be understood. Beginning with nothing, as he explains, is a paradoxical way of generating a story from language and avoiding representing extra-linguistic realities. It also places his texts in the company of Mallarmé's "Un Coup de dés" and "Salut," Nathalie Sarraute's *Martereau* and Flaubert's desire to write a novel from nothing. But a more telling dimension of the word is revealed in the epigraph from Artaud which opens the abovementioned essay: "Un monde nouveau de parturitions non à propos de quelque chose mais de rien..."[20] The word "rien" is the point of departure for *La Prise/Prose de Constantinople*, which gives birth to a "monde nouveau" as I have shown. Ricardou's inscription of his own patronym and his numerical structures based on his name suggest a desire to be born, like Aphrodite, of a "parturition roussellienne" and thereby to transform biological chance into scriptural necessity.

The desire to produce oneself and thus to be one's own author—what Kellman calls "the Modernist ideal of autogeny"—is an existential project when viewed philosophically. Ricardou's goal of reeducating himself and his reading public constitutes a sincere ideological commitment in and outside his fiction. The fantasmatic dimension of that desire emerges as an ambivalent myth of eroticism and of meaning. When a mythical female image is at the same time the desired goal and the feared consequence of writing, and when her birth from waves represents the ideal birth from words while simultaneously reconfirming the impossibility of purely self-begotten texts or authors, the only way she can be erased is to stop writing.

Epilogue

A New Direction? Some Final Speculations

(Cela en somme n'est qu'une parenthèse)
--Ricardou

(Sans parler du cas où écrire fait peur)
--Barthes

If Ricardou has turned away from fiction, it is not difficult to see why. The fundamental contradiction in his work has brought him to an impasse: while his essays persist in extolling the opacity and productive potential of poetic language, these theories are qualified if not falsified by a practice of fiction that cannot seem to avoid representing ideas by means of didactic parables. Ricardou's attempts over two decades to weave fiction and theory together in a seamless web have produced on the contrary a more and more frenzied critical schizophrenia.

Identification of Eros with Mimesis, a cornerstone of his work, has only intensified the problem. Ricardou links representation to an image of ideal but unattainable womanhood (Eros from a male point of view), and his practice of fiction strives to eradicate both together. His work thus produces an effective metaphor while providing a clue to the political repression and violence inherent in an ideology that seeks to liberate. Theory comes to play a policing role, monitoring adherence to rules. Or, to use another image, where sexual desire is a figure for the desire for meaning, theory acts as a sort of superego to curb the excesses of an unruly representational urge.

But to seek meaning is human. The violence required to repress that urge is an indication of its strength. What Freud said about sexuality applies to the Ricardolian ambivalence about meaning. In *Civilization and its Discontents*, Freud argued that civilization provides security and protection in exchange for renunciation of instinctual satisfaction. The principle instincts thus repressed, he goes on to explain, are sexuality and aggression.[1] Similarly, the presence of an anti-mimetic theory in Ricardou's fiction offers a shield against the unsettling mix of sexuality and violence that constantly threatens to bubble up to the surface.

In this light, Sartre was right in the Mutualité debate of 1964, when he claimed that the New Novel offers a reassuring verbal world. He was right, that is, about Nouveau Roman *theory*. The fiction continues to have a mind of its own and to reveal that split between fiction and theory that the latter tries so desperately to overcome. Ricardou wants to create a harmonious blend of two discourses: so far, he has produced fabulous beasts, disturbing hybrids, optical illusions, monsters, sphinxes.

Le Théâtre des métamorphoses contains Ricardou's first published fiction since the impasse of "Jeu." The volume's generic self-classification as a "mixte" signals the writer's renewed effort to bring fiction and theory together. Dominated by a four-part pattern, the book is composed of two short fictions and--by far the bulk of the book--a long theoretical commentary on each. But neither of the two fictive segments is new: "Improbables Strip-teases" reappears more or less as it was in its 1973 special edition, complete with Mallarméan hypogram and new drawings. The other piece, entitled "Communications," Ricardou wrote and produced in 1973 as a radio script. It makes use of some of the same characters, situations and devices as *La Prise/Prose de Constantinople*.

"Communications" is cleverly constructed: in each of four telephone conversations--four "*communications*"--a narrator threatens his listener with a watery and ghastly death. For the writer Basile (author of a novel entitled *La Prise de Constantinople*), he foresees death by transformation into a hideous sea monster. To frighten Marina, he relates an invented story of her son's death by drowning. Eight-year-old Michel, home alone at night, is less easily frightened by a tale of murky monsters emerging from the plumbing to devour him. When the narrator--whose pseudonyms Martin and Marcel echo the story's maritime themes--reports the results of his experiment to Ondine, she turns the tables on him, confessing that she planned to run away with Gilles after poisoning the narrator with moisture-activated poison on his telephone! But the narrator regains control of the situation: appearing suddenly beside Ondine, he threatens to shoot her, or electrocute her in her bath, or lose her in a fiction. This last is exactly what happens as Martin/Marcel, a.k.a. Ed Word, wakes from a dream to find himself part of a Venusian space exploration and a character in *La Prise/Prose de Constantinople*.

Like all Ricardou's fiction, "Communications" is spun from the material givens of its story-telling situation. Here, these are electric conduction and telecommunications of a radio broadcast and the marine setting of Debussy's "La Mer" which serves as background. "Ondine," threatened with electrocution in her bath, suggests both sound and ocean waves. The story's successive loops convey a familiar metafictional message: fiction is the inevitable triumph of words. Disarticulation of the referential illusion intensifies the contradiction, however, and is accompanied by a crescendo in the narrator's fear, madness and violence. He threatens his victims, but the imminent emergence of monsters from the water-text is real only to him. The only escape route open to him is refuge in a concentric series of metafictions.

In "Communications," theory is farther removed from fiction than before. Instead of a character who explicates his own fiction, *Le Théâtre des métamorphoses* gives us theoretical excursions alongside its fictions. The book does not achieve the ideal interweaving for which it strives: although printed on alternate pages, the two segments are as unlike as oil and water and are impossible to read as a single text. It is thus not the two stories that indicate a new direction. They simply restate the problem in a new way.

If the experiment of fiction as parable of theory has perhaps been carried as far as it can go, *Le Théâtre des métamorphoses* opens the possibility of a reverse paradigm: fiction within theory, theory *as* fiction. In yet another shift of a figure/ground illusion, it is not the theory within fiction, but rather and surprisingly, the fictional dimension of theory that points in a new direction. In this, perhaps, Ricardou's itinerary demonstrates the crisis of modern critical discourse.

Theory's tentative acceptance of its own fictionality takes several forms in Ricardou's newest book. First, there is an awareness of the limits of theory. Until now, as I have proposed, his theories used fiction in an attempt to remotivate language and remove its arbitrary quality. Now he seems to be recovering from the Socratic disappointment over a lost linguistic paradise to recognize, at least obliquely, that his theoretical constructions might have become futile attempts to fend off the very arbitrary and unpredictable nature of language that the theories supposedly celebrate. He identifies a "fantasme techniciste qui menace toute manipulation: celui d'une entière maîtrise des contrecoups" (p. 275). As he explicates his own writing, instead of a fantasy of total control, he repeats a more modest refrain: "Il y a davantage, peut-être." The inevitable excess of fiction cannot be pre-theorized. It is no longer that theory has *not yet* accounted for the text, but finally a recognition that theory cannot *ever* account for the text.

Implicit in these remarks is a new hint of self-criticism. Ricardou finally suspects that the theory within his fictions has often been an impediment to its own demonstration. Now he can articulate the contradiction with a certain self-irony:

Nul doute [...], selon le cruel adage 'tel est mot qui croyait mordre,' que l'analyse de l'antireprésentation ne soit victime d'une antireprésentation de son analyse. Ou, plus simplement: *une antireprésentation par autoreprésentation est infligée à la représentation d'une antireprésentation.* (p. 237, Ricardou's emphasis)

Most importantly, there is a suggestion that theory itself can be a source of play. Characters appear on scene to interrupt a logical argument, change the subject, derail the reasoning. Dialogue between Ricardou's habitual theoretical discourse and a new more playful one brings welcome disorder. Ricardou has always given careful attention to the prose in his essays. But the commentaries in *Le Théâtre des métamorphoses* manifest a new non-scientific interest in neologism and wordplay. Technical terminology is less oppressive than before and is even occasionally mocked by concurrent emergence of a different theoretical voice. The theoretical text is less strictly controlled and often follows the initiative of words into digressions, where theory may fade from view and once or twice approaches babble. At times it actually seems true that "les émaux du mot prennent avantage sur les emois du moi" (p. 58). And for the first time, the *pleasure* of reading becomes a subject for meditation.

Le Théâtre des métamorphoses marks, I think, a first step in the direction of a non-logocentric theorizing where theory would no longer explain fiction but play with it and prolong it. Theory itself becomes fiction through play. It is ironic that the intransitive ideal might finally be more possible in theoretical writing than in fiction. As theory approaches babel, it may accomplish what the fiction, so wedded to logos, could not do: become a "texte de jouissance." As Barthes says, "Le texte de jouissance est absolument intransitif." And as if describing the textile metaphore of *Le Théâtre des métamorphoses*, Barthes defines an ideal theory that would be non-representational:

Texte veut dire *Tissu*; mais alors que jusqu'ici on a toujours pris ce tissu pour un produit, un voile tout fait, derrière lequel se tient, plus ou moins caché, le sens (la verité), nous accentuons maintenant, dans le tissu, l'idée générative que le texte se fait, se travaille à travers un entrelacs perpétuel; perdu dans ce tissu--cette texture--le sujet s'y défait, telle une araignée qui se dissoudrait elle-même dans les secrétions constructives de sa toile.[2]

It would seem, then, that in the future it will be more interesting to examine Ricardou's fabulations in theory than his theory of fabulation. The fantasmatic dimension, progressively paralyzed in his *romans* and *nouvelles*, may have migrated into the more personal but less egocentric voice of the essay. The project will not have changed. Ricardou is still trying to realize a balanced interweaving, where fictional elements demonstrate theory and theory reflects on fiction. He may yet succeed. In any case, he will continue to question how--and whether--literature "makes sense."

NOTES

Introduction: Reading Ricardou

[1] John Sturrock, *The French New Novel: Claude Simon, Michel Butor, Alain Robbe-Grillet* (London: Oxford University Press, 1969, p. 56; Leon Roudiez, *French Fiction Today: A New Direction* (New Brunswick, N.J.: Rutgers University Press, 1972), p. 374; Mary Ellis Gibson, "A Conversation with Margaret Atwood," *Chicago Review*, 27, No. 4 (1976), 113.

[2] Roudiez, p. 152.

[3] *Le Monde*, May 22, 1957.

[4] "Description et infraconscience chez Alain Robbe-Grillet," *La Nouvelle Revue Française*, 95 (Nov., 1960), 890-900; "Aspects de la description créatrice--comme postface à 'Description panoramique d'un quartier moderne' de Claude Ollier," *Médiations*, 3 (1961), 13-32.

[5] The proceedings were subsequently published under Ricardou's editorship and with the same title by 10/18, 1972. Books by participants had previously been brought together by Jérôme Lindon at the Editions de Minuit, but the Cerisy colloquium was the first discussion among the writers.

[6] Michel Butor, "Le Roman comme recherche," *Répertoire I* (Paris: Minuit, 1960), pp. 7-11.

[7] Ricardou, "Penser la littérature aujourd'hui," *Sud*, 8 (1972), 38.

[8] For example in Ricardou, *Problèmes du nouveau roman* (Paris: Seuil, 1967), p. 111.

[9] Claude Simon, *Orion Aveugle* (Geneva: Skira, 1970), preface, n. pag.

[10] After Ricardou began writing theory, Robbe-Grillet seems to have abandoned the role of theoretician except for an occasional article. His *Pour Un Nouveau Roman* appeared in 1963.

[11] Ricardou, *Le Théâtre des métamorphoses* (Paris: Seuil, 1982), p. 286.

[12] Ricardou, "Penser la littérature aujourd'hui," p. 33.

[13] Ricardou, *Pour Une Théorie du nouveau roman* (Paris: Seuil, 1971), pp. 62-3.

[14] Ricardou, "Penser la littérature aujourd'hui," p. 38.

[15] Ricardou represents the two dimensions of the text as a graph in *Le Nouveau Roman* (Paris: Seuil, 1973), p. 30.

[16] These terms are explained by Ricardou in "Penser la littérature aujourd'hui."

[17] In other words, he finds them to be what Roland Barthes calls "textes lisibles." See Barthes's *S/Z* (Paris: Seuil, 1970), p. 1.

[18] The entire debate can be read in Simone de Beauvoir et al., *Que Peut la littérature?* (Paris: 10/18, 1965). See also a review of the debate by Mary McCarthy, "Crushing a Butterfly," in *The Writing on the Wall and Other Literary Essays* (New York: Harcourt Brace and World, 1966), pp. 95-101.

[19] *Que Peut la littérature?* p. 57.

[20] *Que Peut la littérature?* pp. 59-60.

[21] *Problèmes du nouveau roman*, pp. 17, 19-20.

[22] Nathalie Sarraute, *Portrait d'un inconnu* (Paris: Gallimard, 3e édition, 1956), pp. 7-8.

[23] Jean-Paul Sartre, "Qu'est-ce que la littérature?" in *Situations II* (Paris: Gallimard, 1948), pp. 63-4.

[24] Paul Valéry, *Oeuvres*, ed., Jean Hytier (Paris: Gallimard, 1960) II, 569.

[25] Valéry, p. 1263.

[26] *Que Peut la littérature?* pp. 51-2.

[27] Valéry, pp. 550 and 678-9.

[28] Valéry, *Cahiers* (Paris: C.N.R.S., 1957-61), X, 713.

[29] Valéry, *Oeuvres*, II, 575.

[30] Valéry, *Oeuvres*, II, 554.

[31] Susan Suleiman, "Ideological Dissent from Works of Fiction: Towards a Rhetoric of the "Roman à Thèse," *Neophilologus*, LX, 2 (April, 1976), p. 164. Suleiman is aware that the term is pejorative, but finds it more precise than the positive label that could also apply: "littérature engagée."

[32] Gérard Genette, "L'Eponymie du nom," in *Mimologiques* (Paris: Seuil, 1976), pp. 11-37; Plato, "Cratylus," in *Collected Dialogues of Plato*, ed. Edith Hamilton and Huntington Cairns (New York: Pantheon, 1963), pp. 421-474.

[33] Plato, p. 469.

[34] Genette, "Au Défaut des langues," in *Mimologiques*, pp. 257-314. See also Genette, "Valéry and the Poetics of Language," in *Textual Strategies: Perspectives in Post-Structural Criticism*, ed. Josué Harari (Ithaca: Cornell U. Press, 1979), pp. 359-373.

[35] Ferdinand de Saussure, *Cours de Linguistique générale* (Paris: Payot, 1971), p. 259.

[36] *Semiotexte*, I, 2 (Fall, 1974), special issue entitled "The Two Saussures."

[37] Jean Starobinski, *Words Upon Words: The Anagrams of Ferdinand de Saussure*, tr. Olivia Emmet (New Haven: Yale U. Press, 1979), p. 122.

[38] Raymond Roussel, *Comment J'ai écrit certains de mes livres* (Paris: Jean-Jacques Pauvert, 1963), pp. 11-35.

[39] Frank Kermode, *The Genesis of Secrecy* (Cambridge: Harvard U. Press, 1979), p. 23.

[40] Pierre Fontanier, *Les Figures du discours* (Paris: Flammarion, 1968), p. 114.

Chapter I

[1] Ricardou, *L'Observatoire de Cannes* (Paris: Minuit, 1961). Further references will be indicated in the text.

[2] Ricardou, "Aspects de la description créatrice--comme postface à 'Description panoramique d'un quartier moderne' de Claude Ollier," *Médiations*, 3 (1961), 13-32. For a different version, see "La Description créatrice: Une Course contre le sens," in *Problèmes du nouveau roman*, pp. 91-111.

[3] Olga Bernal, *Alain Robbe-Grillet: Le Roman de l'absence* (Paris: Gallimard, 1964), pp. 167-8.

[4] Philippe Sollers, *"L'Observatoire de Cannes," Tel Quel*, 6 (1961), 57.

[5] Gérard Genette, *Figures II* (Paris: Seuil, 1969), pp. 49-69.

[6] Alain Robbe-Grillet, *Instantanés* (Paris: Minuit, 1962), pp. 9-13.

[7] Ricardou, *Pour Une Théorie du nouveau roman*, pp. 33-38.

[8] John Huizenga, *Homo Ludens: A Study of the Play Element in Culture* (Boston: Beacon Press, 1950), pp. 35-6.

[9] Roger Shattuck, *Proust's Binoculars* (New York: Vintage, 1963), p. 42.

[10] Shattuck, pp. 49 and 51.

[11] E. H. Gombrich, *Art and Illusion: A Study in the Psychology of Pictorial Representation* (New York: Pantheon Books, 1961), pp. 5-7.

[12] Bernal, p. 205.

[13] Valéry, *Oeuvres*, II, 639.

[14] André Gide, *Journal 1889-1912* (Paris: Gallimard, 1943), pp. 44-45. See also Bruce Morrissette, "Un Héritage d'André Gide: La Duplication intérieure," *Comparative Literature Studies*, 8, No. 2 (1971), 125-42.

[15]Ricardou, "Description et infraconscience chez Alain Robbe-Grillet," *La Nouvelle Revue Française*, 95 (1960), 890-900.

[16]Henri Pevel, "Résonances mallarméennes du nouveau roman," *Médiations*, 7 (1964), 103.

[17]Ricardou's influence can be detected in a similar game with "ulves" in Alain Robbe-Grillet, *Projet pour une révolution à New York* (Paris: Minuit, 1971), p. 67.

[18]The sequence first appeared in chapters XXVIII and XXIX of *L'Observatoire de Cannes*, and the same year as a separate text in *Tel Quel*, 5 (1961), 71-78. Four years later, a variant is read by one of the characters in *La Prise/Prose de Constantinople* (Paris: Minuit, 1965). Another version was published with twelve accompanying drawings by Ricardou under the title *Improbables Strip-teases* (Liège: Cahiers Odradek, 1973). Finally, the text reappeared in *Le Théâtre des métamorphoses*, pp. 197-215, complete with commentary and analysis, pp. 217-297. Only the Cahiers Odradek and the *Théâtre des métamorphoses* versions contain the hypogramme.

[19]Ricardou, *Le Nouveau Roman*, p. 29.

[20]Freud, *On Dreams* (New York: Vintage, 1967), pp. 42-44.

[21]See note 18.

[22]Sollers, p. 56.

[23]Roland Barthes, "Style and Its Image," in *Literary Style: A Symposium*, ed., Seymour Chatman (London: Oxford University Press, 1971), p. 10.

[24]Norman Holland, *Poems in Persons* (New York: W. W. Norton, 1973).

[25]See Ricardou's diagram of geographical and anatomical voyages in *Le Nouveau roman*, p. 68.

[26]Annette Kolodny, *The Lay of the Land: Metaphor as Experience in American Life and Letters* (Chapel Hill: University of North Carolina Press, 1975).

[27]*Colloque de Cerisy: Robbe-Grillet* (Paris: 10/18, 1976), I, 36.

Chapter II

[1]Ricardou, *Les Lieux-dits: Petit Guide d'un voyage dans le livre* (Paris: Gallimard, 1969). Further references will appear in the text.

[2]Germaine Brée, "Novelists in Search of the Novel: The French Scene," *Modern Fiction Studies*, 16, No. 1 (1970), 7.

[3] Umberto Eco, *L'Oeuvre ouverte*, tr., Chantal Roux de Bézieux and Andre Boucourechliev (Paris: Seuil, 1965), p. 59.

[4] Ricardou, *Le Nouveau Roman*, pp. 166-7.

[5] Brée, p. 7.

[6] Ricardou, *Le Nouveau Roman*, p. 80.

[7] Ricardou, *Problèmes du nouveau roman*, p. 156.

[8] Claude Lévi-Strauss, *Anthropologie structurale* (Paris: Plon, 1958), p. 237.

[9] Lévi-Strauss, *Le Cru et le cuit* (Paris: Plon, 1964), p. 20.

[10] Raymond Roussel, *Comment J'ai écrit certains de mes livres* (Paris: Alphonse Lemerre, 1935), p. 4.

[11] See Ricardou, "L'Activité roussellienne," in *Pour Une Théorie du nouveau roman*, pp. 91-117.

[12] Ricardou, *Problèmes du nouveau roman*, pp. 11-15.

[13] Ricardou. *Le Nouveau Roman*, p. 33.

[14] Joseph Campbell, *The Hero with a Thousand Faces* (New York: Meridian, 1949), p. 30.

[15] Françoise Calin and William Calin, "Medieval Fiction and New Novel: Some Polemical Remarks on the Subject of Narrative," *Yale French Studies*, 51 (1975), 238-9.

[16] Chrétien de Troyes, *Le Roman de Perceval ou le conte du Graal*, tr., S. Hannedouche (Paris: Triades, 1969), p. 58; Edwin H. Zeydel, ed. and tr., *The Parzival of Wolfram von Eschenbach* (Chapel Hill: University of North Carolina Press, 1951), pp. 212 and 358.

[17] Hervé Masson, *Dictionnaire initiatique* (Paris: Pierre Belford, 1970), p. 267.

[18] Ricardou, *Le Nouveau Roman*, p. 70.

[19] Ferdinand de Saussure, *Cours de linguistique générale* (Paris: Payot, 1971), pp. 43, 127 and 153.

[20] Gide originally conceived the *mise-en-abyme* in comparison with the blason, which he believed generally to contain a miniature interior replica of itself (See his *Journal 1889-1912*, p. 45). He was, in fact, mistaken, as blasons are rarely thus constructed. By drawing out the interior correspondences of the Pall Mall package illustration, Ricardou's text actually serves as a corrective to Gide's.

[21] Jean-Claude Lebensztejn, *La Fourche* (Paris: Gallimard, 1972), pp. 43-44.

[22] Ricardou, "Naissance d'une fiction," *Nouveau Roman: hier, aujourd'hui* (Paris: 10/18, 1972), II, 379.

[23]Jean Racine, *Andromaque*, Act I, scene 4.

[24]Lebensztejn, p. 74.

[25]For a fuller discussion of Ricardou's anagrams, see Lynn A. Higgins, "Literature 'à la lettre': Ricardou and the Poetics of Anagram," *The Romanic Review*, 73, No. 4 (1982), 473-488.

[26]Villehardouin's account, like Ricardou's novel, begins with an orator calling for recruits. See Geoffroi de Villehardouin, *La Conquête de Constantinople*, ed., Edmond Faral (Paris: Société des Belles Lettres, 1961).

[27]Ricardou, "La Population des miroirs (problèmes de la similitude à partir d'un texte d'Alain Robbe-Grillet)," *Nouveaux Problèmes du roman*, pp. 140-178.

[28]Nicolas Meyer, *The Seven-Per-Cent Solution* (New York: Ballantine, 1972), p. 44.

[29]The etching described bears a close resemblance to Fragonard's "Le Verrou." See Alexandre Ananoff, *L'Oeuvre dessiné de Jean-Honoré Fragonard (1732-1806), catalogue raisonné* (Paris: F. de Nobele, 1970), IV, 43-46 and figures 549 and 550. Ricardou's rendering of the scene repeats and transforms those cited by Ananoff from bibliographic sources and exhibit descriptions.

[30]Ricardou, *Le Nouveau Roman*, p. 70.

[31]Lévi-Strauss, *Le Cru et le cuit*, p. 18.

[32]Anthony Wilden, *System and Structure: Essays in Communication and Exchange* (London: Tavistock, 1972), p. 348-9.

[33]Genette, *Figures III* (Paris: Seuil, 1972), p. 245.

[34]Ricardou, *Le Nouveau Roman*, p. 70.

Chapter III

[1]In order to take both titles into account, I will refer to the novel as *La Prise/Prose de Constantinople* (Paris: Minuit, 1965), or simply as *La Prise/Prose*. In order to locate citations, and rather than paginating the novel as some commentators have done, I have adopted a notation which will identify section, subsection and page. For example II, 4:10 refers to page 10 of the fourth chapter in part II. Such a system preserves the spatial construction of the book (three parts with eight chapters each, all unnumbered), rather than imposing a linear order.

[2]Imbrie Buffum, *Studies in the Baroque from Montaigne to Rotrou* (New Haven: Yale University Press, 1957), pp. 27-45.

[3]See for example Ricardou, *Le Nouveau Roman*, pp. 68 and 106; "Naissance d'une fiction," in *Nouveau Roman: hier, aujourd'hui* (Paris: 10/18, 1972), II, 379-392; "Problèmes de l'élaboration textuelle sur l'exemple de *La Prise de Constantinople*," *Nouveaux Problèmes du roman*, pp. 244-351.

[4]See Villehardouin, *La Conquête de Constantinople*.

[5]It is also interesting, although not well known, that the painter Delacroix authored some short stories which he published under the penname Maxime And*ouin*, thus furnishing a further correspondence for Ricardou.

[6]Stéphane Mallarmé, Oeuvres complètes, ed., Henri Mondor and G. Jean-Aubry (Paris: Gallimard, 1945), p. 53.

[7]Lebensztejn, p. 34.

[8]Roussel, *Locus Solus* (Paris: Pauvert, 1965).

[9]Roussel, *Comment j'ai écrit certains de mes livres*, pp. 3-26. The two generative sentences do not appear in the final text, as Roussel explains.

[10]Don Rice, "The Ex-centricities of Jean Ricardou's *La Prise/Prose de Constantinople*," *International Fiction Review*, 2, No. 2 (1975), 110.

[11]Ricardou, *Révolutions minuscules* (Paris: Gallimard, 1971), pp. 165-6.

[12]Emile Benvéniste, "Communication animale et langage humain," in *Problèmes de linguistique générale* (Paris: Gallimard, 1966), pp. 56-62.

[13]Hélène Prigogine, "L'Aventure ricardolienne du nombre," in *Nouveau Roman: hier, aujourd'hui*, II, 353.

[14]R. D. Laing, *The Divided Self* (London: Penguin, 1965).

[15]Lewis Spence, *Encyclopedia of Occultism* (Secaucus: Citadel Press, 1960), pp. 194 and 241.

[16]Jacques Scherer, *Le Livre de Mallarmé* (Paris: Gallimard, 1957). Scherer includes at the end of his analysis a complete transcription of Mallarmé's notes (*feuillets*).

[17]Mallarmé, *Oeuvres*, p. 70.

[18]Scherer, feuillet 94A.

[19]Feuillet 100A.

[20]Feuillet 194A.

[21]Feuillet 105A.

[22]Feuillet 199.

[23]Feuillet 107A.

[24]Feuillet 107A.

[25] Feuillet 59 and 107 A.

[26] Feuillet 195 A.

[27] Valéry, *Oeuvres*, I, 1467.

[28] Mallarmé, *Oeuvres*, p. 380.

[29] Marc Saporta, *Composition N°. 1* (Paris: Seuil, 1962).

[30] Raymond Queneau, *Cent Mille Milliards de poèmes* (Paris: Gallimard, 1961).

[31] Ricardou, "La Révolution textuelle (rudiments d'une analyse élaborationnelle)," *Esprit*, 12 (1974), 927-945.

[32] Ricardou, "La Révolution textuelle," p. 944.

[33] Rice, pp. 108-9.

[34] Valéry, *Oeuvres*, I, 886-907.

[35] Ricardou, "Naissance d'une fiction," p. 380.

[36] Mallarmé, *Oeuvres*, pp. 474-477.

[37] Mallarmé, *Oeuvres*, p. 370.

[38] Scherer, p. 22.

Chapter IV

[1] Ricardou, *Révolutions minuscules* (Paris: Gallimard, 1971). Further references will appear in the text.

[2] The "nouvelles" first appeared as follows: "Sur la pierre," *Tel Quel*, 2 (1960), 33-6; "Lancement d'un voilier," *Nouvelle Revue Française*, 99 (1961), 555-559; "Réflexion totale," *Tel Quel*, 11 (1962), 77-80; "Gravitation," *Tel Quel*, 16 (1964), 42-51; "Diptyque," *Tel Quel*, 27 (1966), 82-89; "Plage blanche," *Mantèia*, 3 (1968), 44-49; "Autobiographie," *Cahiers du Chemin* (April-July, 1970), 39-45; "Incident," *Lettres Nouvelles* (May-June, 1970), 51-56; "Jeu," *Nouveau Commerce*, 17 (1970), 95-106.

[3] Michel Pierssens, "Un Fantastique sans mystère," *Sub-stance*, 1 (1970), 69; Pierre Caminade, "Vers une nouvelle poétique? la métaphore structurelle de Jean Ricardou," *Courier du Centre International d'Etudes poétiques*, 65 (1968).

[4] Jean Ricardou, "Epitaph," tr., Erica Frieberg, *Chicago Review*, 27, No. 3 (1975), 4-8.

[5] Robbe-Grillet used some of the same themes in his *Projet pour une révolution à New York* (1971).

[6] Julien Besançon, *Journal mural de mai '68* (Paris: Tchou, 1968), p. 62. Another inscription--"L'Anarchie, c'est je" (Besançon, p. 15)--puts

into practice the recommended grammatical subversion. The creative potential of anagram is indicated in another: "L'Action ne doit pas être une réaction mais une création" (Besançon, p. 56).

[7] André Gide, *Romans, récits et soties*, ed., Yvonne Davet and Jean-Jacques Thierry (Paris: Gallimard, 1958), p. 399.

[8] My reading of "Jeu" appeared in Lynn Anthony Higgins, "Typographical Eros: Reading Ricardou in the Third Dimension," *Yale French Studies*, 57 (1979), 180-94.

[9] Wilden, p. 5.

[10] Irwin Panofsky, *Studies in Iconology* (New York: Viking Press, 1958), p. 33.

[11] Roman Jakobson and Morris Halle, *Fundamentals of Language* (The Hague: Mouton, 1971), pp. 67-96.

[12] Genette, *Figures II*, p. 60.

[13] Dorothy Dinnerstein, *The Mermaid and the Minotaur: Sexual Arrangements and Human Malaise* (New York: Harper and Row, 1976), p. 105 and passim.

[14] Gaston Bachelard, *L'Eau et les rêves* (Paris: José Corti, 1942).

[15] Personal interview with Ricardou, August, 1978.

[16] Most notable among these are the essays in *Nouveaux Problèmes du roman* and the numerous "decades" at Cérisy-la-Salle over which he has presided and for which he has edited the published transcripts. See in particular *Robbe-Grillet: Analyse, Théorie*, 2 vols. (Paris: 10/18, 1976) and *Claude Simon: Analyse, Théorie*, (Paris: 10/18, 1975). *Le Théâtre des Métamorphoses* (1982) is also primarily criticism and theory. Its two fictive pieces were in fact written and published separately much earlier: one is *Improbables Strip-teases* (see chapter I, note 18); the other is "Communications," first published as a radio script by Radio-France in 1973.

[17] "Problèmes de l'élaboration textuelle sur l'exemple de *la Prise de Constantinople*," *Nouveaux Problèmes du roman*, p. 259.

[18] My own vocabulary is not innocent either. A section of the article mentioned in note 17 launches into an apparently gratuitous extrapolation about *La Prise/Prose*. Beginning with the letter *i* and *o*, Ricardou devises a new permutation of the novel's last sentence in which "Je suis" is an anagrammatic variant of "Jésus."

[19] Steven G. Kellman, *The Self-Begetting Novel* (New York: Columbia University Press, 1980).

[20] *Nouveaux Problèmes du roman*, p. 244.

Epilogue

[1] Sigmund Freud, *Civilization and its Discontents*, tr. James Strachey (New York: W. W. Norton, 1961).

[2] Roland Barthes, *Le Plaisir du texte* (Paris: Seuil, 1973), pp. 83, 100-101.

Bibliography

I. By Ricardou

A. Books

Les Lieux-dits. Paris: Gallimard, 1969.
Nouveaux Problèmes du roman. Paris: Seuil, 1978.
Le Nouveau Roman. Paris: Seuil, 1971.
L'Observatoire de Cannes. Paris: Minuit, 1961.
La Prise de Constantinople. Paris: Minuit, 1965.
Pour Une Théorie du nouveau roman. Paris: Seuil, 1971.
Problèmes du nouveau roman. Paris: Seuil, 1967.
Révolutions minuscules. Paris: Gallimard, 1971.
Le Théâtre des métamorphoses. Paris: Seuil, 1982.

B. Journal articles. Articles that reappeared in one of the books are followed by a notation PNR, PTNR, NPR or RM. Bibliography does not include newspaper articles.

"L'Activité roussellienne," *Tel Quel*, 39 (Fall, 1969), 78-99. (PTNR)
L'Aqueduc et le piédestal: La Querelle de la métaphore," *Tel Quel*, 18 (summer, 1964), 87-88.
"Aspects de la description créatrice: comme une postface à *Description panoramique d'un quartier moderne* de Claude Ollier." *Médiations*, 3 (Fall, 1961), 13-32.
"Autobiographie." *Cahiers du Chemin*, April-July, 1970, pp. 39-45. (RM)
"Aventures et mésaventures de la description," *Critique*, 174 (Nov. 1961), 937-49.
"L'Aventure d'une écriture." *Magazine Littéraire*, 71 (Dec., 1972), 54-65.
"Belligérance du texte." *La Production du sens chez Flaubert.* Paris: 10/18, 1975, pp. 85-102.
"Le Caractère singulier de cette eau." *Critique*, 24, nos. 243-4 (1967), 718-33. (PNR)
"Communications." Radio France, 1973.
"Cet espace devenu poème: 1-La Subversion du récit; 2-Comme un livre." *Les Lettres Françaises*, 1190 (1967), 13-14.
" 'Claude Simon' textuellement." *Claude Simon: Colloque de Cerisy dirigé par Jean Ricardou*. Paris: 10/18, 1975, pp. 7-19.

"Description d'un strip-tease." *Tel Quel*, 5 (1961), 71-78.

"Description et infraconscience chez Alain Robbe-Grillet." *La Nouvelle Revue Française*, 95 (1960), 890-900.

"deux Livres opposé." *Tel Quel*, 20 (1965), 90-92.

"Diptyque." *Tel Quel*, 27 (1966). (RM)

"Disparition élocutoire." *Actes relatifs à la mort de Raymond Roussel*, ed. Leonard Sciascia. Paris: L'Herne, 1972.

"Le Dispositif osiriaque." *Etudes Littéraires*, 9, no. 1 (1976), 10-79. (NPR)

"Eléments d'une théorie des générateurs." *Positions et oppositions sur le roman contemporain*, ed. Michel Mansuy. Paris: Klincksieck, 1971, pp. 143-62. Also in *Art et science: de la créativité*. Paris: 10/18, 1970, pp. 103-113.

"Un Etrange lecteur." *Les Chemins actuels de la critique*. Paris: 10/18, 1968, pp. 214-221.

"Epitaph." tr. Erica Frieberg. *Chicago Review*, 27, no. 3 (1975), 4-8. (RM)

"Expression et fonctionnement." *Tel Quel*, 24 (1966), 42-55. (PNR)

"Gravitation." *Tel Quel*, 16 (1964). (RM)

"L'Histoire dans l'histoire." *Critique*, 231-232 (1966), 711-729.

"L'Impossible M. Texte." *Synthèses*, 277-278 (1969), 11-24. (PTNR)

"Incident." *Lettres Nouvelles* (May-June, 1970), 51-56. (RM)

"Une Interrogation nommée littérature." *Le Nouvel Observateur*, 6 (1964), 18.

"Jeu." *Nouveau Commerce*, 17 (1970), 95-106. (RM)

"Lancement d'un voilier." *La Nouvelle Revue Française*, 99 (1961), 555-559. (RM)

"Lettre à la rédaction de *Sub-stance*." *Sub-stance*, 1 (1971), 51.

"Miracles' de l'analogie (aspects proustiens de la métaphore productrice)." *Cahiers Marcel Proust*, 7 (1975), 11-42.

"Michel Butor ou le roman et ses degrés." *La Nouvelle Revue Française*, 90 (1960), 1157-1161.

"Naissance d'une fiction." *Nouveau Roman: hier, aujourd'hui*, vol. 2. Paris: 10/18, 1972, pp. 379-392.

"Le Nouveau Roman est-il valéryen?" *Entretiens sur Paul Valéry*, ed. Emilie Noulet. Paris: Mouton, 1968, pp. 69-83.

"Le Nouveau Roman existe-t-il?" *Nouveau Roman: Hier, aujourd'hui*, vol. 1. Paris: 10/18, 1972, pp. 9-20.

"L'Or du scarabée." *Tel Quel*, 34 (1968), 42-57. (PTNR).

"Un Ordre dans la débâcle." *Critique*, 163 (1960), 1011-1024. Also in Claude Simon. *La route des Flandres*. Paris: 10/18, 1960.

"Par delà le réel et l'irréel (simple note sur un fragment d'*Un Régicide.*"
    Médiations, 5 (1962), 17-25.
"Penser la littérature aujourd'hui." *Sud*, 8 (1972), 32-46.
"Plage blanche." *Mantéia*, 3 (1968), 44-49. (RM)
"La Population des miroirs." *Poétique*, 22 (1975), 196-226. (NPR)
"Premières lectures du parc." *Médiations*, 4 (1962), 175-85.
"La Prise de Constantinople." *Tel Quel*, 22 (1965), 14-29.
"La Querelle de la métaphore." *Tel Quel*, 18 (1964), 56-67.
"Réalités variables." *Tel Quel*, 12 (1963), 31-37. (PNR)
"Réflexion totale." *Tel Quel*, 11 (1962), 77-80. (RM)
"Une Réponse de Jean Ricardou." *Les Lettres Françaises*, 1414 (1971),
    2.
"La Révolution textuelle." *Esprit*, 12 (1974), 927-945.
"Sur La Pierre." *Tel Quel*, 2 (1960), 33-36. (RM)
"Sur Une Erreur de Bachelard." *Tel Quel*, 28 (1967).
"Le Symptôme du contradictoire." *Sud*, 4 (1971), 55-57.
"Terrorisme, théorie." *Robbe-Grillet: Colloque de Cerisy*, vol. 1. Paris:
    10/18, 1976, pp. 10-33.
"Textes 'mis en scène'." *La Quinzaine Littéraire*, 38 (1967), 6.
Jean Ricardou with Simone de Beauvoir, Yves Berger, Jean-Pierre Faye,
    Jean-Paul Sartre, Jorge Semprun, Yves Buin. *Que Peut La Littérature?*
    Paris: 10/18, 1965.

II. Selected articles about Ricardou

Albérès, R. M. "Le Culte de l'onirique." *Nouvelles Littéraires*, 2269
    (1971), 5.
Alter, Jean. "Jean Ricardou: *Révolutions minuscules.*" *French Review*,
    45, no. 2 (1971), 486-7.
Bonnet, Henri. "Jean Ricardou et la métaphore proustienne." *Bulletin de
    la Société des Amis de Marcel Proust*, 1976, pp. 286-294.
Calle-Gruber, Mireille. "Effets d'un texte non saturé: *La Prise de
    Constantinople.*" *Poétique*, 35 (1978), 325-335.
Caminade, Pierre. "Analogie et métaphore structurelle de Jean Ricardou."
    Images et métaphore, un problème de poétique contemporaine. Paris:
    Bordas, 1970, pp. 90-96.
--------. "Vers Une Nouvelle Poétique? La métaphore structurelle de Jean
    Ricardou." *Courier du Centre International d'Etudes Poétiques*, 65
    (1968).

Duranteau, Josanne. "Ou Peut-être est-ce un texte qui rêve?" *Lettres Françaises*, 1395 (1971), 7-9.

Fried, Ursula. "Lecture créatrice à base structuraliste de 'Plage Blanche" par Jean Ricardou." *Bonnes Feuilles*, 6 (1976), 3-17.

Galey, Matthieu, "La Carte du tendre des structuralistes." *L'Express*, 927 (1969), 59-60.

Guereña, Jacento-Luis. "Théorie du nouveau roman." *Estafeta Literaria*, 475 (1971), 680-81.

Helbo, André. "Jean Ricardou: transparences et opacité." *Critique*, 331 (1974), 1095-98.

Higgins, Lynn A. "Literature 'à la lettre': Ricardou and the Poetics of Anagram." *The Romanic Review*, 73, No. 4 (1982), 473-488.

--------. "Typographical Eros: Reading Ricardou in the Third Dimension." *Yale French Studies*, 57 (1979), 80-94.

Jean, Raymond. "De La Plage à la page: *Révolutions minuscules* de Jean Ricardou." *Le Monde*, (Mar. 12, 1971), 15-16.

--------. "Une Méthode critique. Jean Ricardou et les problèmes du nouveau roman." *Le Monde* (Jan. 17, 1968).

Jones, Tobin. "In Quest of a Newer New Novel: Ricardou's La Prise de Constantinople." Contemporary Literature, 14, no. 3, pp. 296-309.

Levy, Sydney. "Expression et production." *Sud*, 8 (1972), 67-74.

--------. "Texte moderne et nouvelle critique: *Pour Une Théorie du nouveau roman* de Jean Ricardou." *Sub-stance*, 1 (1971), 59-64.

"Literature, not life." *The Times Literary Supplement*, Nov. 23, 1967.

Ollier, Claude, Philippe Sollers, Claude Simon. "*Problèmes du nouveau roman*: trois avis autorisés." *Les Lettres Françaises*, 1203 (1967), 13.

Piatier, Jacqueline. "Du Critique au créateur: Jean Ricardou et ses 'générateurs.'" *Le Monde* (25 June, 1971).

--------. "Jean Ricardou et ses 'générateurs.'" *Les Critiques de notre temps et le nouveau roman*. Paris: Garnier, 1972.

Pierssens, Michel. "Un Fantastique sans mystère." *Sub-stance*, 1 (1971), 65-70. Also in *Sud*, 8 (1972), 59-66.

Prigogine, Hélène. "L'Aventure ricardolienne du nombre." *Nouveau Roman: hier, aujourd'hui*, vol. 2. Paris: 10/18, 1972, pp. 353-378.

Prigogine, Hélène. "Jean Ricardou ou l'écriture aux prises avec le livre." *Synthèses*, 238 (1966), 290-296.

Raillon, Jean-Claude. "'Une étude perilleusement excessive du texte cité.'" *Sud*, 8 (1972), 47-58.

Rice, Donald B. "The Ex-centricities of Jean Ricardou's *La Prise/Prose de Constantinople*." *International Fiction Review*, 2, no. 2 (1975), 106-112.

Simon, Pierre-Henri. "De Jean Ricardou: *L'Observatoire de Cannes*." *Diagnostic des Lettres Françaises Contemporaines*. Brussels: Renaissance du livre, 1966, pp. 321-326.

--------. "*L'Observatoire de Cannes* de Jean Ricardou." *Le Monde* (Sept. 13, 1961), p. 9.

Sollers, Philippe. "*L'Observatoire de Cannes*." *Tel Quel*, 6 (1961), 56-7.

Thibaudeau, Jean. "La Leçon de l'école." *Critique*, 173 (1961), 835-42.

III. Closely related works (partly about Ricardou)

Brée, Germaine. "Novelists in search of the novel: the French Scene." *Modern Fiction Studies*, 16 (1970), 3-11.

Caminade, Pierre. "Le Nouveau Roman, décade de Cerisy-la-Salle." *Sud*, 5-6 (1971), 44-62.

Jaffé-Freem, E. "Chronique du roman -- 1971." *Rapports Franse Boek*, 42, nos. 1-2 (1972), 1-9.

Lorent, Laure E. "Formalisme ou engagement (à propos de quelques livres récents)." *La Revue Nouvelle*, 49, no. 3 (1969), 303-313.

McCarthy, Mary. "Crushing a Butterfly." *The Writing on the Wall and Other Literary Essays*. New York: Harcourt, Brace & World, pp. 95-101.

Noguez, Dominique. "Lettre d'un jeune homme au vieux Flaubert." *Arts*, 11 (1965), 14-15.

"Un Nouveau Nouveau Roman?" special issue of *Marche Romane*, 21, nos. 1-2 (1971).

Pével, Henri. "Résonances mallarméennes du nouveau roman." *Médiations*, 7 (1964), 95-113.

Pingaud, Bernard. "Où va *Tel Quel*?" *La Quinzaine Littéraire*, 42 (1968), 8-9.

--------. "Le Réflexe de réduction." *La Quinzaine Littéraire*, 43 (1968), 10-12.

Prigogine, Hélène. "Ecritures." *Synthèses*, 291 (1970), 48-54.

Roudiez, Leon. *French Fiction Today*. New Brunswick: Rutgers University Press, 1972.